"*Revolutionary Leadership* will embolden you. It will instruct you and inspire you for the days ahead. Whatever your leadership arena, Pat's stories and revolutionary insights will strengthen you for the fight."

Brian Kilmeade, bestselling author and
Fox News TV and radio host

"The 'shot heard 'round the world' announced the birth of freedom and the death knell of oppression in America. The heroes of the American Revolution set a leadership example for us all. In *Revolutionary Leadership*, Pat Williams uncovers new insights into the lives of these revolutionary leaders and shows us how we can become more effective leaders in every arena of our lives. Learn these principles and become a revolutionary leader!"

Mike Huckabee, 44th governor of Arkansas
and political commentator

"Pat Williams offers a unique and compelling interpretation of the American Revolution. He focuses the lens of leadership on the lives of men and women who made a difference for the cause of liberty. Become a more effective leader in your home, school, workplace, or society. Read *Revolutionary Leadership*."

Alan Mulally, former CEO, Ford Motor Company;
former CEO, Boeing Commercial Airplanes;
former president, Boeing Information,
Space & Defense Systems

"All the lessons we learn from great Revolutionary War leaders can be applied to any leadership arena today. George Washington teaches us that winning is not determined by who your opponent is but by who *you* are. Great tacticians like Nathanael Greene and Francis Marion remind us that winning involves taking your opponent out of the game and making it all about you. Henry Knox, the fighting bookseller, teaches us that bold action produces big gains. And the stories of dedicated old soldiers, teenage Minutemen, and courageous women in combat tell us that victory goes to those who want it most. If you want to be inspired to lead and to win, you *must* read *Revolutionary Leadership* by Pat Williams."

Nick Saban, head football coach of the Alabama Crimson Tide

"In *Revolutionary Leadership*, Pat Williams teaches us that many of the leadership traits that produce victory on the battlefield—teamwork, resilience, and character—also lead to success on the basketball court and in any field of competition. Pat shares powerful lessons from America's early years that are as important and relevant as ever."

Adam Silver, commissioner of the
National Basketball Association

"*Revolutionary Leadership* by Pat Williams, whom I greatly admire, is very interesting as well as inspirational for both students of history and those who desire to know more about the foundation of our great nation. Reading this book will undoubtedly produce many more courageous leaders in our time of great need."

Benjamin S. Carson Sr., MD, professor emeritus of neurosurgery,
oncology, plastic surgery, and pediatrics
at Johns Hopkins School of Medicine

"In *Revolutionary Leadership*, motivational guru Pat Williams tells stories you've never heard before, finds insights you've never thought of before, and presents the American Revolution in a way that will continually surprise you. He tells stories of the great and famous leaders, such as Washington, Jefferson, Franklin, and Lafayette. But he also tells stories of unsung heroes and heroines of the Revolution—people you've never heard of but who made a difference through their courage, dedication, and leadership. A must-read for fans of history—and students of leadership."

John Swofford, former commissioner of the
Atlantic Coast Conference

"In *Revolutionary Leadership*, Pat Williams has captured the soul of the American Revolution and the essential principles of effective leadership. Through stories of early American heroes and heroines, he makes the Revolutionary era come alive. Read this book and you'll have a deeper understanding of what a divinely blessed miracle America truly is—and a deeper understanding of what it takes to be a leader in a time of crisis."

Rick Perry, 14th United States Secretary of Energy
and 47th governor of Texas

Revolutionary LEADERSHIP

Revolutionary
LEADERSHIP

ESSENTIAL LESSONS FROM THE MEN AND WOMEN OF THE AMERICAN REVOLUTION

PAT WILLIAMS
with JIM DENNEY

Revell

a division of Baker Publishing Group
Grand Rapids, Michigan

Published by Revell
a division of Baker Publishing Group
PO Box 6287, Grand Rapids, MI 49516-6287
www.revellbooks.com

Printed in the United States of America

Library of Congress Cataloging-in-Publication Data
Names: Williams, Pat, 1940– author. | Denney, Jim, 1953– author.
Title: Revolutionary leadership : essential lessons from the men and women of the American Revolution / Pat Williams with Jim Denney.
Other titles: Essential lessons from the men and women of the American Revolution
Description: Grand Rapids, Michigan : Revell, a division of Baker Publishing Group, [2021]
Identifiers: LCCN 2020042281 | ISBN 9780800738730 (cloth)
Subjects: LCSH: United States—History—Revolution, 1775–1783—Influence. | United States—Politics and government—1775–1783. | Leadership—Case studies. | Founding Fathers of the United States—Biography. | United States—History—Revolution, 1775–1783—Women. | United States—History—Revolution, 1775–1783—Biography.
Classification: LCC E209 .W55 2021 | DDC 973.3092/2 [B]—dc23
LC record available at https://lccn.loc.gov/2020042281

21 22 23 24 25 26 27   7 6 5 4 3 2 1

In memory of my mother and father,
who were great students of American history and who
passed along to me their love for this country.

Contents

Foreword

Who can deny that America is in crisis today?

We face deepening racial conflict, a fractured political system, corruption in our government, run-amok social media that undermines our democracy, rises in teen suicide and bullying and violence, protests and riots in our streets, extremism in our media, radicalism on our campuses, threats from terrorists and hostile nations, and a skyrocketing national debt that threatens the global economy. I could go on, but you know as well as I do that much of American society appears to be coming apart at the seams.

Who can deny that, at this critical moment in history, America needs leaders of strength and courage and uncompromising principles? Where can we find such leaders in this time of crisis?

Only one place: Look in the mirror.

You're the leader America needs. I'm not saying you need to run for president of the United States. To solve the crises we face, we need new leadership at every level. We need community leaders, religious leaders, youth leaders, campus leaders, business leaders, leaders in journalism, leaders in every arena of society. As Pat Williams tells us, we need all hands on deck.

And that's why you need to read this book.

Revolutionary Leadership is the story of how ordinary people from the unlikeliest of places came together and turned thirteen oppressed and subjugated British colonies into the United States of America. Most of them had little more to offer than a deep love of country and an intense desire to make a difference.

In this book, you'll read the story of an ordinary bookseller, a man without any military training whatsoever, who became one of the greatest generals and artillery engineers in American history. You'll read about an African American sailor who sacrificed his life and ignited the revolution. You'll read about a brave woman in a Massachusetts village who stood guard at a bridge and captured a British spy.

You'll read about a young man who emigrated to America from the West Indies and led a decisive assault at Yorktown—then went on to invent the US economy. You'll read about a Scotsman who came to America and changed the course of naval warfare. You'll read about farmers and shopkeepers, society matrons and country girls, frightened young privates and grizzled old soldiers, all with three things in common: They loved freedom. They stepped up. They led.

Pat Williams knows leadership. As the general manager of the NBA champion 1983 Philadelphia 76ers and the cofounder of the Orlando Magic, Pat has shown that he knows how to achieve great things in the face of overwhelming odds and tough opposition. His leadership ability was recognized by the presentation of the John Bunn Award at his 2012 induction into the Naismith Memorial Basketball Hall of Fame. Throughout Pat's fifty-plus years in pro sports, leadership has been his passion and his wheelhouse.

And Pat Williams knows history. He has visited all the historic sites and battlefields he writes about in this book. He has studied the battles, the politics of the era, the heroes and villains, the famous lives and the obscure but irreplaceable leaders of the revolution.

Most important of all, Pat finds the lessons in the lives of these leaders—lessons that you and I can learn and apply in our own leadership lives today.

Pat is a captivating storyteller. Through the stories in this book, you'll see how the early Patriots came together to build (to paraphrase Lincoln) a new nation, conceived in liberty, and dedicated to the proposition that all people are created equal. Pat shows us how the founding American principles were engraved on the hearts of those early Patriots: liberty, equality, and government by consent of the governed.

And Pat shows how the essential qualities of leadership were demonstrated by those early Patriots—vision, communication skills, people skills, good character, competence, boldness, and a serving heart. Without these seven qualities, we can't lead. But a leader who embodies them all is ready to start a revolution and take on an empire.

The early Patriots and the founding fathers were not plaster saints. They had flaws and foibles and eccentricities—and Pat documents them honestly in this book. And I'm glad he does, because I can't identify with or learn from a plaster saint—but I can learn a lot from the real flesh-and-blood leaders Pat presents to us in *Revolutionary Leadership*.

You and I live in troubled times—times that cry out for bold, dedicated leadership. As James Russell Lowell wrote in his poem *This Present Crisis*, "Once to every man and nation comes the moment to decide, In the strife of Truth with Falsehood, for the good or evil side." When their moment came, the revolutionary era Patriots decided. They met the crisis of their time. They led.

Now it's our time to decide. It's our crisis. It's our turn to lead.

Revolutionary Leadership will embolden you. It will instruct you and inspire you for the days ahead. Whatever your leadership arena, Pat's stories and revolutionary insights will strengthen you for the fight.

Brian Kilmeade, TV and radio host, Fox News;
author, *Sam Houston and the Alamo Avengers*

Introduction

Leadership Forged in Crisis

This book was forged in crisis.

The coronavirus (COVID-19) crisis of 2020 was just starting to rage across the globe as I wrote about the events of 1775 through 1783—the crisis of the American Revolutionary War. At first glance, these two eras seem completely unlike each other. Yet the Revolutionary War crisis and the coronavirus crisis are really not all that different.

The Revolutionary War era was, like our own time, an era of a virulent, deadly epidemic. The smallpox epidemic began in 1775 and terrorized the newborn nation of America for seven years, coinciding almost exactly with the eight-year Revolutionary War.

Conditions were perfect for spreading the disease throughout the thirteen colonies. People were crowded together in military encampments, besieged cities, and ships at sea. Like carriers of COVID-19, smallpox carriers were extremely contagious while showing no symptoms during the two-week incubation period. As a result, the smallpox virus would spread invisibly through a population before anyone suspected its presence. Historians say the smallpox epidemic of 1775 to 1782 claimed five to ten times as many people as were killed by the Revolutionary War.

Then, as now, the epidemic was a leadership challenge. General George Washington, commander in chief of the Continental Army, had to decide how to respond to the smallpox outbreak among his troops. It was his decision alone whether or not to inoculate his troops against smallpox—and it was not an easy decision.

Doctors in the eighteenth century had learned a crude technique for smallpox inoculation called variolation. A small amount of infectious matter was taken from the sores of a smallpox sufferer and introduced to the skin of a healthy person. This would trigger the healthy person's immune system to fight the smallpox infection when the disease was at a weaker stage. Normally this would result in a light case of the disease. People treated with variolation had to be quarantined to avoid giving the disease to others. In a few cases, the inoculation would lead to a full-blown attack of the disease. Some inoculated people died.

At first General Washington hesitated to inoculate his troops. "Should We inoculate generally," he wrote, "the Enemy, knowing it, will certainly take Advantage of our Situation."[1] By 1777 the smallpox epidemic was seriously interfering with the war effort. Battle plans were delayed by illnesses among the troops. Fear of smallpox kept many potential recruits from enlisting. So Washington ordered all soldiers who had never had the disease to undergo variolation. It was a risky decision.

Washington's inoculation plan proceeded in complete secrecy. Large numbers of his troops were incapacitated for weeks as they recovered from the effects of variolation. Fortunately, the British never learned of the vulnerability of the American forces. The rate of illness and death among Washington's troops fell dramatically once his troops were inoculated. The program was a success and the Continental Army emerged as a healthy, full-strength fighting force.

Then, as now, American leadership rose to the challenge of an epidemic. Leadership is forged in crises like this.

The crisis of the American Revolution bears other similarities to the crises we face today. American society in the Revolutionary era was deeply divided between opposing factions—the pro-revolution Patriots and the pro-monarchy Loyalists. There were global tensions and divisions that had to be addressed. Benjamin Franklin and his fellow diplomats had to carry out delicate negotiations with France and other European nations. It was a time of economic crisis in which American money had little value, Great Britain was sabotaging American trade with other nations, and the Continental Congress had no way of feeding, clothing, or paying soldiers. Then, as now, Congress was sharply divided into factions.

The newspapers of that era were divided into Patriot and Loyalist camps, much as the news media today is divided between Conservatives and Liberals. For example, the *Boston Gazette* published news and editorials from a Patriot perspective while the *Boston Chronicle* advocated support for the British Crown. Tensions between the two newspapers and their respective readerships became so inflamed that, on one occasion, *Chronicle* publisher John Mein encountered *Gazette* publisher John Gill on the street and proceeded to beat him with his cane.[2]

Leadership was the crucial factor that transformed the thirteen colonies into the United States of America. The leaders of the American Revolution invented the greatest engine of freedom in human history—the United States of America—and set a leadership example for us all to follow. That's the driving theme of this book.

In *Revolutionary Leadership*, we look at the lives of great leaders and the times in which they lived. We look at the famous leaders—George Washington, Thomas Jefferson, Benjamin Franklin, Paul Revere, John Paul Jones, and Alexander Hamilton—and discover nuggets of leadership wisdom embedded in their lives. We also look at some not-so-famous but vitally important leaders—Crispus

Attucks, Esther de Berdt Reed, Sarah Bradlee Fulton, Sybil Ludington, and Deborah Sampson—and we discover some of the women
and African American leaders and heroes of the Revolutionary War.

In the process of exploring the lives of these leaders, we'll not
only learn the story of America's founding but we'll also learn essential principles of leadership. These principles can be applied in
any setting or in any field of endeavor to achieve any leadership goal.

I've arranged these stories in roughly chronological order. As
you read, you'll gain a deeper understanding of the chronology of
events and the way individual men and women influenced history
by exercising their leadership skills. You'll discover what these
events meant then, what they mean to us today, and how we can
impact the world through our own leadership influence.

While researching and writing this book, one truth stood out
to me again and again: *The United States of America is a miracle.*
It's a nation that, by all odds, should not exist. Yet it does.

During the revolution, the Continental Army was perpetually
short on manpower, short on food, short on clothing, short on
weapons and ammunition, short on everything. The brand-new
American government was weak and indecisive, had no strong executive leadership, and lacked the power to raise revenue. American
society was divided, and the Patriots found themselves fighting not
only the British Army but also Loyalist Americans who supported
the British cause. The Continental Army lost battle after battle.

Yet it miraculously won the war.

America had no business winning. There was simply no way a
ragtag collection of untrained, ill-equipped farmers, grocers, and
shopkeepers could ever defeat the mighty army and navy of Great
Britain, the most powerful empire in the world. There were so
many times when the cause of liberty hung by a thread—and an
American leader stepped up at just the right moment and snatched
victory from the jaws of defeat. All you can do is shake your head
in wonder and say, "America is a miracle of God."

Take a close look at the lives of these leaders and you'll realize that the Revolutionary War was an "all hands on deck" crisis. Subtract just one of these leaders and the entire war effort collapses.

Take, for example, Henry Knox. He was just a bookseller from Boston who studied military science and military history by reading books. Improbably, he became General Washington's indispensable artillery officer. Without Knox at his side, Washington would not have defeated the British at the Siege of Boston. Nor would Washington have defeated the Hessians in Trenton or ended the war at Yorktown. Henry Knox is hardly a household name today, but it's doubtful that the revolution would have succeeded without him.

The same can be said of so many other revolutionary leaders, starting with George Washington himself. What if the Conway Cabal had succeeded in ousting Washington as commander in chief of the army, replacing him with the feckless and cowardly Horatio Gates? Certain disaster!

What if Alexander Hamilton had never left the little Caribbean island of Nevis to become Washington's right-hand man? What if Lafayette had never left France to serve at Washington's side? Hamilton and Lafayette were the indispensable heroes of the decisive victory at Yorktown. What if they had stayed home instead of coming to America and joining the cause?

What if John Paul Jones had not come to America from Scotland to battle the British on the high seas and on the coasts of England? What if Esther de Berdt Reed had not recruited thousands of women to raise money and sew shirts to support the Continental Army? What if Baron von Steuben hadn't arrived from Prussia to show General Washington, during that miserable winter in Valley Forge, a better way to train and care for an army?

And then there's Nathanael Greene, one of my favorite leaders of the Revolutionary War. He's the most underrated general in American history, the man General Washington chose to succeed him if he was disabled. Nathanael Greene was raised a pacifist

Quaker, but he had a lifelong fascination with warfare. The fighting Quaker could easily have chosen the teachings of his church over his yearning for freedom. He wrestled with a deep inner conflict—and ultimately chose to go to war. Had he chosen otherwise, the revolution might have failed.

From the tragedy at Lexington to the triumph at Yorktown, every American leader had to stand up and be counted. Every leader had to make a contribution, make sacrifices, and persevere beyond the limits of human endurance in order to make freedom ring.

I don't believe America was inevitable. I don't believe America just happened. I'm convinced America was a miracle of God. It's inconceivable to me that the chain of events that resulted in American independence could have happened without divine intervention. And it's equally inconceivable that American independence could have happened without great American leadership.

We are living in a time of crisis. I'm not talking about the COVID-19 crisis. I hope and pray that by the time you read this book, the coronavirus pandemic is a thing of the past.

But even after we have ceased to worry about COVID-19, the world will still be in the grip of global crises. America's skyrocketing national debt threatens to plunge the entire world into a global Great Depression. Civilization is threatened by terrorism and unstable governments wielding nuclear weapons. Dangerous authoritarian regimes are vying with Western nations for domination and power. Climate and environmental uncertainties cloud our future. Racial strife and ideological divisions are fracturing our society.

Once again, America needs a miracle from God. Once again, it's "all hands on deck." No one is nonessential. Everyone's indispensable.

Turn the page. Read these stories. Then step up and be the leader America needs now. Be the leader for today's American crises.

Pat Williams
Orlando, Florida
February 1, 2021

★ 1 ★

Samuel Adams

The Father of the Revolution

Most Americans know Samuel Adams as a name on a beer label.

But Sam Adams—a cousin of the second president of the United States, John Adams—was one of the earliest and most important figures in the drive toward American independence. During his lifetime, he became known as the Father of the Revolution.[1] Yet Sam Adams showed very little leadership ability in his youth. In fact, his father, Samuel Adams Sr., was convinced that his young son was destined for failure.

Samuel Adams was born in Boston in September 1722. He was one of twelve children born to Samuel Sr. and Mary Fifield Adams. In those days of high infant mortality, only three of the twelve Adams children survived past age three. Samuel and Mary Adams raised their children in their devout Puritan faith.

A wealthy Boston merchant and landowner, Samuel Adams Sr. sent young Samuel to the best schools—Boston Latin School and

Harvard College. Academically, Samuel was second in his graduating class at Harvard, but the college president, Benjamin Wadsworth, arbitrarily demoted him to sixth in a class of twenty-three because Samuel's father lacked a "gentleman's education."[2] The aristocratic snobbery Samuel encountered at Harvard reinforced his opposition to the rigid class prejudice and elitism of British society.

Samuel's parents sent him to Harvard to study for the ministry, but he chose to study philosophy and politics instead. He graduated in 1740 and earned his master's degree in 1743. His master's thesis statement demonstrated an early desire for revolution against the British Crown. Translated from the Latin, Samuel's thesis question read: "Is it lawful to resist the government if the welfare of the republic is involved? Responding in the affirmative, Samuel Adams."[3]

At that time, three decades before the Declaration of Independence was written, Adams's bold advocacy of resistance to the Crown must have sounded more like treason than patriotism to his fellow colonists. Most colonists considered themselves British subjects, not American Patriots. Though Adams was only twenty years old when he wrote his master's thesis, he was well ahead of his countrymen in pondering resistance and revolution.

The Successful Failure

Samuel worked briefly in a counting house—a bookkeeping and bill-collecting business. He hated the job and wanted to become a lawyer, but his mother talked him out of it. For a while, his parents tried to persuade him to become a clergyman, but their efforts were to no avail.

When Samuel Sr. realized his son would never enter the ministry, he lent him one thousand British pounds—the equivalent of about two hundred thousand dollars today. Samuel was supposed to use the money to launch a business. Instead, he lent half of the money to a friend (the loan was never repaid). He lost the rest on bad business deals.

Samuel Sr. concluded that young Samuel had no enthusiasm for business and was probably unemployable. He gave his son a job in the family malt house business where, he hoped, his bright but financially inept son would do no harm. A malt house is a building where cereal grain (such as barley) is soaked in water, allowed to sprout, then dried as malt. The Adams malt house probably sold malt for brewing beer and distilling whiskey. (It's unlikely that Samuel Adams ever brewed beer, despite his name being a popular beer brand today.)

In January 1748, twenty-five-year-old Sam Adams launched his first successful business, a weekly newspaper called the *Independent Advertiser*. It gave him a platform from which to preach against oppressive British actions, such as "impressment," seizing sailors from merchant ships (including American ships) and forcing the sailors to serve in the Royal Navy. Samuel's writings were heavily influenced by the English Enlightenment philosopher John Locke, who promoted "natural rights," especially the rights of life, liberty, and property.

That same year, Samuel's father died, and Samuel took over the family estate. He discovered that one of his father's business ventures—a failed banking enterprise—had put the entire estate in jeopardy. His father and other investors had established a bank to stabilize the local economy by issuing its own paper money. The British government and the Loyalist governor of Massachusetts had forced the bank to close.

Throughout the 1750s, Samuel Adams battled the commissioners of the Massachusetts General Court who, on behalf of the British Crown, launched scheme after scheme—many of them clearly illegal and corrupt—in a bid to seize the Adamses' estate. That long battle only inflamed Samuel Adams's hatred for oppressive government—and tilted him in favor of revolution.

During the long legal battle, Adams wrote essays in the *Independent Advertiser* denouncing British oppression. He attacked the commissioners for trying to seize his father's estate and exposed the commissioners' profit incentive for corruption and dishonesty. His newspaper essays generated a public outcry—and the commissioners were fired. This cause-and-effect action taught Adams the power of the press in gaining public sympathy and political leverage.

From Tax Collector to Political Leader

In 1749, the year after his father's death, Samuel Adams married his pastor's daughter, Elizabeth Checkley. She gave birth six times, but only two of those children survived. Elizabeth died in 1757 from complications following a stillbirth. In his eulogy for his wife, a grieving Samuel Adams said that Elizabeth had "run her Christian race with remarkable steadiness and finished in triumph."[4]

A year before, the Boston Town Meeting (the citizens' council that governed Boston) appointed Adams tax collector. Because of his strong sense of compassion and fair play, he was reluctant to collect taxes from fellow citizens who were going through financial difficulties. His lenient nature made him popular with the people, but the Town Meeting held him personally responsible for the shortage in collections. After nine years on the job, he was £8,000 behind in his collections (equivalent to $1.6 million today). Adams parlayed his popularity into political support. The people knew that his concern for their well-being was genuine, springing from his Christian and pro-liberty convictions.

Having failed as a tax collector, Adams turned to a career in politics. He served in both the Massachusetts House of Representatives and the Boston Town Meeting during the 1760s. He organized opposition to oppressive British tax schemes such as the Sugar Act of 1764, the Stamp Act of 1765, and the Townshend Acts of 1767. He also led a boycott of British goods.

As a devout Puritan, Sam Adams was a peace-loving man, and he saw armed revolution as a last resort. His hopes for a peaceful solution were dashed in May 1768 when a fifty-gun British warship, HMS *Romney*, sailed into Boston Harbor and began the impressment of Bostonian sailors.

Unrest in the city was already high when, on June 10, 1768, British customs officials seized the *Liberty*, a sloop owned by the popular Boston merchant John Hancock. When British sailors from the *Romney* came ashore to take the *Liberty* in tow, Bostonians rioted, forcing British officials and their families to flee to the *Romney*. The British government sent army regiments to Boston to quell the riots. Reinforcements soon arrived, and a full-scale military occupation of Boston began.

On March 5, 1770, the Massachusetts colony was stunned by the Boston Massacre. During a time of troubled relations between British soldiers and Boston citizens, a mob gathered in front of a British soldier standing guard at the Boston Custom House. As the sentry endured taunts from the mob, he was joined by eight more soldiers. The crowd threw stones and snowballs at the soldiers—and the soldiers fired into the crowd. Five Boston civilians died. The tragic incident stoked revolutionary passions throughout the thirteen colonies.

After the Boston Massacre, Samuel Adams, John Hancock, and other leaders met with the governor of Massachusetts and with Colonel William Dalrymple, the commander of the British troops. The Boston delegation demanded the withdrawal of troops and an end to the occupation. To reduce unrest, Dalrymple agreed to move his soldiers to Castle William on an island in Boston Harbor.

In April 1770, the British Parliament repealed all of the Townshend Act taxes except the tax on tea. In newspaper essays, Adams urged his fellow colonists to continue boycotting all British goods until Parliament removed the tea tax. As long as the British government continued to tax tea, it legitimized the British claim of a right to tax Americans without giving them a say in Parliament. American patriots united behind the slogan "No taxation without representation." Despite Adams's pleas, the boycott failed. People went back to buying British goods and paying the taxes.

The Boston Tea Party

In his continued frustration over taxes on British goods, Samuel Adams decided to take bolder action, a decision that led to the Boston Tea Party. Though Adams's precise role in the Boston Tea Party is debated by historians, we know he was involved in planning the protest. Adams was the founder of the Sons of Liberty, a secret organization with members in all thirteen colonies who were devoted to resisting British oppression.

He was also a leading member of the Boston Committee of Correspondence, one of many committees of correspondence throughout the colonies. Committees of correspondence acted as shadow governments, organizing opposition to the British government and to colonial governors and legislatures who were loyal to Britain.

In late November 1773, the *Dartmouth*, a British cargo ship laden with tea, anchored in Boston Harbor. The ship's owner, the British East India Company, was required to pay the tax for the goods and unload the cargo within twenty days or British customs officials would confiscate the cargo (the tax was passed along to the colonists in the form of higher tea prices).

Adams convened an emergency town meeting, attended by several thousand Bostonians. The meeting passed a resolution demanding that the *Dartmouth* raise anchor and return the tea to England without unloading or paying the tax. At the meeting, twenty-five men were selected to stand guard and prevent the tea from being unloaded.

Massachusetts royal governor Thomas Hutchinson refused to allow the *Dartmouth* to leave without unloading its cargo. Meanwhile, two more British tea ships, *Eleanor* and *Beaver*, dropped anchor in Boston Harbor. On December 16, the eve of the governor's deadline for unloading the *Dartmouth*, Adams called another town meeting. An estimated five thousand people, nearly a third of the city's sixteen thousand citizens, showed up at Boston's Old South Meeting House, despite a bitterly cold rain.[5] Most of the crowd filled the streets as people strained to hear the debate inside.

A number of town leaders rose to give speeches about the critical situation at the wharf. Finally, Samuel Adams stood and said he could see nothing more that the people of Boston could do to save their country. Some historians believe Adams's words were a signal to the Sons of Liberty. A group of men left the meeting, determined to take action, about fifteen minutes after Adams spoke those words.

That night at around six, a large group of men, some dressed as Mohawk Indians, boarded the three British ships and spent the next three hours opening more than three hundred chests of tea and dumping them into the Boston Harbor. The disguises were intended to prevent the men from being recognized and prosecuted by the government.

This was no rioting mob. The men involved in the Boston Tea Party were remarkably efficient and disciplined as they went about their business. There was to be no looting or destruction of property, other than the tea. When one of the men accidentally broke a padlock, a new padlock was brought aboard to replace it. The disciplined and nonviolent nature of this act of resistance was likely due to Samuel Adams's strong Puritan influence.

By around 9:00 p.m., the Sons of Liberty had completed their task and the crowd on the wharf quietly dispersed. As Samuel's cousin John Adams reflected in his diary, "This is the most magnificent

Movement of all. There is a Dignity, a Majesty, a Sublimity in this last Effort of the Patriots that I greatly admire."[6]

"The Man of the Revolution"

The British government responded to the Boston Tea Party with even more tyrannical measures. The Coercive Acts of 1774 were intended to be so harsh and punitive that the colonists would be coerced into surrender. One of the Coercive Acts was the Boston Port Act, which included economic sanctions that would shut down Boston's economy until the city had repaid the East India Company for the lost tea.

Samuel Adams was a key leader in the colonial resistance to the Coercive Acts. In May 1774, he moderated a Boston Town Meeting that organized another boycott of all British imports. This time, his efforts at planning a boycott on British goods succeeded. He later served as a delegate to the First Continental Congress in Philadelphia and in the Massachusetts Provincial Congress, an outlawed resistance organization that created the first companies of minutemen (militiamen who were ready to fight at a minute's notice).

In April of the following year, Samuel Adams and John Hancock hid out in the village of Lexington, Massachusetts, aware that the British were hunting for them in Boston. On the night of April 18, General Thomas Gage, commander of British forces in North America, sent soldiers to Concord and Lexington, Massachusetts, with orders to disarm the rebels and capture Samuel Adams and John Hancock. Sometime after 9:00 p.m., a resistance leader, Dr. Joseph Warren, passed word to Paul Revere, William Dawes, and Samuel Prescott that the king's troops were embarking on boats across the Charles River toward the road to Lexington and Concord. So Revere, Dawes, and Prescott made the famed "midnight ride" to warn colonial militias that the British Army regulars were coming.

Adams and Hancock received the warning in time to make their escape just as the first shots of the Revolutionary War were fired on Lexington Common. Once the Revolutionary War had begun, the British government hoped to end it quickly. On June 12, 1775, General Thomas Gage made an offer to the American colonists: "I do hereby in his Majesty's name, offer and promise, his most gracious pardon in all who shall forthwith lay down their arms, and return to the duties of peaceable subjects, excepting only from the benefit of such pardon, Samuel Adams and John Hancock."[7]

When General Gage singled out Adams and Hancock by name, he made a grave tactical error. He elevated these two men to the status of heroes of the revolution and made it inevitable that Samuel Adams would become known as the Father of the Revolution.

More than twenty years after Samuel Adams's death, Thomas Jefferson eulogized Adams by comparing him to Palinurus, the heroic navigator and helmsman of Aeneas's ship in the *Aeneid* of Virgil: "If there was any Palinurus to the Revolution, Samuel Adams was the man. . . . For a year or two after it began, he was truly the Man of the Revolution."[8]

✳ LEADERSHIP LESSONS ✳ *from Samuel Adams*

What leadership insights can we learn from the life of Samuel Adams?

1. *Great leaders don't always look like leaders in their early years.* As a young man, Samuel Adams was a failure, not a leader. He had no head for business, couldn't manage money, and seemed unable to hold a job. It wasn't because he lacked intelligence or ambition; he simply had no interest in the world of business and finance. But he was passionate about liberty and equality. Once he had a platform for preaching his convictions, he emerged as one of the key leaders of the American Revolution.

2. *Great leaders are people of vision.* At age twenty, long before the Declaration of Independence was written, Adams had a vision of ending British oppression in the thirteen colonies. At first, he hoped the oppression would end through reform, but he eventually realized that armed rebellion was the only option. Samuel Adams envisioned an America of strong, free, self-reliant people. He worked hard for that vision, and he lived to see it fulfilled.

3. *Great leaders are great communicators.* Samuel Adams was an effective communicator as both a writer and a public speaker. He used the power of the press to shape public opinion and gain support for his causes. And he used the power of public speaking to motivate people to action in meetings that were attended by hundreds and even thousands of people. He communicated his vision of America as a land of freedom and equality—and his compatriots caught that vision and helped turn it into a reality.

4. *Great leaders are people of great character.* Samuel Adams never compromised his character. He believed that all people deserved to be treated fairly and equally. He was committed to living out the tenets of his Puritan Christian faith with absolute integrity and insisted that acts of resistance, such as the Boston Tea Party, be carried out honorably, with discipline and restraint—not as explosions of mob violence. His Christian compassion, his generosity, and his loyalty to the cause made him a leader the people could rally around. His uncompromised character, more than any other quality, made Samuel Adams the Father of the Revolution.

★ 2 ★

Crispus Attucks

The First American Martyr

The first man to die in the American Revolutionary War was an African American sailor named Crispus Attucks. His father was an African-born slave named Prince Yonger. His mother, Nancy Attucks, was a Native American member of the Natick language group. Though his year of birth is not known, he is assumed to have been born in 1773 in Framingham, Massachusetts.

Crispus Attucks was raised as a slave but escaped and gained freedom as a young man. Little else is known about his early life. After his escape, he supported himself in Boston by making rope and hiring out as a sailor on whaling ships and merchant ships.

As an experienced sailor, Attucks was at risk of being rounded up and forced to serve in the British Royal Navy. When the British began the impressment of Boston sailors in May 1768, a riot broke out in the city, prompting British officials to impose a full-scale military occupation.

Bostonians bitterly resented the presence of British soldiers in their streets. As a rope maker and sailor, Crispus Attucks was directly impacted by British oppression. Not only did he worry about being forced to serve in the British Navy but he also had to stand by and watch British redcoats taking part-time work away from his neighbors and himself.

The occupation of Boston continued for the better part of two years until the simmering outrage of the colonists reached a rolling boil. On March 2, 1770, an off-duty British redcoat approached a group of men who were employed by a rope seller named John Grey. When the redcoat asked if there was any work, one of the men replied with an insult: "Go and clean my [outhouse]."[1]

The redcoat left and returned a short time later with thirty or forty friends from the 29th Regiment of Foot. A brawl ensued. Crispus Attucks was not involved in the fight, but he heard about it from friends.

Tensions between the British and the Bostonians continued to rise over the next three days. On March 3, soldiers and sailors brawled at MacNeil's Ropeworks. On March 4, British soldiers returned to John Grey's rope shop, searching for a missing sergeant (he later turned up alive and well). As the unrest continued, rumors flew around the city that the British were planning to shed colonial blood.

Between eight and nine on the evening of March 5, a young colonist, a wigmaker's apprentice, went to the Boston Custom House on King Street, where British officials collected import taxes for the Crown. The wigmaker's apprentice stood in the snow-covered street in front of the building and shouted complaints about a British officer who had refused to pay for a powdered wig (in the eighteenth century, aristocratic men wore wigs powdered with white starch and scented with lavender or orange oil).

A British soldier, Private Hugh White, stood guard in the sentry box in front of the Custom House. Private White traded insults with the wigmaker's apprentice. Hearing the shouts, a group of young men gathered around, jeering at the soldier and calling him a "lobsterback" because of his red-coated uniform.

Finally, Private White had enough. He swung the butt of his musket at the wigmaker's apprentice, striking him in the head. Hearing the commotion, more angry Bostonians rushed to the scene. Soon, some fifty to a hundred people surrounded the soldier, throwing stones and snowballs at him, daring him to fire his musket. Shaken and fearing for his life, Private White retreated to the door of the Custom House, fixed his bayonet, and loaded his musket.

Grasping the Bayonet

News of the confrontation spread through the streets of Boston that night. When Crispus Attucks heard of it, he organized a group of sailors in Boston's Dock Square on the waterfront. The sailors armed themselves with wooden clubs, and Attucks led them up King Street. Arriving at the Boston Custom House, Attucks and his fellow sailors made their way to the front of the crowd.

Moments later, the British officer of the guard, Captain Thomas Preston, arrived at the Custom House with a team of six privates and a corporal. All were armed with muskets and bayonets. The soldiers formed a line facing Attucks and the crowd. The captain, standing in front of the line of soldiers, ordered them to load their muskets. He had positioned himself between his troops and the crowd, hoping that the mere threat of loaded muskets would persuade the angry civilians to disperse.

Yet they proceeded to pelt the soldiers with snowballs and advance toward them. The crowd came within arm's reach of the British guns. Attucks and the other sailors batted at the British bayonets with their clubs.

According to some accounts, Crispus Attucks shouted, "Be not afraid! They dare not fire!" Others in the crowd took up the chant, "The wretches dare not fire!" Then Attucks grasped Captain Preston's bayonet with his left hand.[2]

There are differing accounts on who attacked first. According to the most plausible account, one of the sailors with Crispus Attacks threw a wooden club at a soldier, Private Hugh Montgomery. The soldier fell to the snow, then jumped to his feet and fired his musket into the air as a warning shot. His fellow soldiers, frightened and tensed for action, took it as a signal to open fire. The roar and smoke of gunfire filled the air.

Crispus Attucks was the first man shot. Two musket balls struck him in the chest. He fell and died immediately.

The firing continued. Two other Bostonians were killed on the spot, while two more were mortally wounded and died within days. Six wounded colonists recovered from their wounds.

After discharging all of their ammunition into the crowd, the soldiers reloaded hastily, fearing that the crowd would charge at them. Captain Preston ordered the men to cease firing. The soldiers held their fire while the colonists returned to tend their wounded.

News of the slayings spread swiftly throughout the colonies. Americans, who already chafed under British taxation and the impressment of sailors, reacted with howls of outrage over the slaughter. In the days that followed, Samuel Adams gave the incident an appropriate name: the Boston Massacre.[3]

The bodies of Crispus Attucks and his fellow martyrs were taken to Boston's Faneuil Hall, where they lay in state. Hundreds of Bostonians filed by and paid their respects. Crispus Attucks was buried in the Park Street Cemetery alongside his fellow honored heroes. Their deaths in the Boston Massacre propelled the thirteen colonies toward revolution.

The story of Crispus Attucks lived on long after the American Revolution, inspiring antislavery abolitionists in the nineteenth century and civil rights activists in the twentieth century. Dr. Martin Luther King Jr., in his 1963 book *Why We Can't Wait*, cited

Crispus Attucks for his courage in risking—and sacrificing—his life to oppose tyranny during the British occupation of Boston.[4]

★ LEADERSHIP LESSONS ★
from Crispus Attucks

Crispus Attucks has been a controversial figure over the years. Some historians have called him a rabble-rouser. I see him as a patriotic hero who, like his fellow Bostonians, endured all the heavy-handed oppression he could stand. He refused to be impressed into the British Navy, and he organized his fellow sailors into a force of opposition to tyranny.

Among all the colonists who suffered mistreatment from the British Crown, Crispus Attucks was one of the first to raise a defiant challenge. When the British opened fire, he was the first American to die. Crispus Attucks was the first casualty of the revolution—and its first hero. We can learn a lot from his example.

Great leaders are courageous. Anyone who displays timidity and hesitation in a time of moral crisis is, by definition, not leading.

Crispus Attucks reminds me of a courageous young leader of our own era. On June 5, 1989, during the Tiananmen Square uprisings in Beijing, the Communist government of China sent a column of tanks into the city to quell the protests. Video cameras captured the courage of one young protester who stood on Chang'an Avenue and forced the tanks to come to a halt. When the lead tank tried to go around the young man, he moved in front of it. He even climbed onto the tank and talked to the crew. Eventually, Public Security Bureau officers rushed onto the street and dragged the man away and his fate is unknown. History remembers this bold young man as the Tank Man.[5]

And history remembers the courage of Crispus Attucks, the brave young man whose courageous stance against oppression set America on the path to revolution.

★ 3 ★

John Adams

The Conscience of the Revolution

On the night of the Boston Massacre, lawyer John Adams, the younger cousin of Samuel Adams, was sharing drinks and swapping stories with friends in the city's south end. He was too far from the Custom House to hear the sound of gunfire, but just after nine o'clock, he and his friends heard the tolling of church bells—an alarm that usually meant a fire in the city.

Adams soon learned that several Boston citizens had been gunned down by British soldiers. Along with hundreds of other townspeople, Adams made his way to King Street and the site of the massacre.

Upon arriving, he found that additional British troops had arrived to form a cordon around the Custom House. The colonists were angry. The soldiers were tense and afraid. The bodies of three men lay in the street.

After seeing the horrific carnage on King Street, Adams realized there was nothing he could do to help, so he hurried home to his wife, Abigail. John and Abigail had recently buried their little daughter Susanna, and Abigail was pregnant again while still grieving the tragic loss. News of the massacre would upset her deeply, and John needed to keep her calm.

The Boston Massacre had long been a tragedy waiting to happen. Over the years, unrest had grown. There were protests and riots against British oppression throughout the thirteen colonies. But the yoke of oppression was heaviest in Boston, a city that bitterly resented the presence of an occupation force of two thousand soldiers. British troops treated the citizens callously, taking goods and services without paying, roughing up men in the streets, and mistreating the women.

The Sons of Liberty had designated an elm tree near Boston Common as the Liberty Tree. The tree became a staging area for protests, such as the hanging in effigy of British administrator Andrew Oliver. John Adams's cousin Samuel took frequent jabs at the British occupation in his newspaper columns. Throughout the city, passions were inflamed against the British Crown.

A No-Win Proposition

The day after the tragedy on King Street, March 6, John Adams was in his law office when there was a knock at the door. Adams found an Irish-American merchant, James Forrest, on his steps. Forrest was a Loyalist and a friend of Captain Thomas Preston, the British officer of the guard at Custom House. Forrest came begging a favor for Captain Preston.

Preston was one of the few representatives of the British government to earn the respect of Bostonians. And on the night of the massacre, he had not ordered the gunfire and had tried to avoid violence altogether. Now he and his soldiers were accused of murder and no lawyer would defend them. Forrest had approached two other Boston attorneys, Josiah Quincy Jr. and Robert Auchmuty

Jr. Both men refused to consider the case—unless John Adams agreed to join them.

Adams's sympathies were 100 percent with the colonists. The people of Boston had suffered grievously under the British occupation. Freedom-loving, hard-working Bostonians, armed only with snowballs and wooden clubs, were shot and bayoneted by occupation soldiers. The snow in King Street was still stained with their blood. If he took the case, he would put his practice and even his personal safety at risk.

And what about Abigail? She was pregnant and emotionally fragile. Could she withstand the stress of a contentious, highly publicized trial? He and Abigail had everything to lose and nothing to gain. The British soldiers had very little money with which to pay his fee.

Forrest had offered Adams a no-win proposition, but one aspect of the case compelled him. He believed every accused individual had a right to a fair trial. Adams also believed the thirteen colonies and the British Crown were on a course that would one day lead to American independence. He wanted to establish certain principles as the legal foundation of the new American nation. Those principles included a defendant's right to counsel, the right to a vigorous defense, and the presumption of innocence.

With these ideas running through his head, John Adams agreed to take the case.

James Forrest tearfully thanked him, adding, "As God Almighty is my judge, I believe him an innocent man."

Adams was not persuaded. "That must be ascertained by his trial."[1]

"Facts Are Stubborn Things"

As the defense counsel for the British soldiers, Adams took the position that his clients had fired in self-defense. Upon hearing that John Adams was defending the soldiers, the citizens of Boston became enraged. His cousin Samuel Adams wrote newspaper articles designed to inflame public opinion against the redcoats. Silversmith Paul Revere created propaganda engravings that were widely published and depicted the massacre in a prejudicial way. In the drawings, Revere placed Captain Preston behind the row of soldiers, brandishing a sword and ordering the soldiers to fire, when, in fact, Captain Preston stood between the soldiers and colonists, hoping to prevent bloodshed.

While Adams prepared the case for trial, he courageously endured the wrath of the public. He was cursed and insulted in the streets wherever he went. Friends turned their backs on him. Longtime clients abandoned him. On several occasions, people threw rocks through the windows of his house. The people wanted vengeance against Captain Preston, his troops, and the lawyers who defended them.

The trial officially began on October 24, 1770. Though the trial would be conducted according to British law, it featured several uniquely American innovations. In this trial, guilt had to be established beyond a reasonable doubt. It was also the first trial in history in which jurors were sequestered to prevent their opinions from being tainted by outside influences.

Prosecutors Robert Treat Paine and Samuel Quincy argued that Captain Preston and his soldiers were part of an occupation army that treated Bostonians with scorn and malice. They claimed the soldiers fired with premeditated intent. Their motive? To settle grudges following brawls between Bostonians and British soldiers over the preceding three days.

When the prosecutors had stated their case, John Adams and Josiah Quincy Jr. (the younger brother of prosecutor Samuel Quincy) argued that Captain Preston and his troops were confronted with mob violence. They had fired their muskets in self-defense while fearing for their lives. Adams and Quincy Jr. proved that Captain Preston gave no order to fire, because the firing had been haphazard. Well-trained British soldiers would have fired in unison if Preston had given the order.

The trial lasted three days, and John Adams gave his summation on October 27. He reminded the jury of the natural right of all human beings to self-defense. He called the jury's attention to every flaw in the prosecutors' case. To the dismay and outrage of the people of Boston, the jury found Captain Preston not guilty.

The trial of Captain Preston's squad of eight soldiers began on November 27, 1770. Adams's central argument was that the soldiers feared for their lives and, like all human beings, had a legal right to self-defense. As a result, they were innocent of the capital crime of murder. Adams also argued the principle that guilt must be established beyond a reasonable doubt, saying, "It's of more importance to community that innocence should be protected than it is that guilt should be punished."

The most powerful (and often-quoted) statement Adams made to the jury was, "Facts are stubborn things; and whatever may be our wishes, our inclinations, or the dictates of our passion, they cannot alter the state of facts and evidence."[2]

The jury deliberated for just two and a half hours. The jurors found two soldiers guilty of manslaughter and freed the rest. The two convicted soldiers were sentenced to being branded on the thumb with the letter M for manslaughter.

The Conscience of a Nation

When John Adams first undertook the defense of Captain Preston and his men, the city of Boston treated him as a villain and a traitor. By the end of the second trial, his eloquent and principled defense of the British soldiers had won over the jury—and the people of Boston. His decision to defend the soldiers, which at first appeared to be the ruin of his career, elevated his public reputation. Years later, Adams concluded that his defense of the soldiers of the Boston Massacre was "one of the most gallant, generous, manly and disinterested actions of my whole life, and one of the best pieces of service I ever rendered my country."[3]

It's true. His performance in those trials helped secure the principles that still form the foundation of our legal system today. Had Adams not made a courageous decision when approached by James Forrest, the American legal system—and American society—might look very different today, and for the worse.

John Adams went on to serve alongside his cousin Samuel in the Continental Congress, and he organized the Committee of Five—a group that included Thomas Jefferson, Benjamin Franklin, Robert R. Livingston, Roger Sherman, and himself—to draft the Declaration of Independence. As a diplomat, Adams negotiated a treaty that enabled direct trade between the thirteen colonies and France, which proved to be an essential economic lifeline for America in its struggle for independence. At the end of the Revolutionary War, Adams served as chief negotiator of the Treaty of Paris, which ended the revolution and secured American independence from Great Britain.

In addition, Adams served as George Washington's vice president from 1789 to 1797 and was elected the second president of the United States in 1796. He served most of his single term as president at his Quincy, Massachusetts, home called Peacefield. He lost the election of 1800 to Thomas Jefferson, and the two men didn't speak or write to each other from 1801 to 1812, when Adams proposed a reconciliation.

On July 4, 1826, the fiftieth anniversary of the Declaration of Independence, John Adams lay dying at Peacefield. His last words were a tribute to his longtime friend (and sometimes opponent): "Thomas Jefferson survives." John Adams died peacefully on that Independence Day, unaware that Jefferson had passed away a few hours earlier that same day.

Few people of the revolutionary era had a greater impact on the new American nation than John Adams. No act of service was more honorable, courageous, principled, and self-sacrificing than his decision to defend nine British soldiers following the Boston Massacre. He earned the right to be called the Conscience of the Revolution.

★ LEADERSHIP LESSONS ★
from John Adams

The life of John Adams is rich in leadership insights for our lives today.

1. *Great leaders live to serve others.* Leaders must be servants. Many people think of a leader as "the boss," but an authentic leader is the servant of all. John Adams led by serving, by putting the interests of others ahead of his own. He had little to gain and everything to lose by defending the soldiers of the Boston Massacre, but he wanted to establish important American legal principles by giving those soldiers a vigorous defense.

2. *Great leaders have a vision for the future.* They can see over the horizon. They make change happen. John Adams was able to articulate a vision of a legal system founded on a presumption of innocence, in which the state had a burden to prove the defendants' guilt beyond a reasonable doubt. He envisioned such a legal system of the future—then he proceeded to build it, defendant by defendant, argument by argument. Today, we enjoy the liberty and legal protections Adams foresaw. We are the heirs of his vision.

3. *Great leaders demonstrate good character and integrity.* Adams was willing to put his reputation, his income, and his personal safety on the line to do what was right. He knew he would pay a price to defend the British soldiers—but he also knew it was the right thing to do. He endured the threats, the insults, the

defamatory press coverage, and the loss of business in order to keep his conscience clean.

In time, as he made his case in the courtroom, John Adams won over the naysayers and critics. His integrity persuaded the doubters and skeptics to follow him, to elect him, and to revere him as a leader of conscience and character.

Benjamin Franklin

The First American

On July 4, 1776, Congress ratified the Declaration of Independence. That day, Massachusetts delegate John Hancock spoke, stressing the need for unity among all the delegates. "We must be unanimous," he said. "We must all hang together."

Pennsylvania delegate Benjamin Franklin replied, "We must indeed all hang together—or, most assuredly, we shall all hang separately."[1] Ben Franklin earned the title the First American because of his passion for maintaining American unity and his insistence that Americans needed to "hang together."

One of the most important founding fathers of the United States, Franklin was an amazing polymath—a person with expertise spanning a variety of different subjects. Franklin was a writer, printer, innovator, scientist, inventor, musician, statesman, diplomat, and the organizer of the nation's first post office, first fire department, and first lending library.

Born in Boston in 1706, Franklin was the fifteenth child in a family of seventeen children. His father was a maker and seller of candles and soap. As a boy, Franklin worked in his father's shop. Though he disliked candle making and soap boiling, he worked hard and used his earnings to buy books to feed his reading addiction. When he wasn't working or reading, he would go to the river to swim, row, or sail. His boyhood friends looked up to him as a leader.

In his teens, Benjamin Franklin was apprenticed to his older brother James, who operated a print shop in Boston. An apprentice received no wages other than a small allowance for meals. Franklin skimped on food, often making a meal out of just a biscuit and a few raisins. This simple fare saved money for buying more books. He would even eat quickly to save time for reading.

James Franklin was a domineering boss who was sometimes physically violent. After enduring this harsh treatment for a time, Benjamin finally had enough and ran away at age seventeen. He sold some of his books to finance a boat voyage to New York. Unable to find work in New York, he set off on a sailboat to New Jersey. On his way to New Jersey, Benjamin's boat was nearly shipwrecked in a storm. Once he arrived, he walked from Perth Amboy to Burlington, New Jersey—a fifty-mile trek in a bone-chilling rainstorm. At Burlington, he boarded a boat (which the passengers had to row) that took him up the Delaware River to Philadelphia.

He apprenticed himself to a master printer in Philadelphia. His work was so outstanding that the governor of the Pennsylvania colony, Sir William Keith, took note of him. Governor Keith urged him to start his own print shop and offered to help him secure a start-up loan. Franklin sailed to England to select a printing press for his business—but the governor failed to follow through on his promise. Franklin found himself stranded in London without money or friends. He spent the next two years working in a London printing office.

In 1726, Franklin returned to Philadelphia. Four years later, in September 1730, he entered into a common-law marriage with Deborah Read, with whom he would later raise three children. He went deep into debt to set up a print shop in Philadelphia and worked long hours to make enough money to retire the debt early.

A Plan for Moral Perfection

Despite his financial struggles, Franklin was known for his cheerfulness and commitment to self-improvement. In his early twenties, he formulated what he called a "Plan for Attaining Moral Perfection." In his autobiography (published after his death), Franklin wrote,

> I wish'd to live without committing any fault at any time; I would conquer all that either natural inclination, custom, or company might lead me into. As I knew, or thought I knew, what was right and wrong, I did not see why I might not always do the one and avoid the other. But I soon found I had undertaken a task of more difficulty than I had imagined.

He listed thirteen essential virtues and committed himself to living them out each day.

1. TEMPERANCE.
   Eat not to dullness; drink not to elevation.
2. SILENCE.
   Speak not but what may benefit others or yourself; avoid trifling conversation.
3. ORDER.
   Let all your things have their places; let each part of your business have its time.
4. RESOLUTION.
   Resolve to perform what you ought; perform without fail what you resolve.

5. FRUGALITY.

   Make no expense but to do good to others or yourself;
   i.e., waste nothing.

6. INDUSTRY.

   Lose no time; be always employed in something useful;
   cut off all unnecessary actions.

7. SINCERITY.

   Use no hurtful deceit; think innocently and justly;
   and, if you speak, speak accordingly.

8. JUSTICE.

   Wrong none by doing injuries,
   or omitting the benefits that are your duty.

9. MODERATION.

   Avoid extremes; forbear resenting injuries
   so much as you think they deserve.

10. CLEANLINESS.

    Tolerate no uncleanliness in body, clothes, or habitation.

11. TRANQUILITY.

    Be not disturbed at trifles,
    or at accidents common or unavoidable.

12. CHASTITY.

13. HUMILITY.

    Imitate Jesus and Socrates.[2]

Franklin published some of his wisest observations in a reference book series called *Poor Richard's Almanack*. He began the series when he was twenty-six, and he published a new edition annually from 1733 to 1758. Some of the maxims from the *Almanack* are still repeated today: "Early to bed and early to rise makes a man healthy, wealthy, and wise." "He that lies down with dogs shall rise up with fleas." "No gains without pains." "He that cannot obey cannot command." "Little strokes fell great oaks." "Three may keep a secret, if two of them are dead." "Haste makes waste."[3]

Franklin also had a deep fascination with science and knowledge. He established a lending library in Philadelphia and founded an academy that eventually became the University of Pennsylvania. He invented the Franklin stove, a more efficient device for heating a room than the traditional open fireplace. Convinced that lightning was a form of electricity, he set out to prove it by sending a silken kite aloft in a thunderstorm. The kite was tethered by a silk string that would not conduct electricity. An iron key dangled from the kite. He sent the kite aloft for a while, then brought it down and placed his hand near the key. Bright sparks of electricity jumped from the key to his hand. When Franklin published his findings, he became world famous. Several European universities conferred an honorary doctorate on him.

Man of Achievement, Man of Humility

Long before the outbreak of the Revolutionary War, Franklin worried about disunity among the thirteen colonies. He believed that in unity there is strength. In 1754, he proposed the Plan of Union, which he hoped would unite the colonies in a pact of mutual defense against foreign enemies. The plan failed, but the debate over the plan helped push the leaders of the colonies to focus on the need for unity in the struggle against King George and British tyranny. The plan also helped raise Franklin's stature as a political theorist.

In early June 1776, John Adams selected Franklin to serve on the Committee of Five to draft the Declaration of Independence. After the Declaration was adopted on July 4, 1776, the Continental Congress sent Franklin to France to seek its help in the war against Great Britain. Tensions were high between France and Britain, so the French government was eager to see Britain become mired in a revolution across the ocean.

The people of France welcomed Franklin with parades and parties. With his sparkling wit and gracious manner, the seventy-year-old Franklin charmed the leaders and common people of France. He obtained France's pledge of much-needed trade and military support. He served as America's ambassador to France for a decade, returning to America in 1785. He died on April 17, 1790, at age eighty-four.

Though Franklin never held public office and never served in the military, he was one of America's greatest founders and statesmen. Any of his many accomplishments would have been sufficient to secure his enduring fame—his discoveries about electricity; his invention of the Franklin stove, the lightning rod, and bifocals; and on and on. Despite his fame and achievements, he remained a man of humility to the end of his life. Humility was, after all, the thirteenth virtue in his "Plan for Attaining Moral Perfection." He kept his focus on the goal he had set for himself: "Imitate Jesus and Socrates."

When he died, his grave was covered by a simple marble slab with the words, "Benjamin and Deborah Franklin, 1790." A plaque near the grave bears an epitaph he wrote in jest as a young man:

THE BODY OF
B. FRANKLIN,
PRINTER,
LIKE THE COVER OF AN OLD BOOK,
ITS CONTENTS TORN OUT,
AND STRIPT OF ITS LETTERING AND GILDING,
LIES HERE, FOOD FOR WORMS.
BUT THE WORK SHALL NOT BE WHOLLY LOST:
FOR IT WILL, AS HE BELIEV'D, APPEAR ONCE MORE,
IN A NEW & MORE PERFECT EDITION,
CORRECTED AND AMENDED
BY THE AUTHOR.[4]

This great founding father saw himself in the humblest of terms: B. Franklin, Printer. The man who patterned his life after Jesus and Socrates found greatness through humility.

★ LEADERSHIP LESSONS ★
from Benjamin Franklin

Here are four key lessons we can draw from the exemplary life of Benjamin Franklin.

1. *Great leaders are readers.* As a young man, Franklin sacrificed meals to feed his mind with books. President Harry S. Truman once wrote, "Readers of good books, particularly books of biography and history, are preparing themselves for leadership. Not all readers become leaders, but all leaders must be readers."[5]

Though Franklin's formal education was limited, he was one of the best read, best informed, most deeply perceptive men of his time. Why? Because he was a man of many books. His wide range of interests and his long reading list gave him a deep understanding of world history, philosophy, and the lives of great people. It also enriched his speech with a quick and biting wit. Franklin had no university diploma to hang on his wall, but he had a doctorate-level mind, thanks to the countless books he read.

To grow as a leader, invest at least an hour a day reading about great lives and important ideas. An hour a day averages out to a book per week. That's four books a month, fifty-two books per year, five hundred and twenty books per decade. Read five authoritative books on any subject and you'll be a world-class authority on that subject. Like Benjamin Franklin, you'll become a sparkling conversationalist and a leader of impact and influence.

2. *Great leaders grow strong through adversity.* Franklin faced adversity as an apprentice to his abusive older brother. That experience gave him the toughness to strike out on his own, seek his own fortune in New York and Philadelphia, walk the width of New Jersey in a rainstorm, and spend two years stranded in London. Franklin's response to adversity put steel in his spine and prepared him for the storms to come.

The way a leader responds to adversity sets the tone for an entire organization or nation. If a leader folds in tough times, how can the followers keep going? As a leader, use adversity as an opportunity to grow strong. Make sure you outlast any trial life throws at you.

3. *Great leaders are people of virtue, character, and humility.* At an early age, Franklin committed himself to a plan for moral perfection—focusing on thirteen character traits he deliberately built into his life: temperance (self-control), silence (avoiding useless or frivolous chatter), order, resolution (finish what you start), frugality (thriftiness and saving), industry (a strong work ethic), sincerity (honesty), justice (fairness and kindness to all), moderation (avoiding extremes), cleanliness, tranquility (an even emotional keel), chastity (moral purity), and humility.

What is character? It's the accumulation of personality traits we build into our lives over time. These traits determine our response to various situations, including stress, pressure, danger, success, and temptation. Are you honest at all times—or only when the truth is in your best interest? Are you loyal to friends and family or are you unfaithful? Are you self-sacrificing and self-effacing or self-serving? Are you diligent or lazy? Do you face danger with courage or cowardice?

I once heard General Norman Schwarzkopf give a speech in Orlando, Florida. One statement he made has stuck with me through the years: "Leadership consists of two vital ingredients: strategy and character. If you must do without one or the other, do without the strategy."

How do we become people of incorruptible character? We build character gradually, day by day, as we make courageous, honest, moral decisions. We accumulate good character traits by choosing the harder path, by accepting responsibility instead of shifting blame, by setting aside our own interests to serve others. Every selfless, moral choice we make helps to build our character.

4. *Great leaders are team builders.* Benjamin Franklin was committed to the unification of the thirteen colonies. Remember

he once said, "We must indeed all hang together or, most assuredly, we shall all hang separately." He was the first American because he was the first to see that he and his fellow colonists were not merely citizens of Massachusetts or Pennsylvania but citizens of a new nation, the United States of America—with the emphasis on *united*.

When people of different backgrounds, talents, skills, creeds, and beliefs come together to pursue a common goal, it's called *teamwork*. Industrialist Andrew Carnegie said, "Teamwork is the ability to work together toward a common vision, the ability to direct individual accomplishments toward organizational objectives. It is the fuel that allows common people to attain uncommon results."[6] And as author Ken Blanchard has often said (quoting the wisdom of a lady named Miss Weatherby), "None of us is as smart as all of us."[7]

To be a leader of excellence, be a team builder like Benjamin Franklin.

★ 5 ★

Sarah Bradlee Fulton

The Mother of the Boston Tea Party

Born in 1740, Sarah Bradlee was a leader in the Daughters of Liberty, a movement of ninety-two women from the thirteen colonies who supported the American Revolution. She helped put economic pressure on Great Britain by organizing a boycott against imported British goods. She married John Fulton in 1762, and they lived in Medford, Massachusetts, five miles north of Boston.

In late November 1773, the tea-laden cargo ship *Dartmouth* dropped anchor in Boston Harbor, throwing the colony of Massachusetts into crisis. Bostonians were ready to riot.

Then on December 16, just before the governor's deadline for unloading the *Dartmouth*'s cargo of tea, Samuel Adams called a town meeting and five thousand Bostonians showed up. A group of men left the meeting early and went to the home of Nathaniel Bradlee, the brother of Sarah Bradlee Fulton and a leader in the Patriot movement. There the men prepared to launch a powerful yet peaceful act of protest, the Boston Tea Party.

Sarah Bradlee Fulton proposed disguising the men as Mohawk Indians to prevent them from being recognized. In the kitchen of Nathaniel Bradlee's home, Sarah applied war paint to the faces of her brother, her husband, and their Tea Party companions.

According to some accounts, a British spy peeked in the window of the house that night, but the only sight he saw was Sarah and her mother-in-law working in the kitchen. The women were "moving about so quietly and naturally that he passed on, little dreaming what was really in progress there."[1]

At the agreed-upon hour, the Tea Partiers headed toward the wharf where three tea-filled British ships—*Dartmouth*, *Eleanor*, and *Beaver*—were anchored. Spectators lined the wharf as the men boarded the ships, struck open the tea chests, and filled Boston Harbor with tea.

"Shoot Away!"

On June 17, the British and American armies met on Breed's Hill and Bunker Hill, overlooking Boston Harbor. In the battle, the British forced 1,200 colonial troops to retreat, leaving the British in control of the peninsula. Though the British won the battle, they suffered a much higher casualty rate than the Americans. In fact, the Americans might have won had they not run out of ammunition. Even in retreat they proved they were the equal of highly trained British regulars.

At sunset after the battle on June 17, the American militiamen brought their wounded to Medford. There was a grassy green around Wade's Tavern on South Street that the Patriots turned into a field hospital. Because there were few surgeons to tend to the wounded, Sarah Bradlee Fulton organized a group of women into a team of nurses. As the Medford Historical Society records, "The steady nerves of Sarah Fulton made her a leader. One poor fellow had a bullet in his cheek, and she removed it; she almost forgot the circumstances until, years after, he came to thank her for her service."[2]

On one occasion during the British siege of Boston, Americans were moving a load of wood by oxcart, trying to get the desperately needed fuel to the beleaguered troops at Cambridge. The shipment was supposed to come through Medford, but Sarah learned that British soldiers had taken up positions on the road in order to seize the shipment.

Fearing the fuel would end up in enemy hands, Sarah sent her husband out to meet the shipment, purchase the load, and bring it to their Medford home, where they would keep the wood until it was safe to move it to Cambridge. John Fulton met the American wood haulers, purchased the wood, and was bringing it back to Medford when he encountered the British soldiers. John returned home empty-handed and told Sarah that the redcoats had seized the load.

Furious, Sarah put on a shawl and went out on foot. She found the troops on the road and ran in front of their oxen. She grasped the oxen by the horns and turned them around as the British threatened to shoot her.

She shouted defiantly, "Shoot away!"[3]

The British troops lowered their muskets and allowed her to take both the oxen and the wood. Had her husband tried such a bold act, the British soldiers would have certainly carried out their threat to shoot. But they didn't know how to respond to a bold, take-charge woman like Sarah. She succeeded where a man would have failed.

On another occasion, Major John Brooks of Medford wanted to send dispatches from General Washington to a unit operating behind enemy lines in Boston. Major Brooks approached John Fulton with the assignment because Fulton knew the city of Boston better than anyone. Sarah listened as Major Brooks explained the assignment to her husband—then she volunteered to go instead.

A man would attract suspicion, she said, but a woman would not be seen as a threat. Major Brooks accepted her offer.

Sarah walked four miles by night to the waterfront village of Charlestown. Finding a rowboat tethered to the dock, she got in and rowed across the Charles River to Boston. She found the address she'd been given and delivered the dispatches. Then she returned home, arriving at her own doorstep as dawn was breaking, exhausted but elated.

A few days later, General Washington himself stopped by the Fulton home in Medford and personally thanked Sarah. John Fulton served up a beverage from Sarah's new punch bowl and silver ladle. She would always remember that day as the proudest moment of her life. Years later, General Lafayette also came to visit the Fultons, and he sat in the "General Washington chair" and was served a beverage from the same punch bowl.

Sarah Bradlee Fulton lived to see the founding of the United States of America and the inauguration of several presidents. She died peacefully in her sleep in November 1835, just one month short of her ninety-fifth birthday.

★ LEADERSHIP LESSONS ★
from Sarah Bradlee Fulton

Sarah Bradlee Fulton was a Patriot and a leader who more than lived up to the title of the Mother of the Boston Tea Party. Some of the leadership lessons we learn from her life include:

1. *Great leaders are team builders and unifiers.* Sarah Bradlee Fulton was a leading member of the Daughters of Liberty, a group that used their influence to organize support for the boycott on British goods. She was also part of the team that planned and launched the Boston Tea Party. Leaders accomplish great goals through teams of people.

2. *Great leaders are creative thinkers.* Sarah Bradlee Fulton identified potential problems and found innovative solutions. If not for Sarah's idea of disguising the Tea Partiers as Mohawk Indians, the men might have been recognized, rounded up by the authorities, and put on trial for the destruction of the tea. The British might have been able to suppress or stamp out much of the patriotic fervor in Boston and throughout the thirteen colonies.

3. *Great leaders remain calm and think clearly in times of crisis.* Sarah Bradlee Fulton organized a team of nurses to tend the wounded after the Battle of Bunker Hill. She maintained a sense of calm efficiency in the midst of every crisis that came her way.

4. *Great leaders are courageously willing to sacrifice themselves for the cause.* While facing the muzzles of British guns, she said, "Shoot away!" and got the job done. And when General Washington needed to send dispatches into enemy-occupied Boston, Sarah summoned the physical courage to cross behind enemy lines in the dead of night. She did what needed to be done at great personal risk.

Leaders take counsel of their courage, not their fears. When others are paralyzed with indecision, leaders find creative, innovative solutions. When a crisis looms, leaders throw themselves into the battle and set an example for others to follow. The name of Sarah Bradlee Fulton may not be well-known, but we can be grateful for her example of bold leadership.

Patrick Henry

The Voice of the Revolution

F ew Americans know much about the life of Patrick Henry
beyond the famous line he spoke in a speech in 1775: "Give
me liberty or give me death!" But we owe an enormous debt to
Patrick Henry for many reasons—especially for his role in creating
the Bill of Rights, the first ten amendments to the Constitution,
which guarantee our liberties as citizens of the United States.

Patrick Henry was born on a farm in Hanover County, Virginia,
in 1736. He was homeschooled by his father, Colonel John Henry,
a Scottish-born, college-educated planter. In his early adulthood,
Patrick Henry failed as a farmer and a shopkeeper. He married
sixteen-year-old Sarah Shelton in 1754. The first of their six children, daughter Martha, was born almost a year later. While working as a bartender at his father-in-law's inn, Patrick taught himself
the law by reading books. At age twenty-four, he opened his law
practice in 1760.

In the courtroom and on the political stump, Henry built a reputation as a public speaker who could move hearts and minds with his reasoning and passionate persuasion. His speaking style was often likened to that of the evangelical revival preachers of his time.

Henry came to prominence for his role in a 1763 trial known as the Parson's Cause. The case involved a dispute over the wages paid to Anglican clergy in the colony of Virginia. Because the clergy served in the Church of England—the British state-sponsored church—their pay was set by the government. Virginia was a tobacco-producing colony, so the ministers were paid in tobacco, which they could then sell for income.

Back in 1748, Virginia's legislature passed a law that set the Anglican ministers' wages at sixteen thousand pounds of tobacco per year. In the late 1750s, however, Virginia suffered a drought that caused a tobacco shortage. The shortage pushed the price per pound of tobacco from two cents a pound to nearly six cents a pound. This meant the ministers' salary would be nearly tripled. To prevent this, the Virginia legislature enacted the Two Penny Act, which capped the ministers' wages at two pennies per pound of tobacco instead of the inflated price.

The clergy took their case to King George III of Britain. He agreed with the ministers and vetoed the Virginia law. He also urged the ministers to sue for back pay.

The Reverend James Maury sued on behalf of all Anglican ministers in Virginia—and, in effect, on behalf of the British Crown. So the ministers went to court. The presiding judge in the case was Patrick Henry's father, Colonel John Henry. At the time, Patrick was a young, unknown attorney in charge of representing the colony of Virginia, arguing in favor of the Two Penny Act. Over the course of the trial, he gained fame for arguing that the British Crown had no legal or moral right to meddle in colonial affairs. He argued that "a King, by disallowing Acts of this salutary nature, from being the father of his people, degenerated into a Tyrant, and forfeits all right to his subjects' obedience."[1]

Patrick Henry's argument was rebellious in tone and revolutionary in substance. And it was persuasive. Though the jury awarded Reverend Maury only one penny in damages, the verdict nullified the king's veto. It was a major victory for Patrick Henry.

The Parson's Cause brought the young lawyer to the attention of the thirteen colonies and elevated his stature in the growing groundswell for independence. The Parson's Cause was one of the first legal challenges to Britain's authority over the colonies—and a stepping-stone to the revolution.[2]

Liberty or Death

When Great Britain imposed the Stamp Act on the thirteen colonies in 1765, Americans viewed it as an oppressive and unacceptable precedent. Patrick Henry responded with a powerful speech before the Virginia legislature in which he proposed a series of resolutions in opposition to the Stamp Act. These resolutions were then published in the other colonies. Patrick Henry's ideas set forth the principle that taxes should be imposed only by a vote of elected representatives and that there should be no taxation without representation.

In March 1775, the Second Virginia Convention met at St. John's Episcopal Church in Richmond. The delegates were bitterly divided. Some urged reconciliation with the king. Others, such as Patrick Henry, believed that war with Britain was inevitable. George Washington, Thomas Jefferson, and five other future signers of the Declaration of Independence attended the convention.

Patrick Henry rose and spoke passionately and without notes, concluding with these words:

> Gentlemen may cry, peace, peace—but there is no peace. The war is actually begun! The next gale that sweeps from the north will

bring to our ears the clash of resounding arms! Our brethren are already in the field! Why stand we here idle? What is it that gentlemen wish? What would they have? Is life so dear, or peace so sweet, as to be purchased at the price of chains and slavery? Forbid it, Almighty God!—I know not what course others may take; but as for me, give me liberty or give me death![3]

That speech persuaded the leaders of Virginia to prepare for war.

Patrick Henry and the Bill of Rights

Patrick Henry's wife, Sarah Shelton Henry, started showing signs of acute mental illness after the birth of their sixth child, Edward (nicknamed Neddy). Sarah's doctor urged Henry to send her to the newly built Eastern State Hospital in Williamsburg, but Henry refused to commit his wife to an asylum. He kept her confined at home until her death in the spring of 1775.

Sarah's death left him a single parent to six children. But two years later, Patrick Henry married Dorothea Dandridge, and they went on to have eleven children together.

Patrick Henry served as Virginia's first governor from 1776 to 1779. He later served another term as governor from 1784 to 1786.

After America won its eight-year war for independence, there was a deep division between the Federalists, who wanted a strong central government, and the anti-Federalists like Patrick Henry, who feared a powerful central government. The anti-Federalists wanted the strongest power to reside with the states, and they opposed the ratification of the Constitution. The office of the president was not clearly defined at that point, and Henry was concerned that a strong presidency could devolve into a monarchy.

Though Henry and his anti-Federalist friends were unable to prevent the ratification of the Constitution, their influence helped shape the first ten amendments to the Constitution—the Bill of

Rights. These amendments protected the rights of individual citizens by limiting the powers of the federal government.

Patrick Henry died at age sixty-three on June 6, 1799. His plantation in southern Virginia is now a popular historic tourist destination, the Red Hill Patrick Henry National Memorial.

★ LEADERSHIP LESSONS ★
from Patrick Henry

Patrick Henry was the Voice of the Revolution. We can learn a lot about leadership when we look at his life.

1. *Great leaders are passionate.* Henry demonstrated a contagious and fiery passion for liberty—a passion that inspired and motivated his listeners. His words resonated in the hearts of his Virginia compatriots, including some who went on to fight in the war and sign the Declaration of Independence. He laid out the stark choice before his fellow Virginians: Liberty or death? Neutrality was not an option. In times of crisis, leaders must take a stand.

2. *Great leaders are always great communicators.* They speak with authority and clarity, with boldness and conviction. A speaker who seems timid or hesitant undermines his or her own authority. As the Bible tells us, "If the trumpet does not sound a clear call, who will get ready for battle?"[4]

No one who heard Patrick Henry speak could remain on the fence. His words forced every hearer to take a side. He sounded an unmistakable call to arms, saying in effect, "Liberty or death—who's with me?" With that clear call to action, the Voice of the Revolution summoned the people to battle and helped give birth to a new nation.

Paul Revere

The Midnight Rider

Listen, my children, and you shall hear
Of the midnight ride of Paul Revere,
On the eighteenth of April, in Seventy-Five:
Hardly a man is now alive
Who remembers that famous day and year.

He said to his friend, "If the British march
By land or sea from the town to-night,
Hang a lantern aloft in the belfry-arch
Of the North-Church-tower, as a signal-light,—
One if by land, and two if by sea;
And I on the opposite shore will be,
Ready to ride and spread the alarm
Through every Middlesex village and farm,
For the country-folk to be up and to arm."

So begins "Paul Revere's Ride," a poem by Henry Wadsworth Longfellow that was first published in the *Atlantic Monthly* in January 1861. Much of what we know—or think we know—about Paul Revere's ride comes from Longfellow's poem, which was written eighty-five years after the event. Revere's role in the Revolutionary War was scarcely discussed until Longfellow made him a household name.

Though that poem was memorized by generations of school-children, it does not provide a completely accurate portrayal of the events that took place on the night of April 18, 1775. The poem speaks of one rider, Paul Revere, but Revere was joined in his mission by two other Patriots, William Dawes and Samuel Prescott. Also Revere never reached the town of Concord, as the poem claims, because he was detained by British troops.

But the truth about Paul Revere's ride is every bit as exciting as the legend enshrined in Longfellow's poem. Who was this man who gained fame as a symbol and a leader of American resistance to British tyranny?

Paul Revere was born on New Year's Day 1735. By profession, he was a silversmith and an engraver, though he later became an ironsmith and coppersmith. He learned his trade from his father, an immigrant French Huguenot metalsmith named Apollos Rivoire who Americanized his surname to Revere.

Paul Revere was a devout Christian who never missed a Sunday service at Boston's New Brick Church. He and all his children were baptized there. He was a believer, a leader, and a Patriot. As a young man, he adapted his family coat of arms by adding a Latin motto that expressed a typical American attitude: *Pugna pro patria*, "Fight for your country."

In his early career as a Boston silversmith, Paul Revere was well-known and prosperous, but his business suffered disastrously after Great Britain imposed the Stamp Act of 1765. The act caused a depression of the Massachusetts economy. Like many Boston merchants and artisans of the time, Paul Revere was cash-strapped and went into debt to keep his business afloat. The same year the

Stamp Act was enacted, creditors sued Revere and tried to seize his property over a debt of ten pounds sterling. He settled the matter out of court and managed to keep his business going in a troubled economy.[1]

Revere earned extra money by learning dentistry from a surgeon who roomed in the home of a friend. His skill at crafting delicate engravings in metal served him well as a dentist. He carved false teeth from animal teeth or imported walrus ivory—though he never made wooden dentures for George Washington, as some legends claim. One client of Paul Revere's dental practice was Dr. Joseph Warren, a patriotic resistance leader who would later play a key role in Revere's midnight ride.

Paul Revere, Secret Agent

When the British Parliament continued to levy additional taxes on an already-struggling American economy, Paul Revere responded by joining a new movement founded by Samuel Adams, the Sons of Liberty. Revere made a special silver medal, engraved with an image of Boston's Liberty Tree and the words "Sons of Liberty." Members of the group used the medal and a series of passwords to identify themselves to one another.

Revere also created engravings, which he printed and sold, with a theme of resistance to oppression. Those pictures included depictions of the arrival of British occupation troops in 1768 and the Boston Massacre in 1770. As an act of defiance to the British Crown, he boldly affixed his name to the Boston Massacre print.

When the tea-laden merchant ship *Dartmouth* docked in Boston Harbor, Paul Revere and Dr. Joseph Warren organized a citizens' watch at the wharf to keep the ship from being unloaded. Revere took turns with the other Patriots standing guard. He was not only involved in keeping the British-taxed goods on their ships but he was also one of the leaders and planners of the Boston Tea Party.

The Central Intelligence Agency credits Paul Revere as one of America's first and foremost spies because of his work with a revolutionary group called the Mechanics. The CIA's website tells us,

> The first Patriot intelligence network on record was a secret group in Boston known as the "Mechanics." Their activities in the 10 years before the outbreak of the Revolution in April 1775 included some of the earliest uses in America of warning, surveillance, and intelligence collection. One of the Mechanics was Boston silversmith Paul Revere.[2]

There were more than thirty members of the Mechanics. They held regular meetings at the Green Dragon Tavern and kept tabs on the activities of British soldiers, the strength of their fortifications, and the movement of weapons, munitions, and supplies. The Mechanics managed to gather valuable intelligence—especially on the night before the Battles of Lexington and Concord—even though one of their members, Dr. Benjamin Church, was a traitor.

On one occasion, in December 1774, the Mechanics received word that British troops would be landing at Portsmouth, New Hampshire. Paul Revere rode from Boston to Portsmouth to alert the locals of the impending British landing. His ride became known as the Portsmouth Alarm. Unfortunately, as it turned out, the report was false.

But Paul Revere and the Portsmouth Alarm did move the local Patriots to action. The Portsmouth Patriots raided Fort William and Mary (held by just six British soldiers) and seized its store of gunpowder. The action prompted colonials in Rhode Island and Connecticut to stage similar raids and deprive British forces of munitions.[3]

The Midnight Rider

Paul Revere worked for the Boston Committee of Correspondence and the Massachusetts Committee of Safety. These committees worked together and acted as a shadow government, organizing opposition to British oppression. Revere served the committees as an express rider, taking messages and documents wherever they were needed throughout Massachusetts and neighboring colonies.

The evening of April 18, 1775, Dr. Joseph Warren gave Paul Revere a special assignment. Revere was to ride to Lexington, Massachusetts, and deliver the news that British troops were on the march. Warren told Revere that the troops intended to arrest Samuel Adams and John Hancock, who were houseguests of Parson Jonas Clarke, pastor of the Church of Christ of Lexington. Some historians question whether the British were actually planning to arrest Adams and Hancock, but regardless of their full intentions, the British were certainly planning to capture military supplies in Lexington and Concord.

Revere had instructed a friend (most likely Robert Newman, the sexton of Christ Church in Boston, now known as the Old North Church) to place two lanterns in the church steeple. In case Revere was stopped by the British, the lanterns would serve as a backup signal, indicating that the British planned to row across the Charles River to Cambridge instead of taking the long way around through Boston Neck.

After putting on an overcoat and boots, Paul Revere went to the waterfront on Boston's North End. Friends rowed him through the darkness past a British warship to Charlestown. There he met with a militia colonel, William Conant, and members of the Sons of Liberty. Revere gave them the latest news of events in Boston, and they confirmed seeing the lanterns in the church steeple. They also warned that British officers in Charlestown might try to stop him.

A Charlestown shopkeeper, John Larkin, lent Revere a mare named Brown Beauty, and Revere set off on his mission around eleven o'clock. He was nearly captured on the outskirts of Charlestown, so he altered his route and rode through Medford instead. There he gave the word to the captain of the Medford militia, Isaac Hall. He stopped at Patriot houses along the road to Lexington, spreading the news that the British Army regulars were on the march.

One of the most widely misunderstood aspects of Paul Revere's ride is the notion that he shouted, "The British are coming!" as he rode through the countryside. This is a false depiction of true events. In fact, Revere rode in silence, being careful not to attract the attention of small units of British troops who were scattered throughout the Massachusetts countryside. When he reached a Patriot home, he would deliver the message—then continue discreetly on his way.

Paul Revere reached the Lexington home of Parson Jonas Clarke sometime after midnight. Once in Lexington, he had little need for stealth, so he shouted to the occupants of the house. A militiaman who stood guard told him to stop making so much noise.

"Noise!" Revere said. "You'll have noise enough before long. The regulars are coming out!"[4]

John Hancock heard Paul Revere's raucous arrival and invited the midnight rider inside. As Revere was having food and drink in preparation for the ride to Concord, Revere's friend William Dawes arrived. He had seen the lanterns in the church steeple and carried the word to the minutemen, just as Revere had.

Dawes and Revere set off together for Concord. Their mission was to make sure that the munitions were relocated to a place where the British couldn't find them. They had not gone far outside of Lexington when they were stopped by Dr. Samuel Prescott, a fellow Patriot. The three rode together until a squad of British soldiers intercepted them. Prescott and Dawes made their escape— but Revere was not so fortunate.

The British soldiers forced him into a pasture. Revere later recalled, "Just as I reached it [the pasture], out started six officers, seized my bridle, put their pistols to my breast, ordered me to dismount, which I did. . . . One of them . . . clapped his pistol to my head, and said he was going to ask me some questions, and if I did not tell the truth, he would blow my brains out."[5] The British questioned him—then they confiscated Brown Beauty and left him standing in the road.

Feeling grateful he wasn't shot or captured, Revere turned his steps toward Lexington. As he walked on that morning of April 19, 1775, Lexington militiamen filed out of Buckman Tavern, which sat next to the town green. They formed two rows and waited. As the morning sun peeked through the trees, the British troops, commanded by Major James Pitcairn, marched into town at double-quick time. Pitcairn, on horseback, assembled his troops in two ranks at the south end of Lexington Green. Then he rode up in front of his troops and demanded that the militiamen disarm themselves and disperse.

There were only forty militiamen lined up on the Green, though another thirty militiamen were scattered in the street or in buildings along the Green. They faced hundreds of well-trained British regulars. The militia leader, Captain John Parker, knew his men didn't have a fighting chance. He ordered his men to disperse—but not to let go of their weapons. As the militiamen started to withdraw from the Green, a gun was fired. Whether it was an accident or a deliberate act is unknown—and no one knows if it was a British soldier or an American militiaman who fired the shot.

But it was "the shot heard 'round the world"—the first shot of the Revolutionary War, the shot that drove freedom-loving Americans to beat their plowshares into swords.

The British soldiers fired on the Americans from a range of forty yards. Pitcairn shouted at his men to cease firing but was unable to regain control. The militiamen scattered but some returned fire. When the British had spent their ammunition, they made a bayonet charge and forced the Americans off the Green. The British troops then broke ranks and were chasing militiamen into their homes when Pitcairn's superior, Lieutenant Colonel Frances Smith, arrived with more troops.

Paul Revere arrived to see Pitcairn and Smith trying to reestablish order over the British troops. He saw the bodies of the dead and dying on the Green. The British formed into columns, fired a victory volley in the air, shouted "Huzzah!" three times, and continued marching on their way toward Concord.

Eight militiamen were killed, while the British regulars suffered one minor wound. It was a crushing blow for Paul Revere to see the dead and wounded on Lexington Green. His warning had given Samuel Adams and John Hancock time to get away—but eight brave Patriots died in the opening battle of America's war for independence. Unfortunately, many more brave Patriots would soon be added to that number.

★ LEADERSHIP LESSONS ★
from Paul Revere

Paul Revere had no way of knowing, much less controlling, his impact on future generations. He didn't make his midnight ride to gain fame. But eighty-five years after the event and more than forty years after his death, this unsung hero of the revolution became a symbol of liberty, thanks to his publicist, Henry Wadsworth Longfellow. The life of Paul Revere teaches us several key leadership lessons.

1. *Great leaders are effective communicators.* You and I may never have a poet sing the praises of our leadership efforts, but we can expand our influence through communication—through public speaking, through writing, and through projecting our influence

on social media. We can give interviews on broadcast, online, and print media. We can talk about our values, our leadership goals, our team's accomplishments, and our passions.

2. *Great leaders can come from any background and rise to become a revolutionary leader.* A leader is someone who takes the initiative to lead. Many Revolutionary War–era leaders came from aristocratic backgrounds and had wealth and education. Paul Revere was not an aristocrat but an artisan—or, as he called himself, a "mechanic." Today he would call himself a "blue-collar worker."

He joined the independence movement not because he had great wealth to contribute but because the taxation policies of the British Crown deprived him of his livelihood. He craved the freedom to simply make a living on his own terms, and that's why he became a revolutionary leader. You don't need wealth, education, or status to be a great leader. You just need to be passionate about your cause and be willing to serve.

3. *Great leaders are nimble, innovative, and creative.* When the British government closed the door on his livelihood as a silversmith, Paul Revere probably asked himself where else his skills could be put to good use. The answer: dentistry. He added a new line of work to his panoply of skills, reinvented himself as a dentist, and saved himself from bankruptcy. If high taxes or a bad economy or a global pandemic have you down, don't accept defeat. Lead like Paul Revere. Be innovative, reinvent yourself, and keep moving forward.

Paul Revere demonstrated his nimble, creative leadership by having a backup plan in case he was unable to get through to Lexington. He arranged for the two lamps in the Christ Church steeple—and two other riders, William Dawes and Samuel Prescott, also made the ride to Lexington. Though Revere was stopped on his way to Concord, Dawes and Prescott continued the mission. They warned the Concord militiamen of the approaching British regulars.

This stunning American success might never have happened if Paul Revere had not had the foresight to have a backup plan in place: two lamps in the church steeple and two extra riders to make sure the alarm reached Concord.

4. *Great leaders build a reputation of dependability.* Historian Richard Frothingham referred to the midnight rider as "the steady, vigorous, sensible, and persevering Paul Revere."[6] This intensely dedicated man served the revolution in countless ways, including spying, casting cannons, and printing currency.

But perhaps his most valuable service was as an express rider, carrying messages and dispatches wherever they were urgently needed. He knew the lay of the land and was skilled at avoiding British patrols. He could get the job done when no one else could. Paul Revere was a leader and a problem solver. We owe a debt of gratitude to the midnight rider for our American way of life.

Parson Jonas Clarke

The Chaplain of the Revolution

The destination of Paul Revere's midnight ride was the home of Parson Jonas Clarke, pastor of the Church of Christ of Lexington and host to John Hancock and Samuel Adams. Parson Clarke was a firebrand preacher who loved the words of St. Paul: "Where the Spirit of the Lord is, there is freedom."[1]

The night Paul Revere arrived at Parson Clarke's home, Hancock and Adams asked him if the men of Lexington would fight. Parson Clarke replied, "I have trained them for this very hour; they would fight and, if need be, die, too, under the shadow of the house of God."[2]

At sunrise on April 19, 1775, when British soldiers entered Lexington, they were met by militiamen and villagers, almost all of them parishioners of Jonas Clarke. After the battle, Clarke tended to the dying and wounded, saying through tears, "From this day will be dated the liberty of the world."[3]

Shoot Only in Self-Defense

Reverend Jonas Clarke was ordained as a pastor of the Church of Christ in 1755, three years after his graduation from Harvard College. He married Lucy Bowes, a cousin of John Hancock, and he farmed sixty acres in addition to his duties as the shepherd of his Christian flock. Clarke was a community leader as much as a spiritual leader, and he regularly denounced tyranny and extolled liberty from his pulpit. He offered his church as a meeting place for revolutionary leaders—and he offered his home as a place of refuge.

The Lexington militia was headed by Captain John Parker, one of Clarke's deacons. When word went out that the British regulars were coming, Parker assembled his militiamen on the lawn of the church and had them load their guns. When it was time to assemble on Lexington Green, the signal was given by the staccato beat of drums and the pealing of church bells, rung by Clarke.

The militiamen demonstrated Christian restraint. They had been taught by Clarke to shoot only in self-defense. They held their fire until they heard the shot from an unidentified gun. Historian George Bancroft records what happened next.

> In the disparity of numbers, the common was a field of murder, not of battle; Parker, therefore, ordered his men to disperse. Then, and not till then, did a few of them, on their own impulse, return the British fire. These random shots of fugitives or dying men did no harm, except that Pitcairn's horse was perhaps grazed, and a private of the tenth light infantry was touched slightly in the leg.[4]

Bancroft also records the fate of eight militiamen—most of them parishioners of Jonas Clarke's church—beginning with another man named Jonas.

> Jonas Parker, the strongest and best wrestler in Lexington, had promised never to run from British troops; and he kept his vow. A

wound brought him on his knees. Having discharged his gun, he was preparing to load it again, when as sound a heart as ever throbbed for freedom was stilled by a bayonet, and he lay on the post which he took at the morning's drum beat. So fell Isaac Muzzey, and so died the aged Robert Munroe, the same who in 1758 had been an ensign at Louisburg. Jonathan Harrington, junior, was struck in front of his own house on the north of the common. His wife was at the window as he fell. With the blood gushing from his breast, he rose in her sight, tottered, fell again, then crawled on hands and knees towards his dwelling; she ran to meet him, but only reached him as he expired on their threshold. Caleb Harrington, who had gone into the meeting-house for powder, was shot as he came out. Samuel Hadley and John Brown were pursued, and killed after they had left the green. Asahel Porter, of Woburn, who had been taken prisoner by the British on the march, endeavoring to escape, was shot within a few rods of the common.[5]

Eight God-fearing Patriots poured out their blood on Lexington Green for the cause of liberty. Their bravery and dedication to their cause altered the course of human events. In a sermon delivered on April 19, 1776, one year after the Battle of Lexington, Parson Clarke told his congregation,

> Next to the acknowledgement of the existence of a Deity, there is no one principle of greater importance in religion, than . . . to realize that God is Governor among the nations, that his government is wise and just, and that all our times and changes are in his hands. . . . Yea, however dark and mysterious the ways of providence may appear; yet nothing shall overwhelm the mind, or destroy the trust and hope of those that realize the government of heaven.[6]

He added that, in the Bible, nations such as Egypt and Edom, which had enslaved and slaughtered the people of Israel, had been left desolate by God's judgment. Clarke urged his congregation to courageously oppose "the enemies and oppressors" in the confidence that "God himself will plead their cause and both cleanse and avenge their innocent blood."[7]

★ LEADERSHIP LESSONS ★
from Parson Jonas Clarke

As a man who dedicated his life to the church, Parson Jonas Clarke also played a part in the revolutionary fight for the independence of his country. We can learn a lot from his example.

1. *Great leaders are prepared for anything.* Parson Clarke saw the gathering storm clouds of war, and he prepared his people for battle. Week after week, he preached a message of encouragement and determination in the face of oppression and opposition. And when the British regulars arrived with muskets loaded and bayonets fixed, the people he led were ready for the fight. "I have trained them for this very hour," he said.

2. *Great leaders are mentors and encouragers who train their followers for battle.* Who is your congregation? Who are the people you are leading into battle? How are you preparing them and encouraging them to be strong in battle? How are you training them to respond when the hour comes?

When the time came for war, Parson Jonas Clarke himself rang the church bell, summoning the militiamen to battle. But the church bell was more than an alarm. It was the bell of freedom, announcing that the liberty of the world was at hand.

★ 9 ★

Jonathan Trumbull

The Prophet of the Revolution

In March 1775, Jonathan Trumbull Sr., the governor of the colony of Connecticut, asked his people to join him in a day of fasting and prayer. He set April 19, 1775, as the date for this day of prayer and fasting. In his proclamation, he asked the people to pray that

> God would graciously pour out his Holy Spirit on us, to bring us to a thorough Repentance and effectual Reformation that our iniquities may not be our ruin; that He would restore, preserve, and secure the Liberties of this and all the other British American colonies, and make the Land a mountain of Holiness and Habitation of Righteousness forever.[1]

Governor Trumbull could not have known that the day he selected for his people to fast and pray would be the very day the Revolutionary War would begin. The same day the people of Connecticut devoted themselves to prayer and fasting, war erupted in

Massachusetts. The timing of the day of prayer and the timing of the battle could not have been a mere coincidence. The hand of God was involved in these events.

Trumbull was born in 1710 in Lebanon, Connecticut, which was little more than a wide spot in a forest footpath. He graduated from Harvard College in 1727 and earned a master's in theology under the Reverend Solomon Williams. Trumbull planned to become a congregationalist minister. He was also highly trained in mathematics, astronomy, and Hebrew. He was invited to serve as a minister in Colchester, Connecticut, but after his brother was lost at sea, Trumbull returned home to operate the family farming business.

King George III appointed Trumbull deputy governor of the colony of Connecticut in 1766, and he became governor when the previous governor, William Pitkin, died in 1769. Trumbull is the only person who has served as the chief executive of both a British colony and an American state.

A Blistering Rebuke

For about five years prior to the Battles of Lexington and Concord, Governor Trumbull became increasingly troubled by Great Britain's growing oppression of the colonies. Laws passed by the Connecticut legislature had to be sent to Great Britain, where they were often nullified by a whim of King George or a vote of Parliament. Meanwhile, Britain imposed laws and taxes on the colonies without listening to the voice of the people who lived in them. Though Governor Trumbull had long hoped for a peaceful relationship with "the Mother-Country," he could see that British oppression was becoming increasingly intolerable—most acutely in neighboring Massachusetts but also in Connecticut.[2]

In May 1774—before the war had started—British General Thomas Gage stepped onto Long Wharf in Boston, determined to put an end to the protests in the city. The top British military officer in Massachusetts, Gage had also been appointed the new royal governor of the colony. Within a week of arriving, he sent a message to Governor Trumbull in Connecticut, expressing his readiness to cooperate with Trumbull "for the good of his Majesty's service."[3] Eleven months later, Governor Trumbull learned of the slaughter in the Battles of Lexington and Concord. He opened his family store in Lebanon and gave free food and supplies to the militiamen who were going to Massachusetts to fight the redcoats. He even convened a Council of Safety and held meetings in the store. Through a network of Patriot spies, Trumbull collected a great deal of useful information about British troop strength.

Soon after the Battles of Lexington and Concord, General Gage sent Governor Trumbull a request for assistance. In an act of courageous defiance, Trumbull sent Gage a blistering rebuke and pointedly refused to send assistance. In a letter to the British general, he made it clear that his sympathies were with the Patriots, not the British Crown.

> By the best intelligence that we have yet been able to obtain, the late transaction [the bloodshed in Lexington and Concord] was a most unprovoked attack upon the lives and property of his Majesty's subjects; and it is represented to us that such outrages have been committed as would disgrace even barbarians. . . .
>
> It is feared, therefore, . . . that you have it in command and intention to ravage and desolate the country. If this is not the case, permit us to ask, why have these outrages been committed? Why is the town of Boston now shut up? To what end are all the hostile preparations that are daily making? And why do we continually hear of fresh destinations of troops to this country? The people of this Colony, you may rely upon it, abhor the idea of taking up arms against the troops of their sovereign, and dread nothing so much as the horrors of a civil war. But, sir, at the same time, we beg leave to assure your Excellency, that as they apprehend themselves justified

by the principle of self defence, they are most firmly resolved to defend their rights and privileges to the last extremity.[4]

On July 6, 1775, Governor Trumbull commissioned Nathan Hale of Coventry, Connecticut, as a first lieutenant in the Seventh Regiment of the Continental Army. Hale later volunteered for an intelligence-gathering mission. He was captured in New York City by the British and hanged on September 22, 1776, at the age of twenty-one. His last words were, "I only regret that I have but one life to lose for my country."

Though Governor Trumbull had been appointed by King George III, the outbreak of war between Great Britain and the thirteen colonies meant that the king had no way to remove him from office. Trumbull had won the admiration of the people of Connecticut, and he became a leader in the revolution.

He was a trusted friend to General George Washington throughout the Revolutionary War. He served as paymaster general of the Continental Army for a time, and Washington knew he could always turn to "Brother Jonathan" in a moment of need. When Trumbull resigned from that position, he had his back pay distributed to needy soldiers. After his death in 1785, General Washington wrote to Trumbull's son, Jonathan Trumbull Jr.

> You know too well the sincere respect and regard I entertain for your venerable father's public and private character. . . . *A long and well-spent life in the service of his country places Governor Trumbull among the first of patriots.* In the social duties he yielded to no one; and his lamp, from the common course of nature, being nearly extinguished, worn down with age and cares, yet retaining his mental faculties in perfection, are blessings which rarely attend advanced life. All these combined, have secured to his memory unusual respect and love here, and, no doubt, unmeasurable happiness hereafter.[5]

Governor Jonathan Trumbull died in Lebanon, Connecticut, where he was born, and he was buried at the Old Cemetery. He was the Prophet of the Revolution, the godly man who called his followers to a day of prayer and fasting—on the day the Revolutionary War began.

✦ LEADERSHIP LESSONS ✦
from Jonathan Trumbull

Jonathan Trumbull was a great leader because of his commitment to God and his spiritual sensitivity. He knew that war was coming and that the people of the colonies needed to prepare themselves through prayer and fasting. And somehow, God led him to choose April 19, 1775—the date of the outbreak of war—as the day he asked his fellow Americans to join him in prayer and fasting.

The example of Governor Trumbull teaches us an all-important principle:

Great leaders—whether in politics, business, or any other field—should also be moral and spiritual leaders. No matter what our leadership arena may be, we should always strive to exemplify excellent moral character and a deep spiritual commitment.

Governor Trumbull must have been an extraordinarily committed Christian. He originally planned to join the clergy and serve as a pastor—a worthy leadership goal—but God had other plans for Trumbull's life. His education in theology and science prepared his mind for a life in leadership.

Trumbull reminds me of the prophet Ezra, of whom the Bible says, "Ezra had devoted himself to the study and observance of the Law of the Lord, and to teaching its decrees and laws in Israel."[6] Trumbull's experience operating the family farming business prepared him to be a trusted friend and advisor to General George Washington. He is a role model of the biblical principle found in the book of Proverbs.

> Do you see someone skilled in their work?
>> They will serve before kings;
>> they will not serve before officials of low rank.[7]

Trumbull knew he needed a flawless character and an unblemished reputation. He lived out the leadership admonition of the apostle Paul: "Now the overseer is to be above reproach, faithful to his wife, temperate, self-controlled, respectable, hospitable, able to teach."[8]

And in his sharp rebuke to General Gage, he demonstrated a fearlessness that can come only from a deep faith in God. He exemplified the admonition of God to the prophet Isaiah.

> So do not fear, for I am with you;
>> do not be dismayed, for I am your God.
> I will strengthen you and help you;
>> I will uphold you with my righteous right hand.[9]

Great leaders are usually people of great faith, great moral character, and great devotion to God. Such a leader was Jonathan Trumbull, the Prophet of the Revolution.

★ 10 ★

Samuel Whittemore

The Oldest Soldier of the Revolution

One of the most underreported stories of the colonial era is the account of Samuel Whittemore, the oldest known soldier to fight in the American Revolutionary War. Born in 1696, Whittemore was seventy-eight and a veteran soldier when America's war for independence began.

While in his late forties, he had enlisted in Colonel Jeremiah Moulton's Third Massachusetts Regiment. During the capture of the French fortress at Louisbourg, Nova Scotia, in 1745, Private Whittemore captured a sword from a French officer. Almost twenty years later, while in his sixties, he led British troops against the Odawa War Chief Pontiac in the Great Lakes region. He acquired a pair of dueling pistols in that battle.

In peacetime, Whittemore was a farmer and a public servant. In 1768, the town of Cambridge, Massachusetts, chose him as a delegate to the Massachusetts Committee of Convention, a group that actively resisted Britain's taxation policies and the quartering of British troops in colonial homes. And in 1772, the same townspeople elected seventy-six-year-old Whittemore to the local Committee of Correspondence, which opposed the tea tax and other oppressive acts.

On April 19, 1775, American militiamen harassed British forces as they retreated from Lexington and Concord. Samuel Whittemore was farming in his field when he saw a brigade of British Grenadiers of the 47th Regiment of Foot moving down the road. Whittemore positioned himself behind a stone wall, loaded his musket, and fired his single-shot musket, killing one soldier. Then he drew his dueling pistols—the same pistols he had won in Pontiac's War—and felled two more British soldiers.

The Grenadiers spotted Whittemore and realized he was out of ammunition. As they approached him from the road, he drew his sword—the same sword he had won in the siege at Louisbourg—and ran straight at his attackers. One of the Grenadiers fired, shooting Whittemore in the face. As he fell, the other Grenadiers bayonetted him and beat him in the head with musket butts. They left him in a crimson pool, bleeding from six bayonet wounds and one bullet wound.

When a team of American militiamen came upon Whittemore, he was on his knees, attempting to load his musket. The militiamen persuaded him to go to Dr. Cotton Tufts in Medford. The doctor treated Whittemore but was sure he wouldn't last the night.

Samuel Whittemore recovered, however, and went on to live eighteen more years, dying of natural causes at the age of ninety-six.[1]

★ LEADERSHIP LESSONS ★
from Samuel Whittemore

Who is too old to lead?

Samuel Whittemore joined the military as a private while in his late forties and was still soldiering on in his late seventies.

In peacetime, the townspeople who knew him chose the septua-
genarian Whittemore as their representative in two important
political committees. They knew he had the character, the physical stamina, and the intellect to represent their interests, even at
his advanced age.

The lesson of Samuel Whittemore's life is this:

Great leaders are not limited by age. Prepare yourself. Read
books on leadership. Accept challenging leadership roles. Find
ways to put your leadership talent to good use. Don't let anyone
intimidate you or tell you your best days are behind you.

If you feel you are too old or too young to make a difference, remember Samuel Whittemore, crouched behind his stone wall, taking potshots at the British Grenadiers. Remember how he wielded
his sword and charged at his attackers. Remember how, even after
they bloodied him and left him for dead, he was reloading and
ready to get back in the fight.

Courage. Preparation. Perseverance. That's the stuff of leadership at any age.

★ 11 ★

Henry Knox

The Gold Standard of American Know-How

The Fort Knox army post in Kentucky is the site of the United States Bullion Depository, which stores the government's gold reserves. It is named for Henry Knox, a Boston-born Patriot who made a solid-gold contribution to the Revolutionary War.[1]

Henry Knox was born in 1750. His father was a financially troubled ship captain who died when Henry was nine years old. As the oldest son, Henry left school to support his family, earning a living as a bookstore clerk in Boston. The owner of the shop became a father figure to young Henry, and he allowed the boy to take any of the store's books home to read. Through these books, Henry taught himself French, mathematics, and philosophy.

On March 5, 1770, Knox witnessed the slaughter of five townspeople in the Boston Massacre. He testified at the trials of the British soldiers, saying he had urged the redcoats to return to their quarters in the hope of averting tragedy.

Just a year later, twenty-one-year-old Henry Knox opened his own shop, the London Book Store. It became a favorite haunt of British military officers and aristocratic men and ladies. The store also supported his avid reading habit. Henry's favorite subjects were history and military science, and he had a special interest in artillery.

Knox later joined the Sons of Liberty in their resistance to British policies. In 1772, he cofounded the Boston Grenadier Corps, a militia group committed to resisting British tyranny. He served as second-in-command.

During the Boston Tea Party, twenty-three-year-old Henry Knox served guard duty on the wharf to prevent the unloading of the tea. He may have been one of the participants in the bold protest action against the British taxes.

In June 1774, Henry married Lucy Flucker over the objections of her Loyalist father. Thomas Flucker was the royal secretary of the province of Massachusetts Bay. He knew of Knox's involvement with the Sons of Liberty and often debated politics with him. Flucker even tried to persuade Knox to join the British Army, thinking the discipline of British military life might knock some sense into him. But Henry and Lucy were deeply devoted to each other, and Lucy's father was no match for their love.

When the Revolutionary War broke out in 1775, Knox knew he could no longer remain in British-occupied Boston. He and Lucy closed up the bookstore and escaped from the city as American forces were laying siege to Boston. Knox joined the militia forces that besieged the city. In his absence, Loyalist gangs broke into his bookshop and looted his stock.

On May 10, three weeks after the Battles of Lexington and Concord, the Green Mountain Boys, led by Ethan Allen and Colonel Benedict Arnold, captured Fort Ticonderoga, a large British-held fort on the La Chute River in northern New York. The capture of Fort Ticonderoga was the first American offensive to seize control of British-held territory. The Green Mountain Boys captured nearby Fort Crown Point the next day. Both forts were well stocked with cannons and other armaments and would soon play a major role in the leadership career of Henry Knox.

Upon joining the militia, Knox placed his engineering knowledge at the service of General Artemas Ward. Since the Knoxes had lost their home in Boston, a Watertown Patriot named John Cook invited Lucy Knox and other Boston refugees into his home. Lucy often visited her husband on the battlefield, where he helped train artillerymen. During the Siege of Boston, the Americans were encouraged when a company arrived from Rhode Island, bringing twelve heavy cannons, both eighteen- and twenty-four-pounders (a reference to the eighteen- and twenty-four-pound cannonballs they fired).

Meanwhile, the British troops occupying Boston were eyeing Charlestown, which was held by American Patriots. On June 12, General Thomas Gage, commander of British forces, sent soldiers to Charlestown with a demand that the rebels lay down their arms and swear allegiance to King George. All who refused would be considered traitors. The Patriots scorned Gage's demand.

Tested at the Battle of Bunker Hill

The Patriots knew that Gage's demand to lay down their weapons was a prelude to an attack. The American commanders, led by General Ward, decided to seize Charlestown's two unoccupied strategic heights, Bunker Hill and Breed's Hill. Ward sent Henry Knox to reconnoiter the two hills. On June 16, at Knox's direction, 1,200 American militiamen quietly moved onto Breed's Hill and began building a line of fortifications.

The next morning, British generals in Boston gathered to plan an assault against the Patriots' fortifications. General Thomas Gage placed General William Howe in command of the operation.

Henry Knox was inspecting the unfinished fortifications on the afternoon of the seventeenth when he saw twenty-eight British barges crossing the river from Boston to Charlestown. Those barges carried three thousand British troops. The assault had begun.

Knox ordered the artillery pieces be brought up, and he began directing fire against the onrushing British troops. Meanwhile, on the Charles River, cannons opened fire from four British battleships—the *Somerset*, the *Cerberis*, the *Glasglow*, and the *Lively*, along with other smaller vessels. The precision-aimed British guns rained destruction on Breed's Hill, to Henry Knox's dismay. Yet the Patriots tenaciously held their position atop Breed's Hill.

Much of the British cannon fire fell on Charlestown. British soldiers passing through the town torched the wooden buildings and set the town aflame.

The British land assault approached Breed's Hill in two wings, with General Howe personally leading the right wing of the charge. The bright-red British uniforms painted an unmistakable target on the grassy slope. The combination of American musket fire and Knox's expertly aimed artillery blasted through the British troops, felling hundreds. The survivors retreated, scrambling over the dead and wounded.

After a few minutes' rest, the British troops launched a second charge up the hill. Again, they were forced back by cannon and musket fire. The British commanders realized, however, that the American gunfire was weaker this time. The rebels were running out of gunpowder.

The redcoats fixed bayonets and prepared for a third charge up Breed's Hill. The Americans had no bayonets. Without gunpowder, they'd be defenseless before the British soldiers.

From the top of the hill, the Americans saw the redcoats charging. The Patriots met the British at the hilltop and the two armies fought with lunging blades, musket butts, clubs, fists, and chokeholds. When the Americans finally retreated, the British were too exhausted to give chase.

Though the battle took place almost entirely on Breed's Hill, it became known as the Battle of Bunker Hill. The Americans suffered 115 dead, 305 wounded, and 30 captured. The British suffered 226 dead (including 19 officers) and 828 wounded (including 62 officers). They suffered a total of 1,054 casualties. The British had taken Breed's Hill—but they had paid dearly for it.

The day after the battle, General Howe wrote to his brother, a naval admiral, "I freely confess to you, when I look to the consequences of it, in the loss of so many brave officers, I do it with horror. The success is too dearly bought."[2]

Many historians believe the Battle of Bunker Hill cast a lifelong shadow over General Howe. Though the British general exhibited extreme courage on the battlefield, his confidence was shattered by the carnage he witnessed. American historian Thomas Fleming wrote,

> Many of his contemporaries blamed Howe's failure to win the Revolutionary War on his experience at Bunker Hill. . . . Again and again, in the two years he was commander in chief, he failed to follow up smashing victories, or he let Washington slip away because he could not bring himself to send his men against the Americans when they entrenched themselves behind even the flimsiest walls.[3]

British historian George Otto Trevelyan wrote that, for General Howe, the losses in the Battle of Bunker Hill "exercised a permanent and most potent influence. . . . That joyous confidence, and that eagerness to bring matters to an immediate issue, which had been his most valuable military endowments, thenceforward were apt to fail him at the very moment when they were especially wanted."[4]

Much of the credit for Howe's loss of command ability goes to Henry Knox for his expert use of artillery at the Battle of Bunker

Hill. Knox's cannons denied the British an easy victory, raised the cost of war to unacceptable heights, and left General Howe shaken and tentative for the rest of his career.

Knox's "Noble Train of Artillery"

On July 2, 1775—two weeks after the Battle of Bunker Hill—General George Washington arrived at the siege emplacements near Boston. Just a few weeks earlier, on June 14, the Second Continental Congress had appointed him commander in chief of the Continental Army. Washington was impressed by Knox's effective and scientific use of artillery. The forty-three-year-old Washington and the twenty-five-year-old Knox soon formed a bond of friendship that would outlast the war.

Though Knox lacked formal military training and had no commission in the army, fellow Bostonian John Adams persuaded the Second Continental Congress to grant Knox a commission as a colonel.

Meanwhile, the capture of Fort Ticonderoga and Fort Crown Point in May gave Henry Knox an idea. He went to General Washington with a plan. The forts in New York bristled with cannons. Meanwhile, the siege fortifications around Boston were lacking in cannons. If Knox could go to Forts Ticonderoga and Crown Point and bring back those cannons, the Americans could break the stalemate and force the British out of Boston.

It was a daring, almost foolhardy plan. Knox would have to haul the cannons on wooden sleds across the length of Massachusetts, from west to east, across roughly three hundred miles of backwoods trails, untracked forests, and swamps, plus two rivers topped with treacherous ice. Though planning began in July 1775, the expedition could not start for Fort Ticonderoga until late fall. The rivers in their path would be unfordable until they had frozen over in winter.

Washington put Henry Knox in charge, even though Knox's commission had not yet arrived from Congress. General Washington placed great faith in the twenty-five-year-old bookseller whose knowledge of artillery science came entirely from books. Washington authorized the expenditure of a thousand British pounds to finance the venture.

On November 17 of that year, Henry Knox and his troops left Washington's camp for New York City to obtain supplies. Then they traveled overland to Fort Ticonderoga, arriving on December 5. Knox and his troops took possession of one brass twenty-four-pounder cannon, thirteen eighteen-pounder cannons, and ten twelve-pounder cannons, as well as two howitzers, fourteen mortars, and an assortment of smaller cannons. Their haul amounted to an estimated 119,000 pounds of artillery: some brass, some iron. Knox didn't take any ammunition from Ticonderoga, reasoning (correctly) that the Massachusetts militiamen could seize ammunition and gunpowder from British stores.

On December 6, Knox and his men moved the artillery by boat on Lake Champlain, then overland a short distance to nearby Lake George, where the guns were loaded on three boats. One of the boats was overloaded and sank in shallow water, but they managed to refloat it and get all the guns safely across the lake. Reaching the far end of Lake George, Knox was pleased to see snow falling—a good omen for taking the guns overland by sled.

Knox dubbed his gun caravan a "Noble Train of Artillery." In a letter to General Washington on December 17, 1775, he spoke of constructing forty-two sleds and securing "eighty yoke of Oxen to drag them as far as Springfield."[5] That was his plan—but he was forced to resort to plan B.

Most history books record that Henry Knox obtained eighty yoke of oxen (that is, 160 individual oxen, yoked in pairs) to haul the sleds. But historian Derek W. Beck, author of *Igniting the American Revolution: 1773–1775*, carefully examined the original text of Henry Knox's diary and made a surprising discovery. All the books, paintings, and encyclopedia entries that depict the sleds being pulled by oxen are wrong. Knox's diary shows that when he tried to buy the oxen, greedy livestock dealers tried to gouge him on the price, so Knox bought horses instead. Apparently, most historians only checked the letter Knox wrote to Washington on December 17. They failed to check Knox's own diary as Derek W. Beck did.[6]

In his letter, Knox told Washington he expected to reach Boston in sixteen or seventeen days. He was overoptimistic, to say the least. The journey from Ticonderoga to Boston would ultimately take more than six weeks. One reason is that the river crossings were more treacherous than expected. Several times, heavy cannons broke through the river ice. Miraculously Knox's troops were able to recover the guns from the near-freezing water each time.

Reaching Albany, New York, Knox's caravan turned east and began climbing the Berkshires into Massachusetts. The uphill journey was far more difficult than Knox expected. On January 11, 1776, Knox located two teams of oxen for the steepest, hardest part of the journey. So yes, Henry Knox did employ four oxen to give his "Noble Train of Artillery" some extra oomph—but far fewer than the 160 oxen he told General Washington he planned to use.

Finally, on January 27, Henry Knox strode into Washington's siege camp overlooking Boston. Villanova historian Victor Brooks wrote that Henry Knox's achievement was "one of the most stupendous feats of logistics in the entire War of Independence."[7] Upon arriving, Knox learned that his commission as a colonel in the Continental Army had arrived at camp shortly after he had left. He had carried out the entire mission thinking he was still a civilian bookseller when in fact he was a full-fledged army officer.

In March of that year, Washington seized Dorchester Heights, with its commanding view of Boston Harbor. General Washington put Colonel Knox in charge of placing the artillery pieces around the Heights. The artillery that Henry Knox hauled from Fort Ticonderoga enabled the American forces to break the stalemate in the Siege of Boston.

General Howe saw that the Americans had gained an overwhelming strategic advantage and were in a position to rain artillery fire on British positions throughout Boston. On March 17, Howe ordered his troops onto their ships, and they retreated to Halifax, Nova Scotia. The British occupation of Boston had ended.

Always at Washington's Side

Henry Knox went on to shore up the defenses of Rhode Island and Connecticut, as well as New York City. He also directed the Christmas night 1776 operation when Washington crossed the Delaware to surprise the Hessian troops at Trenton, New Jersey. (The Hessians were German auxiliary troops, primarily from the German states of Hesse-Kassel and Hesse-Hanau, who served under the command of the British Army.)

General Washington would not have been able to capture Trenton if not for the genius of Henry Knox. On that Christmas night, a blizzard blanketed the region with snow. The Delaware River was choked with jagged ice floes. At Henry Knox's direction, Washington's troops loaded soldiers, horses, and eighteen pieces of artillery onto boats. Historian David Hackett Fischer observed, "Washington had given command of the crossing to Knox. . . . Many men remembered his [Knox's] 'deep bass voice,' which they could hear above the roar of the nor'easter. Several commanders of the army believed that the crossing would have failed 'but for the stentorian lungs of Colonel Knox.'"[8]

Not a single man or artillery piece was lost in the crossing. The troops arrived in New Jersey soaked to the skin but in good spirits because they trusted their leaders. Knox directed the unloading of the artillery pieces from the boats and coordinated the movement of the guns up the snow-clad hills toward Trenton. Washington later reflected that Knox's "genius supplied the deficit of means."[9] As a result of that leadership, Washington's forces caught the Hessian defenders of Trenton by surprise. For his role in the successful mission, Knox was promoted to brigadier general.

(Another soldier who crossed the Delaware and fought at Trenton alongside Washington was future president James Monroe. Though the surprise attack against the Hessians succeeded, Monroe was shot and nearly died due to a severed artery. Washington cited Monroe for heroism and promoted him to captain.)

Henry Knox was also with Washington at Valley Forge, Pennsylvania. There he designed fortifications to protect the American encampment from attack. He also placed the artillery pieces that enabled the Americans to force the surrender of General Charles Cornwallis at Yorktown, Virginia, on October 19, 1781. For his actions in that decisive victory, Knox was promoted to major general in March 1782, effective retroactively to November 1781.[10]

Henry Knox was appointed commander of West Point in 1782. (West Point was a military post at that time; the military academy was not established there until 1802.) He remained at West Point until the end of the war. Knox was at Fraunces Tavern in New York City on December 4, 1783, standing at General Washington's side, as the commander in chief delivered his farewell address to his officers. That same month, he succeeded Washington as commander in chief of the army. He later served as secretary of war in Washington's presidential cabinet.[11]

After retiring from public service, Major General Henry Knox settled his family on an estate near Thomaston, Maine. He operated several businesses from 1796 until his death in 1806. He left behind a solid-gold legacy of good old American know-how. Whenever General Washington needed a job done, he could always count on the Boston bookseller Henry Knox.

★ LEADERSHIP LESSONS ★
from Henry Knox

Who is too young to lead?

In the previous chapter, we learned about the oldest soldier of the revolution, Samuel Whittemore, who demonstrated amazing physical courage, determination, commitment, and perseverance as a leader. In the life of Henry Knox, we see a young leader who, at just twenty-five years old, demonstrated a level of ingenuity, persistence, and strategic intelligence far beyond his years.

Though he is not the most famous revolutionary leader, Henry Knox's contributions to the war effort were vital, even decisive. If Knox had not brought the Ticonderoga cannons to Boston, could Washington have broken the stalemate in the Siege of Boston? Not likely. And what of Knox's indispensable role in directing the artillery at Trenton and Yorktown? Clearly Henry Knox was a key figure in the revolution, though few Americans know his name. What are the leadership lessons we learn from his life?

1. *Great leaders can step up at any age.* Older leaders need to inspire young people with the confidence to take great risks and believe in their ability to influence the world for good. And young people should study the example of Henry Knox and take on leadership challenges at school, at church, and in their communities. Young leader, if a leadership opportunity comes your way, accept it. If you fail, learn the lessons of that experience, correct your mistakes, and keep going. You are never too young to gain leadership experience.

2. *Great leaders can come from anywhere.* A young bookseller with scarcely any formal education became a major general. Henry Knox went to work to support his family at age nine. No one would have imagined that such a boy would become one of the greatest military engineers of the Revolutionary War. No matter what your background is, you can be a leader.

3. *Great leaders have mentors*. Henry Knox came from a deprived background. He was the son of a poor sea captain who died young and left his family destitute. But nine-year-old Henry found employment with a kindhearted, fatherly bookseller who mentored him in the bookselling trade. Later, Henry found other mentors, including General George Washington himself.

4. *Great leaders are readers*. We've seen this principle in the life of Benjamin Franklin, who sacrificed meals to feed his mind with books. What Henry Knox lacked in formal education, he more than made up for through reading. He became a bookseller to support his reading habit and learned military and artillery science from books. His eager mind was so chock-full of knowledge that he became Washington's go-to guy for military know-how.

5. *Great leaders are innovators*. Henry Knox's brilliant idea of bringing cannons by sled from Fort Ticonderoga to Boston is one of the best examples of outside-the-box thinking in military history. Knox's career, and especially his so-called Noble Train of Artillery, should be studied not just in courses on military history but also in courses on business leadership, sports management, government, and artistic creativity.

Picture British General William Howe stepping out of his Boston headquarters one morning, looking to the south, and finding Dorchester Heights bristling with cannon muzzles. History records that, upon discovering the guns on the Heights, Howe briefly considered an assault to take out the guns—but a blizzard convinced him it was time for a strategic withdrawal. Henry Knox's artillery had punished Howe's troops once at Breed's Hill. General Howe had no wish to repeat the experience on Dorchester Heights. Thanks to whiz kid Henry Knox, Washington took Boston without firing a shot.

6. *Great leaders encourage the creativity of their people*. Washington welcomed Knox's innovative approach to artillery science. The general knew that some of the best information, insights,

and ideas come from the people on the front lines. This is an important principle whether you are leading an army, a corporation, or a religious organization. Encourage your people to be observant, creative, and boldly innovative. Instead of punishing failure, urge your people to think of it as feedback that points the way to future success. Praise initiative. Empower people to take risks. Consider every off-the-wall idea. Washington listened to Henry Knox's guns-of-Ticonderoga idea—and Boston fell into his hands like overripe fruit.

7. *Great leaders judge people by their achievements, not their résumé.* Many people who look great on paper tend to fold in real-life crises. And sometimes the most impressive people you hire have completely unimpressive résumés. Henry Knox had one of the worst résumés imaginable. His formal education ended at age nine. His only military training, if you could call it that, was a brief stint spent drilling with the Boston Grenadier Corps. He had no army commission and no combat experience prior to the Siege of Boston. But after the siege, Henry Knox went on to amass an impressive record—and that was all the "résumé" Washington needed to see.

When you face your next "impossible" leadership challenge, draw inspiration and strength from Henry Knox—the gold standard in leadership know-how.

★ 12 ★

Esther de Berdt Reed

The Crowdfunder of the Revolution

Esther de Berdt was born in London in 1746. The daughter of a wealthy English businessman who traded with the American colonies, Esther was widely admired as a fair-haired beauty. She was a lover of books and widely read on many subjects, including political events on both sides of the Atlantic. Appalled at Britain's mistreatment of its American cousins, she became convinced that the Americans had a moral right to be independent.

In 1763, at age seventeen, Esther met Joseph Reed, a graduate student from Philadelphia who had come to London to study law. They fell in love and wanted to marry, but Esther's father wouldn't consent to it. Though he was fond of Reed, Mr. de Berdt didn't want his daughter to move away from him to America. Reed returned to the colonies with plans to eventually emigrate to England and marry Esther. They maintained their romance through letters carried between continents by oceangoing ships.

Joseph Reed returned to England in 1769. Upon his arrival, he learned that Esther's father had died. Mr. de Berdt suffered serious financial setbacks before his death, and Reed helped to settle the family's finances—a chore that required the de Berdt estate to file for bankruptcy. Esther and Joseph were married on May 31, 1770, at Saint Luke's Church in London. In October, the young couple, along with Esther's mother, set sail for America in order to settle in Philadelphia.

In a November 1774 letter to her brother Dennis in England, Esther wrote, "The people of New England . . . are prepared for the worst event, and they have such ideas of their injured liberty, and so much enthusiasm in the cause, that I do not think that any power on earth could take it from them but with their lives."[1]

Esther's husband was elected to the First Continental Congress, which met in Philadelphia in the fall of 1774. During that time, the Reeds entertained many delegates to the Congress, including John Adams and George Washington.

The Battles of Lexington and Concord erupted in Massachusetts on April 19, 1775. After the outbreak of war, Esther wrote to her brother,

> You see every person willing to sacrifice his private interest in this glorious contest. Virtue, honor, unanimity, bravery—all conspire to carry it on, and sure it has at least a chance to be victorious. I believe it *will*, at last, whatever difficulties and discouragements it may meet with at first.[2]

Raising Money, Sewing Shirts

In 1775, Joseph Reed joined General George Washington's staff as an aide. Joseph was appointed adjutant general of the army in 1776, then returned to Washington's side in 1777. He remained with Washington during the devastating winter of 1777 in Valley Forge.

Esther stayed home in Philadelphia and raised their six children. She had an escape plan ready in case British troops came to Philadelphia. And she was forced to use that plan several times, escaping to Norristown, Pennsylvania, on one occasion; Burlington, New Jersey, on another; and a country farmhouse near Evesham Township, New Jersey, on yet another. While Esther and the children took refuge in New Jersey, one of her daughters contracted smallpox and died. In late 1778, her husband was elected governor of Pennsylvania, and the family was reunited in Philadelphia.

In 1780, the Revolutionary War was in its fifth year. General Washington's forces were exhausted and demoralized due to shortages of food and supplies, lack of pay, and ragged clothing and shoes. Seeing the need, Esther de Berdt Reed, as the first lady of Pennsylvania, published a pamphlet, "Sentiments of an American Woman," in June 1780. The pamphlet explained how women could show their patriotism by working and donating money to support the troops. Female volunteers took the pamphlets from door to door, reaching every home in the city.

The effort inspired thousands more women to join the Ladies Association of Philadelphia, which Esther founded to raise funds for the Continental Army. She also enlisted the support of some of the most influential women in the colonies, including Benjamin Franklin's daughter, Sarah Franklin Bache.

The Ladies Association raised more than seven thousand dollars for the soldiers—the equivalent of more than two hundred thousand dollars today. General Washington suggested that the funds be used to purchase linen to clothe the troops, so Esther organized volunteer seamstresses to make shirts and she encouraged the women to sew their names into the clothing as a show of personal support for the troops. (Sending notes of support and encouragement to the troops is an American tradition that continues to this day.) The Ladies Association made more than 2,200 shirts for soldiers in the Continental Army.[3]

Chapters of the Ladies Association soon formed in New Jersey, Maryland, and Virginia. Esther's leadership resulted in more fundraising and more clothing for the troops.

Tragically, Esther de Berdt Reed would not live to see the victory she worked so hard for. In early September 1780, she contracted dysentery during an epidemic that swept through Philadelphia. She died on September 18, 1780, just one month before her thirty-fourth birthday. Her husband, her mother, and her children—the oldest just ten years old—were at her side as she died. Her body was buried in the Arch Street Presbyterian Cemetery in Philadelphia, but her courageous, self-sacrificing spirit and her leadership example live on.

⋆ LEADERSHIP LESSONS ⋆
from Esther de Berdt Reed

In that prefeminist era of the eighteenth century, Esther de Berdt Reed transcended the traditional role of women to become a leader in the Revolutionary War. She didn't take up a musket on the front lines, but General Washington invited her to play a vital leadership role nonetheless.

When she organized the Ladies Association of Philadelphia, Esther created opportunities for American women to help secure the blessings of liberty for themselves, their children, and generations yet unborn. There were many times when the American war effort hung by a thread—and Esther de Berdt Reed's loyalty and hard work made a huge difference. We can learn from her efforts.

Great leaders are innovators. They see a need and they invent new ways to meet it. That's what Esther de Berdt Reed did—and that's why we acknowledge her as one of the great leaders of the Revolutionary War. Her name may not be as famous as

Washington, Jefferson, Adams, or Hamilton, but she led hundreds of women who sacrificed time, money, and energy for liberty.

Crowdfunding is the practice of financing worthy projects by collecting small donations from vast numbers of people. If Esther de Berdt Reed were alive today, you might find her on the internet, using a crowdfunding website to raise money for veterans or needy children. That's why I consider Esther de Berdt Reed the Crowdfunder of the Revolution. She is a leadership model for us all.

★ 13 ★

Thomas Paine

The Popularizer of the Revolution

Thomas Paine was an Englishman who loved America.

Born in 1737 in the village of Thetford in county Norfolk, England, Thomas Paine spent the first thirty-seven years of his life in his home country. He tried a number of professions, from making corsets to teaching school to selling tobacco to privateering (practicing piracy against foreign ships under a commission from the government)—all without notable success. He was married twice—to Mary Lambert in 1759 (she died in childbirth along with the baby) and Elizabeth Ollive in 1771 (they separated three years later).

He also worked for a while as an excise officer (a tax inspector and collector) in several English towns, including Lewes in Sussex. There he became known for his political debates and speeches in the tavern at the White Hart Hotel. A plaque at the hotel reads:

THOMAS PAINE 1737–1809
HERE EXPOUNDED HIS REVOLUTIONARY POLITICS.
THIS INN IS REGARDED AS A CRADLE OF

AMERICAN INDEPENDENCE WHICH HE HELPED
TO FOUND WITH PEN AND SWORD.[1]

In 1774, George Lewis Scott—the commissioner of the excise
(and Paine's boss in His Majesty's Customs and Excise Office)—
introduced Paine to Benjamin Franklin in London. Franklin was
on an extended diplomatic stay in Great Britain, and the two men
bonded over their shared revolutionary views. Franklin suggested
that Paine, who had recently separated from his wife, emigrate to
colonial America. Franklin gave Paine a letter of recommendation
to help him find work and suggested he look first in Philadelphia.

In October of that year, Paine boarded a ship for America. Unfortunately, the ship's water stores were tainted, and five passengers
died of typhoid fever. Paine became desperately ill. On November 30, Paine's ship sailed up the Delaware River and docked in
Philadelphia. Benjamin Franklin's personal physician met Paine
at the ship and found him too sick to walk. The doctor had Paine
carried ashore on a stretcher and, over the next six weeks, helped
Paine regain his health.

In March 1775, Paine landed a job as managing editor of the
Pennsylvania Journal. By this time, America's relationship with
Mother England had reached a critical stage. After the Seven Years'
War—an incredibly costly global conflict—Great Britain was neck-
deep in debt. Parliament inflicted an array of oppressive taxes on
the colonies—and Americans murmured about revolution. Just
five months after Paine had arrived in America, and one month
after he began his new job at the *Journal*, the Battles of Lexington
and Concord took place. America and Great Britain were at war.

The Power of *Common Sense*

In January 1776, Benjamin Franklin printed the first hundred copies of Thomas Paine's "pamphlet" *Common Sense*. (The word
pamphlet is misleading; it was a short book, fifty pages and 21,000

words in length.) The author was originally identified only as "An Englishman," though Paine's name was added to the book for the second edition.

Common Sense sets forth a strong case for American independence and is filled with passion, irony, and watertight reasoning such as this:

> There is something very absurd, in supposing a continent to be perpetually governed by an island. In no instance hath nature made the satellite larger than its primary planet, and as England and America, with respect to each other, reverses the common order of nature, it is evident they belong to different systems: England to Europe, America to itself.

Common Sense also contains flights of powerful, inspiring rhetoric that filled Paine's readers with a sense that America *can and must* become free.

> We have it in our power to begin the world over again. A situation, similar to the present, hath not happened since the days of Noah until now. The birthday of a new world is at hand, and a race of men, perhaps as numerous as all Europe contains, are to receive their portion of freedom from the event of a few months.[2]

Paine gave eloquent voice to American outrage over oppression and American longing for independence. When *Common Sense* was published, there were roughly two million people living in the thirteen colonies. In its first three months of publication, the book sold one hundred thousand copies—an unheard-of success. That's one copy sold for every thirty Americans at that time. It's the equivalent of selling more than ten million copies in America today. By the end of the Revolutionary War, more than five hundred thousand copies of *Common Sense* were sold in its various editions, spreading a passion for revolution throughout the colonies. The book's influence was expanded by public readings in town halls and even in taverns.

One reason for the book's vast influence was that Paine renounced his copyright and royalties so that anyone with a printing press was permitted to publish *Common Sense*. The result, according to historian David McCullough, was that the book was "more widely read than anything yet published in America."[3]

Whereas most political and philosophical writings of the era were written in a bland and scholarly style, Paine wrote in a passionate, direct, popular style. He wrote for the masses, and the masses eagerly bought *Common Sense* and spread its revolutionary ideas. While many colonists still considered themselves Loyalists and hoped for a reduction in taxes and a peaceful accord with Mother England, *Common Sense* made a devastating case for America's destiny as a free and independent nation. Historian Gordon S. Wood wrote, "*Common Sense* was the most incendiary and popular pamphlet of the entire Revolutionary era; it went through twenty-five editions in 1776 alone."[4]

Common Sense was praised and championed by none other than General George Washington, who had become a friend and ally of Thomas Paine. Washington viewed the book as a turning point in the American Revolution, writing that "the sound doctrine and unanswerable reasoning contained in the pamphlet *Common Sense*" would enable Americans "to decide upon the propriety of separation."[5] Years later, Paine would dedicate another book, *Rights of Man*, to Washington.

But in time their friendship would be dashed to pieces.

Rights of Man and the Reign of Terror

During the revolution, Thomas Paine served as personal assistant to General Nathanael Greene. During his travels with the Continental Army, Paine wrote a series of sixteen "crisis papers." The first, *The Crisis Number I*, was published on December 19, 1776. It began with the famous lines:

These are the times that try men's souls. The summer soldier and the sunshine patriot will, in this crisis, shrink from the service of their country; but he that stands it now, deserves the love and thanks of man and woman. Tyranny, like hell, is not easily conquered; yet we have this consolation with us, that the harder the conflict, the more glorious the triumph. What we obtain too cheap, we esteem too lightly: it is dearness only that gives every thing its value. Heaven knows how to put a proper price upon its goods; and it would be strange indeed if so celestial an article as FREEDOM should not be highly rated.[6]

The first crisis paper appeared after Washington's forces suffered a series of morale-bruising setbacks. It was published just six days before the general intended to make the perilous crossing of the Delaware and the attack on Trenton. Washington had copies of Paine's crisis paper distributed to his officers, with orders that they read the paper to the troops. The reading of Paine's words inspired the Continental Army to fight on with a renewed sense of mission and purpose.

The war formally ended on September 3, 1783. British rule in America came to an end. Thomas Paine had helped popularize the cause of freedom—but by the end of the war, his contribution was all but forgotten.

In April 1787, Paine sailed back to England. He had taken an interest in the French Revolution, which sought to overthrow the monarchy and aristocracy of France. Paine's longtime friend Benjamin Franklin gave him letters of introduction so that Paine could make contacts in London and Paris.

The publication of his 1791 book *Rights of Man* set off a firestorm of controversy—and the book sold nearly a million copies. *Rights of Man* supported revolution in France and attacked the aristocratic class. Great Britain banned the book and indicted Paine for seditious libel—writings intended to incite insurrection against the established order. By this time, Paine had moved to Paris, so Britain tried Paine *in absentia*. The court found him guilty and condemned him to death, but because Paine was in Paris, he could not be punished.

Because of Paine's support for the French Revolution, the provisional French government granted him honorary citizenship. But Paine didn't realize what a snake pit of bloodthirsty rogues the revolutionary movement had become. He served for a while on the Constitutional Committee for the French Republic as it hammered out a Constitution for postmonarchy France. When Paine argued that the deposed French king, Louis XVI, should be exiled instead of guillotined, he found himself in hot water with the power-mad radicals, the Montagnards, and their cult leader, Maximilien Robespierre, architect of the Reign of Terror.

French revolutionary authorities arrested Paine on December 28, 1793. But Paine claimed immunity from arrest as a citizen of the United States (the US was an ally of revolutionary France). The French, however, insisted he was a citizen of France's enemy, England. Paine narrowly escaped being executed because of a chance accident.

While Paine was in prison, the jailer was ordered to make a chalk mark on Paine's cell door, indicating that the prisoner was to be removed and beheaded. The jailer made the chalk mark on the inside of the door instead of the outside (the door was left open while Paine received a visitor), and Paine missed his appointment with the executioner.

He spent nearly a year in prison, from December 1793 to November 1794. Finally, the American minister to France, future president James Monroe, obtained his release. By that time, the mass insanity of the Reign of Terror had largely subsided, and Paine felt free to resume his life as a citizen of France.

Just two years later, Thomas Paine damaged his reputation by publishing an open letter to George Washington—a long and scathing attack on the character of America's first president. Paine felt that Washington should have come to his defense when he was facing execution in France.

Thomas Jefferson invited Paine to return to America in 1802. Unfortunately, his arrival was greeted with either indifference or outright hostility. If Paine was remembered at all, he was thought of as a rabble-rouser—not a hero.

Final Years

Thomas Paine lived out his final years in obscurity. On the morning of June 8, 1809, he died at age seventy-two in an apartment in Greenwich Village, New York. He had arranged to be buried in a cemetery in New Rochelle, but the Quakers who operated the cemetery would not allow Paine, an unbeliever, to be interred there. His remains were later buried under a walnut tree on a piece of rural property he owned. Only six people attended his funeral.

His obituary notice in the *New York Citizen* was cruelly dismissive: "He had lived long, did some good and much harm."[7] But the truth is that Thomas Paine led, and he did much good. Through the power of his words, he helped lead a nation to independence.

★ LEADERSHIP LESSONS ★
from Thomas Paine

According to the *US History Online Textbook* at USHistory.org, at the start of the Revolutionary War, about 20 percent of American colonists were Loyalists who supported Mother England and King George. Another small percentage were Patriots, who were committed to the fight for independence. The vast majority of American colonists were "fence-sitters,"[8] the undecideds who may not have liked Britain's oppressive policies but were not convinced that war was the answer.

Regardless of public opinion, the war had begun. The British had forced the matter with the occupation of Boston and the

Battles of Lexington and Concord. The founding fathers desperately needed a way to sell the revolution to the American public. Enter Thomas Paine. He was the difference maker the founding fathers had hoped for. As John Adams observed, "Without the pen of the author of *Common Sense*, the sword of Washington would have been raised in vain."[9] Here are some of the leadership lessons we learn from Thomas Paine.

1. *Great leaders are persuasive and communicate with both logic and passion, speaking to both the intellect and the emotions.* Some speakers and writers make well-reasoned, logically airtight arguments—but their presentations are dry, lifeless, and unpersuasive. Other speakers make impassioned emotional appeals, tell powerful stories, and wring people's emotions—but their communication is manipulative. It lacks substance, logic, and evidence.

Paine's logic was unassailable—and he drove his arguments home with powerful metaphors. He compared Great Britain to an abusive and untrustworthy parent, making war on its American children. He told the story of the senseless bloodshed in Lexington and Concord—events that demanded revolution and separation. And he promoted a commonsense view of government in which the people were free citizens who chose their own destiny—not oppressed subjects of a distant tyrant.

To lead effectively and persuasively, make sure your written and spoken words are well reasoned, supported by evidence, rich in metaphors and stories, and brimming with passion. Reach for both the intellect and the emotions of your readers and listeners.

2. *Great leaders communicate bold, compelling ideas.* Paine used powerful, attention-getting words that gripped the imaginations of his readers: "We have it in our power to begin the world over again." "The birthday of a new world is at hand." "These are the times that try men's souls." "Society in every state is a blessing, but government even in its best state, is but a necessary evil; in its

worst state an intolerable one."[10] "If there must be trouble, let it be in my day, that my child may have peace."[11]

When you write or speak, eliminate words and phrases that make you seem hesitant or ambivalent. Communicate bold ideas in powerful language. Rid your language of "weasel" words that undermine the strength of your message: *basically*, *often*, *probably*, *it is said*, *some people say*, *experts claim*, *it stands to reason*, and *so forth*. Avoid jargon. Speak plainly and forcefully in language everyone understands.

3. *Great leaders communicate with clarity.* When *Common Sense* was first published, the author was identified only as "An Englishman." The mystery of the book's authorship sparked a storm of speculation. Some were convinced that John Adams had written it. In response, Adams said, "I am innocent of it as a Babe. I could not reach the Strength and Brevity of his style. Nor his elegant Simplicity nor his piercing Pathos."[12]

To communicate persuasively, communicate clearly, directly, and simply. Avoid language that is flowery or showy. Whether talking to an audience of one or one million, have a relaxed conversation with your reader or listener. As Paine himself said, "I offer nothing more than simple facts, plain arguments, and common sense."[13]

4. *Great leaders keep communication uplifting and life affirming.* Thomas Paine's personal attack on George Washington did nothing to undermine Washington's reputation—but it destroyed Paine's influence. He had gone to France to support the French Revolution—and the revolution had turned on him. It was the most frightening time of Paine's life—and he couldn't understand why Washington didn't try to free him. Paine's wounded feelings are understandable. But when Paine attacked Washington's unassailable character, he destroyed his own credibility.

So learn this lesson from the tragedy of Thomas Paine's mistake: Communicate to build up, not to tear down. Be a leader who communicates to inspire, to motivate, to persuade. Be a popularizer of grand ideas and change the world for the better.

★ 14 ★

Thomas Jefferson

The Author of the Declaration of Independence

In December 1962, President John F. Kennedy hosted a White House dinner for recipients of the Nobel Prize. He honored the Nobel laureates in his welcoming remarks, telling them that they comprised the most distinguished gathering of intellects to ever dine at the Executive Mansion—"with the possible exception of when Mr. Jefferson dined here alone."[1]

Like Benjamin Franklin, Thomas Jefferson was a polymath—a person with knowledge spanning many fields. He took a keen interest in science, mathematics, the arts, philosophy, education, history, literature, politics, architecture, and religion.

Jefferson was born on April 13, 1743, the third of ten children born to Peter and Jane Jefferson. At age nine, he attended a boarding school where he learned Latin, Greek, French, Italian, and Spanish—languages that prepared him for a career as a statesman and diplomat. When Jefferson was fourteen, his father died, and he inherited five thousand acres of land and a number of slaves.

In the spring of 1760, sixteen-year-old Thomas Jefferson began his studies at William and Mary College. He was mentored by Dr. William Small, who deeply impacted Jefferson's life. Through Dr. Small's influence, Jefferson discovered the writings of the British empiricists—Isaac Newton, Francis Bacon, and John Locke. Jefferson later recalled Dr. Small's influence:

> It was my great good fortune, and what probably fixed the destinies of my life, that Dr. William Small of Scotland, was then professor of mathematics, a man profound in most of the useful branches of science, with a happy talent of communication, correct and gentlemanly manners, and an enlarged and liberal mind. . . . From his conversation I got my first views of the expansion of science, and of the system of things in which we are placed. . . . He was the first who ever gave, in that college, regular lectures in ethics, rhetoric and *belles lettres*.[2]

Dr. Small introduced Jefferson to the intellectual rigors of mathematics and science and inspired him with a love of philosophy, theology, and *belles lettres*—aesthetic literature such as poetry and drama. Dr. Small also introduced Jefferson to legal scholar George Wythe and Francis Fauquier, the governor of Virginia.[3]

Jefferson completed a four-year course in just two years, graduating in 1762. He studied law while clerking for George Wythe and was admitted to the Virginia bar in 1767.

In 1770, when Jefferson was twenty-six, his family home in Shadwell, Virginia, burned to the ground, along with the family's two-hundred-book library. Within three years, Jefferson replaced the lost library and expanded it by more than a thousand titles. Years later, after the British burned the Library of Congress in 1814, he sold them most of his collection for $23,950. Within days of the sale, he began rebuilding his library again.

In 1768, Jefferson began construction of his neoclassical hilltop home, Monticello ("Little Mountain" in Italian). As a boy, he had often hiked and played on that hill, and imagined living in a house on its summit. Monticello fulfilled a cherished boy-hood dream.

Self-Evident Truths

Jefferson served in the Virginia House of Burgesses from 1769 until 1775. Though he owned slaves, Jefferson sought to reform slavery. In 1769, he proposed a law permitting slave owners to emancipate slaves without the approval of the royal governor and the court, but he was unable to get the law passed.

As a lawyer, Jefferson took seven cases representing slaves. One such case was his April 1770 defense of Samuel Howell. The opposing counsel was Jefferson's mentor George Wythe. Howell was scheduled by law to be emancipated at age thirty-one because of his mixed race (his grandmother was white). Jefferson claimed that Howell should be freed at once. Making an argument from natural law, Jefferson said, "All men are born free [and] everyone comes into the world with a right to his own person."

The judge cut Jefferson off midsentence and ruled against Samuel Howell. Not only did Jefferson take no fee for defending Howell but he also gave money to the man, which Howell later used to finance his escape.[4]

In that same year, Jefferson began courting Martha Wayles Skelton, a young widow who was still in her early twenties. They married on January 1, 1772.

As things heated up between America and the British government, Jefferson became increasingly incensed over British tyranny. After Parliament passed the Intolerable Acts of 1774, Jefferson proposed a resolution declaring a day of fasting and prayer and a boycott of British imports.

On March 27, 1775, three weeks before the outbreak of the Revolutionary War, Jefferson was elected to the Second Continental Congress, which served as the provisional government of the United States during the revolution. He arrived as a delegate in June. At age thirty-three, as one of the youngest members of Congress, he sought out John Adams, who was eight years older than he. The two men became close friends and allies.

Even after the Battles of Lexington and Concord in April 1775 and the Battle of Bunker Hill in June of that same year, Congress sought to avoid an all-out war with Britain. On July 8, Congress ratified the Olive Branch Petition, which affirmed the thirteen colonies' loyalty to the British Crown and asked the king to prevent further violence. By the time King George III received the Olive Branch Petition, he had already responded to the Battle of Bunker Hill. On August 23, the king declared that America had "proceeded to open and avowed rebellion," and he threatened retribution.

In June 1776, John Adams organized a five-person committee to draft a Declaration of Independence. Jefferson urged Adams to write the first draft of the document, but Adams believed Jefferson was better suited to the task. Adams observed, "Mr. Jefferson . . . brought with him a reputation for literature, science, and a happy talent of composition."[5] He recalled a conversation with Jefferson.

"You should do it," Jefferson said.

"Oh! No. . . . I will not," Adams replied.

"Why?"

"Reasons enough."

"What can be your reasons?"

"Reason first, you are a Virginian, and a Virginian ought to appear at the head of this business. Reason second, I am obnoxious, suspected, and unpopular. You are very much otherwise. Reason third, you can write ten times better than I can."

"Very well," said Jefferson, "if you are decided, I will do as well as I can."[6]

Jefferson drew inspiration from many sources, including his proposed draft of the Virginia Constitution, George Mason's

Virginia Declaration of Rights, and the enlightenment writings of philosophers John Locke and Montesquieu. He also consulted regularly with the Committee of Five.

When Jefferson completed an initial draft, he submitted it to the committee for review. He was distressed when committee members struck out phrases here and entire paragraphs there.

Seeing the look of alarm on Jefferson's face, Franklin took the young author aside and told him a story about a friend who opened a hat shop. He wanted a sign over the shop that read, "John Thompson, Hatter; Makes and Sells Hats for Ready Money," along with a picture of a hat. He showed the wording to friends, who said, "Hatter" and "Makes and Sells Hats" were superfluous because of the picture of the hat. "For Ready Money" was also superfluous because few shopkeepers sold on credit, and so on. In the end, the sign read, "John Thompson" with a picture of a hat.

After hearing Franklin's story, Jefferson realized that the committee's edits were making the Declaration leaner, clearer, and stronger, and he agreed to the changes.[7]

The draft of the Declaration was introduced to the Second Continental Congress on June 28, 1776, and Congress began debating the text on July 1. The members deleted roughly a fourth of the text that the Committee of Five had approved, including a passage that criticized King George III for his support of the slave trade. Jefferson was heartbroken over these changes.

He later recalled that the Declaration was ratified and signed in surprisingly short order because the rooms where the Declaration was examined and debated were near a stable. Members of Congress found themselves continually annoyed by aggressive swarms of biting flies. The members were so eager to get out of those fly-infested rooms that they agreed to ratify with very little debate.

Congress voted to ratify the Declaration on July 4, 1776, and all the delegates signed it on August 2. The final text listed twenty-seven grievances against King George III and asserted the natural right of revolution against tyranny. It also contained one of the most famous and influential statements of human rights in history: "We hold these truths to be self-evident, that all men are created equal, that they are endowed by their Creator with certain unalienable Rights, that among these are Life, Liberty and the pursuit of Happiness." That statement is the centerpiece of American political doctrine, and it strongly influenced Lincoln's Gettysburg Address in 1863 and Martin Luther King Jr.'s "I have a dream" speech, which I was privileged to attend with my family on the National Mall in 1963.

Upon its adoption by Congress, the Declaration of Independence was published as a large-format, single-page broadside. It was widely distributed throughout the colonies, inspiring Americans to fight for freedom.

Governor Jefferson versus Benedict Arnold

In 1778, events were brewing in Philadelphia that would soon impact Jefferson's life. In June, the British withdrew from Philadelphia, and General Washington appointed Benedict Arnold as military commander of the city. Though a brilliant field tactician, Benedict Arnold was a self-seeking opportunist. He cashed in on his powerful position, engaged in numerous war-profiteering schemes, and lived an extravagant lifestyle.

When accusations were lodged against him, Arnold demanded a court-martial to clear his name. Instead of being cleared, he was convicted on two minor charges of profiteering. Washington let him off with a public reprimand. Believing he was being unfairly persecuted, Arnold opened secret negotiations with British agents.

Meanwhile, the Continental Army offered him command of the fort at West Point, New York. He accepted the post—and secretly informed the British that he could hand over the fort without any loss of life. Arnold took command in August 1780 and settled on a price for his betrayal: twenty thousand British pounds, the equivalent of about half a million dollars today.

Benedict Arnold's plot was exposed in September 1780 and he fled to British-occupied New York City. General Washington sent spies to capture him, but Arnold eluded them and joined the British Army.

While Arnold was selling secrets to the British, Thomas Jefferson was serving as governor of Virginia. He moved Virginia's state capital from Williamsburg to Richmond, believing Richmond's central location made it easier to defend. Jefferson had no inkling of the disaster that awaited Richmond.

The British gave Arnold a brigadier general's commission and command of 1,600 troops in Virginia. Arnold went on a rampage through Virginia, burning, killing, and looting.

In early January 1781, Arnold's fleet sailed up the James River to Richmond, which was defended by a tiny force of two hundred militiamen. One of Arnold's objectives was to capture the government officials of Virginia, including Jefferson.

The city was caught by surprise. The militiamen fired one volley, then fled at the sight of Arnold's superior force. Jefferson ordered an evacuation of Richmond, including the removal of the town's stores of military supplies. Jefferson took his family to Tuckahoe, northwest of Richmond.[8] At noon, Benedict Arnold's forces entered Richmond without firing a shot. Arnold sent a letter by messenger to Governor Jefferson, offering to spare the city if he would hand over the hidden stores of tobacco and military supplies.

A furious Jefferson replied that he refused to bargain with a traitor. On January 6, Jefferson's reply reached Arnold. Enraged, Arnold ordered his troops to loot every building, including churches, and load the plunder aboard the ships. Then he ordered his men to torch the town. Strong winds sent flames exploding through the wooden structures of Richmond, and the city burned to the ground.

News of Richmond's destruction devastated Jefferson. He ordered a militia force under Colonel Sampson Mathews to pursue Arnold. Using the guerilla tactics taught by General Nathanael Greene, Mathews located Arnold's slow-moving army and inflicted heavy casualties on the troops, forcing them to retreat to Portsmouth.

The destruction of Richmond so angered General Washington that he placed a large bounty on Arnold's head and ordered the Marquis de Lafayette to find the traitor and hang him on sight. Targets printed with Arnold's likeness were distributed to soldiers for target practice to make sure they would recognize him.

Six months later, British Lieutenant Colonel Banastre Tarleton made another attempt to capture Jefferson, this time at his home at Monticello. Tarleton and his troops were spotted making camp near Louisa Courthouse the evening of June 3. A Patriot named Jack Jouett saw the British soldiers and figured they were headed to Charlottesville and Monticello. He rode forty miles to warn Jefferson and the Virginia Assembly that the British were coming. Jefferson and his family escaped from Monticello mere minutes before the British arrived. For his actions, Jack Jouett is remembered as "the Paul Revere of the South."[9]

The Virginia General Assembly convened in June 1781 and inquired into Jefferson's actions, including the evacuation of Richmond. Though the inquest concluded that Jefferson had acted honorably, he declined to seek a third term as governor.

The Jefferson Paradox

The troubling paradox of Thomas Jefferson's life is that he was a slaveholder who wanted to eliminate slavery. As he set forth that inspiring, self-evident truth that "all men are created equal," his plantation was being worked by enslaved men and women. Though the words of the Declaration of Independence contradicted Jefferson's way of life, so did his work as an attorney. He represented seven slaves who were seeking their emancipation. He worked as a Virginia legislator to permit slave owners to free their slaves without government interference.

Yet he continued to own more than two hundred slaves.

Thomas Jefferson feared what slavery was doing to America. In *Notes on the State of Virginia* (1781), he wrote:

> Can the liberties of a nation be thought secure when we have removed their only firm basis, a conviction in the minds of the people that these liberties are of the gift of God? That they are not to be violated but with his wrath? Indeed I tremble for my country when I reflect that God is just: that his justice cannot sleep for ever. . . . The spirit of the master is abating, that of the slave rising from the dust.[10]

How did Jefferson reconcile his Enlightenment ideals with his ownership of slaves? Historian Andrew Burstein explains:

> Jefferson saw African-Americans as noble human beings. In the abstract, he could appreciate the African-American's humanity. . . . Jefferson occupied a particular moral space and within that moral space, he was a liberal who believed that the most humane thing that could be done with the slavery problem was to re-colonize African-Americans back in Africa. . . . Jefferson wanted slaves to have decent lives. He wanted to be the best slaveholder in America. . . . He did not think that America was politically ready [to abolish slavery]. . . . Jefferson . . . was a political pragmatist.[11]

It is easy to judge Thomas Jefferson by today's moral standards, but his perception was shaped by the times in which he lived. His father was a slave owner and his father-in-law, John Wayles, was a slave trader. His friend George Washington was also a slave owner. The slaveholding culture was all he knew. To acknowledge those cultural attitudes does not excuse slavery, but it does help us to understand the contradiction in Jefferson's thinking. We all tend to be products of our times.

Something happened to Jefferson that enabled him to transcend his times and write the timeless words of the Declaration of Independence. Someday, Jefferson believed, America would live out those ideals—but unfortunately, not in his lifetime.

The Third President

Thomas and Martha Jefferson were married for only ten years. During that time, Martha bore six children, only two of whom survived to adulthood. In 1782, after the birth of their last child, Martha died at age thirty-three. Jefferson had her headstone inscribed with these words: "torn from him by Death, September 6, 1782." Jefferson was devastated. For weeks, he holed up in his room, pacing and weeping.[12]

In 1784, Congress sent Jefferson to Paris. There he joined John Adams and Benjamin Franklin in negotiating treaties with the various nations of Europe and North Africa. His friends felt the change of scenery would help the recently widowed Jefferson regain his joy. He spent five years in Paris and helped guide American foreign policy. He also became a close friend of the Marquis de Lafayette.

Jefferson returned to America in September 1789. Though he originally planned to return to France, President George Washington appointed him secretary of state—a cabinet post that required him to remain in the nation's capital. Washington served two presidential terms, from April 30, 1789 to March 4, 1797. In the election of 1796, Thomas Jefferson ran for president against his old friend John Adams, Washington's vice president. It was the first contested presidential election in history. Adams won by a slim margin, and Jefferson became vice president.

In the 1800 election, Jefferson opposed Adams, whose popularity had been eroded by higher taxes and the passage of the unpopular Alien and Sedition Acts. Historian Joyce Oldham Appleby called the 1800 election campaign "one of the most acrimonious in the annals of American history."[13]

Adams and Jefferson tied in the electoral college, and the election had to be decided by the House of Representatives. On the thirty-sixth ballot, Jefferson was elected president, and Aaron Burr was elected vice president. Jefferson took the oath of office on March 4, 1801. He rode into Washington, DC, on horseback, dressed in the simple clothes of a farmer, completely unnoticed. He rejected the regal trappings of high office and became known as "the people's president."

The Sally Hemings Question

In 1802, a hard-drinking, scandal-mongering journalist named James Callender approached President Jefferson for a job as postmaster. Jefferson refused, so Callender took his revenge by publishing a rumor that President Jefferson had fathered children with one of his slaves, Sally Hemings. Callender died by drowning the following year, apparently from falling off a bridge over the James River while drunk. But the rumor he started lives on.[14]

Few historians took Callender's accusations seriously until 1974, when Fawn M. Brodie published *Thomas Jefferson: An Intimate History*, which claimed (on the basis of Freudian analysis) that Jefferson fathered all six of Hemings's children. Prominent Jefferson scholars, including Dumas Malone, Merrill Peterson, and Julian Boyd, were aghast. Malone said that Brodie's book "runs far beyond the evidence and carries psychological speculation to the point of absurdity," adding that the book was a "mishmash of fact and fiction, surmise and conjecture." Boyd noted that among all the favorable reviewers of Brodie's book, "not a single Jefferson scholar is to be found."[15]

In 1998, Dr. Eugene Foster, a retired pathologist, ran DNA tests on living male descendants of Sally Hemings and Jefferson's uncle on his father's side. Y chromosomes are passed from male to male, so if Fawn M. Brodie's claims were true, Hemings's male descendants should have the Y chromosome of Jefferson's family lineage. The tests showed that, in contrast to Brodie's claim, Hemings's firstborn son, Tom, was, *not* related to Thomas Jefferson or any other Jefferson male.[16]

It is important to note that Foster did show that Hemings's lastborn son, Eston, was a Jefferson relation. However, it is impossible to determine if Eston's father was Thomas Jefferson or another Jefferson male. At the time Eston was conceived, more than twenty of Jefferson's male relatives lived in Virginia and seven lived near Monticello.

Though Foster's findings were inconclusive regarding the paternity of Eston Hemings, *Nature* magazine ran the misleading headline "Jefferson Fathered Slave's Last Child." Many newspapers repeated the unverified claim as fact.[17] I confess that I fully believed this claim myself for more than twenty years—until I began researching this book.

In 2011, a panel of thirteen scholars issued a report called *The Jefferson-Hemings Controversy: Report of the Scholars Commission*. Twelve of the thirteen scholars on the panel concluded that the father of Eston Hemings was probably *not* Thomas Jefferson but his younger brother Randolph instead. There are a number of compelling reasons why Eston's father was almost certainly Randolph Jefferson.

1. We know that Thomas wrote Randolph about an impending visit to Monticello at the very time Eston was conceived. (The letter is dated August 12, 1807, nine months before Eston's birth on May 21, 1808.) In the letter, Thomas assumes that Randolph will arrive soon: "Our sister [Anna Scott] Marks arrived here last night and we shall be happy to see you also."[18] Randolph carried the same Y chromosomes as Thomas and the other Jefferson men, and he was a frequent visitor at Monticello.

2. Randolph is believed to have fathered children with his own slaves and had a reputation for socializing with Jefferson's slaves when he came to visit. One Monticello slave, Isaac Jefferson, said of Randolph, "Old Master's brother, Mass Randall . . . used to come out among black people, play the fiddle and dance half the night."[19]

3. Randolph, a widower, was just fifty-one at the time Eston was conceived. His brother Thomas was sixty-four and in ill health at the time. These age and health factors weigh against the notion that Jefferson fathered Eston.

4. Everything we know about Thomas Jefferson tells us it would have been a violation of his character to have sexual relations with slaves. The fact that Jefferson took great pains to live a moral and ethically principled life weighs heavily against the theory that he fathered a child with Sally Hemings.

5. Significantly, Randolph was again at Monticello six days after Eston was born. At that time, he had Thomas draw up his will, leaving his estate to his five legitimate sons—something Randolph would have done if he wanted to make sure Eston could make no claim against his estate.

Based on these facts, I've concluded that Thomas Jefferson is innocent of the accusation that he fathered children by Sally Hemings. We can't know for sure—but the evidence I see weighs against the claim.

Journey's End

Thomas Jefferson called his election "the Revolution of 1800." He slashed taxes (his elimination of the whiskey excise tax made him especially popular) and cut defense spending. The only declared war during his presidency was the First Barbary War, when Jefferson sent American warships to defend merchant shipping against North African pirates.

In 1803, Jefferson made a deal with France, the Louisiana Purchase, that doubled the size of the United States. America paid about fifteen million dollars for 828,000 square miles of land (about four cents an acre), clearly the best real estate bargain in US history.

After Jefferson left office in March 1809, he made a three-day, hundred-mile journey home to Monticello. He traveled by carriage and lodged in country inns along the way. For years afterward, when Jefferson traveled around Virginia, innkeepers and others recognized him and called him "The Squire."

On one occasion, he stopped at Ford's Tavern in rural Virginia for the night. He exchanged first names with another guest at the inn, a clergyman. The clergyman didn't realize that the man who introduced himself as Thomas was the former president of the United States.

The two men chatted about mechanical engineering, and the clergyman thought this stranger was a mechanical engineer. Then they talked about agriculture, and the clergyman decided that his fellow conversationalist must have been an accomplished farmer. Then they talked about religion, and the clergyman decided that the stranger was surely a preacher at one time.

After Jefferson retired to his room, the clergyman asked the innkeeper the identity of this man who had so much knowledge in so many different fields.

The innkeeper said, "Don't you know the Squire? That was Mr. Jefferson."

"Not *President* Jefferson?"

"The same."

The clergyman was Reverend Charles Clay of Bedford, Virginia. The next morning, Reverend Clay introduced himself to the former president. They became good friends and maintained a long exchange of letters over the years.[20]

Jefferson devoted his postpresidential years to the planning and construction of the University of Virginia in Charlottesville, which welcomed its first students in 1819.

In 1812, John Adams wrote a brief note to Jefferson, wishing him a prosperous new year. Jefferson responded with a friendly reply. They continued their correspondence over the next fourteen years, exchanging more than one hundred and fifty letters. They sometimes praised each other and sometimes debated each other, but their friendship remained strong and unshakable to the end of their lives.

By May 1826, Jefferson lived as a shut-in after suffering a series of illnesses. He declined an invitation to attend the fiftieth anniversary of the Declaration of Independence in Washington, DC. On July 3, Jefferson went to bed with a fever.

Sensing the approach of death, he told his daughter his wishes for a simple private funeral, adding, "I have done for my country and for all mankind all that I could do, and I now resign my soul without fear to my God."[21]

He slept through most of the day. Late that evening, he awoke and said his last words, "Is it the fourth?"

His doctor said, "It soon will be."

At age eighty-three, Jefferson slept through the night and died in the early afternoon of July 4.[22]

Five hours later, in Quincy, Massachusetts, a dying John Adams spoke his last words, "Thomas Jefferson survives." He was unaware that his friend had preceded him in death.

★ LEADERSHIP LESSONS ★
from Thomas Jefferson

We find instructive lessons in both the brilliance and the blind spots in Thomas Jefferson's leadership legacy.

1. *Great leaders are readers.* There was no possession Thomas Jefferson treasured more than his library. Like Benjamin Franklin and Henry Knox, Jefferson was an avid and eclectic reader. The books he read became a part of who he was as a leader. The

wisdom he used to pen the Declaration of Independence and the leadership skills that made him one of our greatest presidents came largely from books. Through reading, we gain understanding—and as King Solomon wrote, "Like the horizons for breadth and the ocean for depth, the understanding of a good leader is broad and deep."[23]

2. *Great leaders seize opportunities.* Soon after becoming president, Jefferson learned that France was interested in selling the Louisiana Territory to raise cash for a possible war with Britain. Jefferson sent James Monroe and Robert R. Livingston to negotiate with representatives of Napoleon. The new territory effectively doubled the size of America—not by war but by purchase. Jefferson had to persuade his Federalist opponents in Congress to ratify and fund the deal. The Federalists challenged the constitutionality of the purchase at the time, but today no one questions Jefferson's wisdom in acquiring the Louisiana Territory.

How do you respond to new and unexpected opportunities? Don't wait too long. Be bold! Seize your leadership opportunities and make the most of them.

3. *Great leaders support exploration and the growth of knowledge.* In 1803, Jefferson appointed Meriwether Lewis and William Clark to lead an expedition westward. Jefferson personally tutored Lewis in the sciences he would employ in his travels—mapping, astronomy, navigation, natural history, minerology, zoology, and botany. He gave Lewis access to his personal book collection at Monticello. The expedition took place from May 1804 to September 1806, and Lewis and Clark returned with a wealth of new geographic knowledge, including the location of many previously unreached Native American tribes.

Are there bold explorers and adventurers in your organization, your church, or your family? Encourage them, mentor them, support them, and empower them as Jefferson empowered Lewis and Clark.

4. *Great leaders integrate their private life and their leadership life.* Make sure that there is total alignment between your
public principles and the way you live your life. Thomas Jefferson was an opponent of slavery—yet he was also a slave owner.
This contradiction in his life is hard to understand—and it is
easy to see why many people today want to tear down Jefferson's legacy.

During the 2020 presidential primary, one candidate advocated
removing Jefferson's name from buildings, honors, and events.
Also in 2020, the city council of Charlottesville, Virginia (which
Jefferson called home), voted to stop observing Jefferson's birthday
as a holiday. In 2017, students at New York's Columbia University
draped a Klan hood over a statue of Jefferson and called him "the
epitome of white supremacy." In 2015 students at the University of
Missouri circulated a petition calling for the removal of a statue
of Thomas Jefferson.

I don't believe Jefferson was a hypocrite. I believe he was a man
who felt trapped by the times in which he lived. Slavery, in his
era, was the cultural norm. Yet he wanted a section condemning
King George III for the slave trade inserted into the Declaration
of Independence. He wrote in the Declaration that "all men are
created equal." I believe he wrote those words hoping that someday
America would live up to their meaning. Slowly, reluctantly, at the
cost of a civil war and a civil rights movement and the assassination of Dr. Martin Luther King Jr., America has moved closer and
closer to the fulfillment of Jefferson's words.

We are blessed to live in a nation founded on the principle that
we are all equal, that we have God-given rights to life, liberty,
and the pursuit of happiness. Thomas Jefferson believed in those
principles to the marrow of his bones. But people are complicated
creatures. As Jefferson himself once said, "For none of us, no, not
one, is perfect. And were we to love none who had imperfections
this world would be a desert for our love."[24]

To those who think that Jefferson's legacy should be utterly erased from memory, let me ask you: What steps have we taken to eradicate slavery in our world? Some of the products in our homes were probably made, in part, by forced labor in communist China. Indentured servitude—enslavement to pay off a debt—is legal in India. Cotton from Uzbekistan is harvested in large part by slave labor. More than 4 percent of North Korea's population lives in slavery. According to the Global Slavery Index, some 45.8 million people are enslaved in 167 countries—and 25 percent of them are children.[25] Instead of trying to erase the past, shouldn't we focus on building a future without slavery?

Let's acknowledge Jefferson's blind spot honestly, even as we celebrate the greatness of his contributions to humanity, including the Declaration of Independence. And let's work to eliminate our own blind spots so that our private life and public leadership life are in perfect alignment. That may be the most important leadership lesson from the life of Thomas Jefferson.

★ 15 ★

John Hancock

The Wealthy Servant of the Revolution

The Declaration of Independence was adopted by the Second Continental Congress on July 4, 1776, and it was formally signed by all members of Congress nearly a month later, on August 2. As president of the Congress, John Hancock had the honor of being the first to sign the document. He famously wrote his name in a bold script, underscored with a flourish, easily twice the size of any other signature on the page.

In those days, Great Britain was symbolically referred to as "John Bull" in the same way we call the US government "Uncle Sam" today. According to some accounts, "John Bull" had placed a bounty on Hancock's head—five hundred pounds sterling (equal to more than one hundred thousand dollars today). After inscribing his name in such large, flowing letters, Hancock reportedly said, "There! John Bull can read my name without spectacles and may now double his reward of five hundred pounds for my head. *That* is my defiance."[1]

The act of signing the Declaration of Independence—whether in large letters or small—was, in fact, an act of bold, courageous defiance. If the American Revolution failed, its leaders—including every signer of the Declaration—would be treated as traitors and subject to execution by hanging. The war was entering its seventeenth month at the time of the signing, and British general William Howe and his brother, Admiral Richard Howe, were engaged in a massive counteroffensive, which led to the capture of New York City. American morale was at a low ebb.

So the signatures on the Declaration were symbols of courage, patriotism, and a near-fatalistic defiance of the immense power of the British Empire. The fifty-six members of Congress who signed that document, led by John Hancock, understood the historical significance of that act—and they knew that they were laying their lives down on that beautifully inscribed piece of parchment.

Who was this American leader who was sought by King George III and the British Parliament? Who was John Hancock?

President of Congress—and a Wanted Man

Born in January 1737 in Braintree (later called Quincy), Massachusetts, John Hancock was the son of a clergyman. His father died when he was a boy, so he was raised by his uncle Thomas Hancock, a wealthy Boston merchant.

Thomas Hancock and his wife were childless, and they raised John as their own son. John graduated from Harvard College in 1754 and went to work for his uncle. When Uncle Thomas died in 1764, John inherited the mercantile business and became one of the wealthiest people in the thirteen colonies.

John Hancock was known for his lavish lifestyle but also for his generosity. He saw how British taxation policies depressed the economy of Boston, and he wanted to throw the British yoke off the neck of his people. In part because of his political views,

Hancock became a friend and political protégé of Samuel Adams, a rising Boston politician. Hancock's political and economic views meshed perfectly with those of Adams, and he began using his wealth to fund the American resistance groups and militias.

In 1765, John Hancock won election as a Boston selectman. The following year, he was elected to the legislature of Massachusetts. During this time, the British Parliament passed a series of oppressive tax measures—the Stamp Act in 1765, the Townshend Acts in 1767, and an enforcement bureau called the Board of Customs. The colonists stridently opposed these tax laws, complaining of the injustice of "taxation without representation"—being taxed by Parliament yet having no voice in Parliament.

On June 10, 1768, during a time of increasing tension in Boston, the king's customs officials seized Hancock's sloop, the *Liberty*. This act triggered protests across the city. The British accused Hancock of smuggling, a trumped-up charge that was later dismissed in court. Hancock was so beloved by Bostonians that angry crowds forced British officials to flee to the British ship *Romney*. To quell the riots, Britain sent troops into Boston and began a full-scale military occupation of the city.

In March 1770, British soldiers killed five citizens of Boston during the infamous Boston Massacre. John Hancock was incensed when he learned of the incident the following day. Together with Samuel Adams, Hancock formed a committee to meet with Massachusetts governor Thomas Hutchinson and the commander of British troops, Colonel William Dalrymple. The committee demanded the withdrawal of troops and an end to the occupation of Boston. To quiet the unrest in the city, Dalrymple agreed to move his soldiers to Castle William, an island fortress in Boston Harbor. Because of his role in getting the British troops removed from the city, Hancock was easily reelected to the Massachusetts legislature in May.

Boston became a center of the resistance movement and set an example for all thirteen colonies. Meanwhile, John Hancock was revered among Patriots because he was an effective leader of the movement—and he was reviled by the British for the same reason.

He was elected president of the Massachusetts Provincial Congress in 1774. The Provincial Congress functioned as a provisional government with emergency powers. The rebellious portions of the Massachusetts colony viewed the Provincial Congress as the legitimate government while ignoring the demands of the British royal government.

In December 1774, the Provincial Congress sent John Hancock as a delegate to the Second Continental Congress. Hancock's actions in support of the American rebellion made him a wanted man.

On May 24, 1775, Hancock's fellow delegates unanimously elected him president of the Second Continental Congress, succeeding Peyton Randolph. Hancock had experience presiding over the Massachusetts Provincial Congress, and he was well-liked by all the delegates. Though his position didn't give him much executive power—he essentially presided over meetings and handled official correspondence—he wielded his influence to unify the delegates and focus them on the goal of victory in the Revolutionary War.

In June 1775, in an attempt to bring the war to an early conclusion, British general Thomas Gage offered amnesty to all Americans who would lay down their arms—but Gage's offer of amnesty excluded Samuel Adams and John Hancock by name. In fact, Great Britain had been trying to capture John Hancock even before the Battles of Lexington and Concord. But when the British Empire focused its wrath on these two Patriots, they raised Adams and Hancock to the status of heroes throughout the thirteen colonies.

Also in June 1775, the Second Continental Congress chose George Washington as commander in chief of the Continental Army. Throughout the war, John Hancock used his wealth and influence to fund Washington's army and advance the revolution.

Congress recessed on August 1, giving Hancock time to marry his fiancée, Dorothy Quincy, whom he called Dolly. They were married on August 28 in Fairfield, Connecticut. They would later have two children together, a daughter named Lydia in 1776 and a son named John in 1778. Tragically neither child reached adulthood. Lydia died of an illness at just ten months, and John suffered a fatal head injury while skating at age nine.

Synonymous with "Signature"

On July 4, 1776, the Second Continental Congress, with John Hancock presiding, adopted the Declaration of Independence. The document, handcrafted by Thomas Jefferson in consultation with the Committee of Five, went far beyond making the case that the thirteen colonies ought to be independent from Great Britain. In soaring language, the Declaration made an impassioned case for human liberty and individual rights.

The first version of the Declaration distributed to the public was the so-called Dunlap Broadside, named for John Dunlap, a twenty-nine-year-old Irish immigrant printer in Philadelphia. An estimated two hundred copies were printed on the night the Declaration was adopted. The Committee of Five was present in Dunlap's print shop that night, proofreading and correcting the text as Dunlap set the type.

Copies of the Dunlap Broadside were distributed throughout the thirteen colonies, and some were given to General Washington so that it could be read to the troops. The Dunlap Broadside did not bear any signatures, but it did conclude with the typeset words, "Signed by Order and on Behalf of the Congress, JOHN HANCOCK, PRESIDENT." When the Declaration of Independence was first published, it had one signer—John Hancock.

By order of Congress on July 19, 1776, a parchment copy of the Declaration was handwritten (probably by clerk Timothy

Matlack) with the title, "The Unanimous Declaration of the Thirteen United States of America." At the signing of the parchment document on August 2, John Hancock affixed the first, largest, and boldest signature to the document. Ever since, people have colloquially spoken of a legal signature as a "John Hancock," as in, "Put your John Hancock on the dotted line."

In October 1777, Hancock requested a leave of absence from his duties as president of the Congress. Massachusetts was forming a state government and Hancock believed his political prospects were better in Boston than in Philadelphia. By this time, John Hancock and Samuel Adams—once the closest of allies—were estranged. The humble and unpretentious Adams, who despised the arrogance of the English aristocracy, saw an aristocrat's vanity in Hancock's extravagant lifestyle. Adams believed that the leaders of the revolution should live modestly and simply, like the people they led.

On Hancock's final day in the Second Continental Congress, one of the delegates made a motion to give him a vote of thanks for his service as president of the Congress. That motion was opposed by the entire Massachusetts delegation, including Samuel Adams. Delegates from four other states also opposed. The grounds for this opposition were Hancock's well-known vanity. It was a bitter humiliation for Hancock on his final day in office.

On March 11, 1779, a writer in the *Pennsylvania Ledger* identified only as "A Gentleman from the Eastward" scornfully observed,

> John Hancock, of Boston, appears in public with all the pageantry and state of an Oriental prince; he rides in an elegant chariot. . . . He is attended by four servants, dressed in superb livery, mounted on fine horses richly caparisoned, and escorted by fifty horsemen with drawn sabres, the one-half of whom precede and the other follow his carriage.[2]

Many historians, including the highly esteemed Richard M. Ketchum, have concluded that this disparaging description of Hancock could only have been written by Hancock's former friend and ally, the spartan-minded Samuel Adams.[3] (Adams, in fact, once rode with Hancock in his carriage and was horrified by the pomp and pretentiousness of the experience.)

Hancock's move from Philadelphia back to Boston paid rich dividends for his political ambitions. As Ketchum concludes,

> Elected governor by a huge majority in 1780, Hancock proceeded to turn the state into a private political fief and for all the anguished cries from his opponents became the most popular man in Massachusetts. His inauguration was celebrated with such a round of parties and balls as had not been seen, Sam Adams complained, since the salad days of royal governors and customs officials.[4]

In Boston, Hancock's generous financial support of the war and of widows and orphans increased his popularity. He briefly rejoined the Second Continental Congress in Philadelphia in June 1778. On July 9, he signed the Articles of Confederation on behalf of Massachusetts. The Articles created a weak, nearly powerless central government that functioned more like the United Nations than the United States of America. The Articles were not ratified by all thirteen states until March 1, 1781. Unhappy in Philadelphia, Hancock returned to Boston later that month.

Leadership Disaster in Rhode Island

John Hancock held the rank of a major general in the Massachusetts militia—a mostly honorary title he had received in 1776. In July 1778, General George Washington and General John Sullivan of the Continental Army laid plans for an attack on the British garrison at Newport, Rhode Island, to take place the following month. General Sullivan called upon Hancock to lead a force of six thousand Massachusetts militiamen. Hancock was eager to serve in the war, though he chose to be a figurehead leader. He left the operational details to the professional soldiers.

The operation, known as the Battle of Rhode Island, was a disaster. It was conducted as a joint mission of French and American forces (France had recently entered the war on the side of the Americans). Cooperation between French and American commanders was abysmal. French admiral d'Estaing despised General Sullivan and threatened to return to France and urge the French government to end support for the American Revolution. The French admiral was forced to abandon the Battle of Rhode Island when a hurricane snapped the masts off three of his vessels, including his flagship.

The same storm swept through the Continental Army and militia encampments, leaving (in Hancock's words) "scenes of blood and carnage." As the Americans watched Admiral d'Estaing's fleet depart from the battle, five-sixths of John Hancock's poorly trained militiamen deserted in terror. Hancock had no forces left with which to engage the enemy. Historian Harlow Giles Unger wrote that, on August 26, Hancock "conceded defeat and left for Boston. He recognized he was not a soldier. He had not devised a single strategy or originated a single order." Hancock's "ineffectual bluster" could not "prevent his men from losing confidence in his leadership."[5]

Though Hancock was criticized for the military debacle at Newport, he remained popular with the people of Massachusetts. He went on to help write the Massachusetts Constitution, which was adopted in 1780, the same year he was overwhelmingly elected governor. He resigned in 1785 due to failing health but, after recovering, won reelection in 1787, and he presided over the Massachusetts convention that ratified the United States Constitution.

Hancock was a candidate for the first United States presidential election in 1789, but he came in a distant third to George Washington and John Adams, who were elected president and vice president, respectively. Hancock remained in office as Massachusetts governor until his death (possibly from a stroke or heart attack brought on by chronic gout) on October 8, 1793. He was fifty-six years old. His funeral procession included his former friend and frequent adversary Samuel Adams (who succeeded Hancock as governor), Vice President John Adams, and Secretary of War Henry Knox. He was buried in Boston's Old Granary Burying Ground.

Years later, John Adams wrote a kind remembrance of John Hancock, the man he and his cousin Samuel long viewed as an adversary: "I could melt into tears when I hear his name. . . . If benevolence, charity, generosity were ever personified in North America, they were in John Hancock."[6]

✶ LEADERSHIP LESSONS ✶
from John Hancock

John Hancock's leadership life is instructive, not only through his successes but also through his failures. Here are some of the lessons we find in his life story.

1. *Great leaders should adopt a bold style.* Great leaders should have a personal trademark, a signature image that announces to the world, "This is who I am; this is what I stand for." John Hancock's famous signature was more than a trademark; it was a statement of his boldness and courage. With style and a calligraphic flourish, he taunted the British Parliament and King George, daring them to arrest him and hang him. His flamboyant personal style seemed vain and ostentatious to the astringent Samuel Adams, but it helped establish Hancock's image in the public mind. It gave him the appearance of a leader.

Without question, John Hancock took his bold—and sometimes vain—personal style too far. On one occasion, for example, he kept President George Washington waiting, insisting that the president of the United States was of lower rank than the governor of Massachusetts.[7] And, of course, there was the matter of Hancock's pageantry, his lavish carriage, his servants, his horsemen with drawn swords—all were over-the-top. A leader can have a bold personal style without being vain and showy.

2. *Great leaders are willing to take personal risks.* Knowing he risked execution if the revolution failed, Hancock tweaked the nose of "John Bull" and boldly signed his name to the Declaration of Independence. "*That* is my defiance," he said.

When people see a leader take bold risks, they are emboldened to put themselves at risk for the cause. Courage inspires courage. Boldness generates boldness. The people of Massachusetts were willing to walk through walls for John Hancock, because his courageous example inspired and motivated them.

Let your followers see you putting everything on the line for your cause. Don't take foolish gambles, but once you make a decision, go all in. Boldly and courageously lead your people to victory.

3. *Great leaders are generous servants of the people they lead.* Though John Hancock was known for his wealth and his self-indulgent lifestyle, he was even more well-known for his generosity. He used his wealth to support the war effort—and to support widows, orphans, and the poor. People respect generous leaders. John Hancock won the hearts of the people of Massachusetts because they knew he had a generous heart.

4. *Great leaders know their limitations.* John Hancock failed this test. Because he held the honorary rank of major general in the Massachusetts militia, Hancock fancied himself a military leader. But when the battle began and it was time to lead his men into battle, Hancock discovered he was not the military leader he imagined himself to be. His political leadership skills didn't transfer to the battlefield, and he found he was unable to inspire and motivate his troops. He couldn't devise a strategy. He couldn't issue an order. He was out of his depth.

There is a principle in psychology known as the Dunning-Kruger effect, in which people overestimate their ability because they don't know how much they don't know. John Hancock was so successful in political leadership that he thought he would make a great military leader as well. He didn't realize how little he actually knew about leading men into battle. He didn't know how much he didn't know, so he wildly overestimated his ability as a major general.

It takes a lot of self-awareness to be an effective leader. You must know the limits of your knowledge, training, and experience. When you face a leadership challenge that is above your skill level, don't bluff your way through. Recruit people who can supply the knowledge and experience you lack.

Learn from John Hancock's greatest mistake. In the end, he realized he was not a military leader. He returned to Massachusetts sadder but wiser, and he remained an effective and beloved civilian leader to the end of his days.

★ 16 ★

John Paul Jones
The Ranger of the Sea

Jones was not his real last name. The son of a Scottish landscape gardener was born John Paul Jr. on July 6, 1747. But the gardener's son grew up dreaming of adventure on the high seas.

John Paul Jr. was a natural leader as a boy. He and his friends would go to the shore to play. The other boys would get in rowboats and paddle out into the water, and Paul would climb onto a rock, shouting orders to them, pretending to be a Royal Navy admiral sending his fleet into battle.

In the strict class system of eighteenth-century Britain, the sons of the poor had no way to better themselves except through naval service. So John Paul Jr. dreamed of a career in His Majesty's Royal Navy. Later in life, he wrote about his boyhood dreams in a letter to his mentor, Benjamin Franklin: "I had made the art of war at sea in some degree my study, and had been fond of the navy, from boyish days up."[1]

Though he never joined the Royal Navy, he did enter the British merchant marine at age thirteen, serving as a cabin boy on a slave ship. According to *The Sextant*, the official blog of the US Navy's Naval History and Heritage Command, "The teenage Jones grew disgusted with the slave trade after three years working on a slaver."[2] By age fifteen, he managed to sign on to a cargo ship. On one voyage, a virulent disease spread through the ship, killing the captain and the first mate. The youngest crewman aboard, John Paul Jr., gave orders to the weakened and terrified crew and got the ship safely into port. As a reward, the ship's owners placed him in command of his own vessel.

In 1773, the teenage captain's crew mutinied off the island of Tobago in the West Indies. Perhaps the mutineers thought that such a young man would lack the nerve to defend his captaincy and his life. But John Paul Jr. acted quickly, killing the ringleader and quelling the rebellion. Though killing in self-defense is no crime, John Paul Jr. didn't want to take a chance at trial. He jumped ship and fled to Fredericksburg, Virginia, where his brother lived. He took the surname Jones to hide his identity and avoid arrest.

In the Continental Navy

When the American Revolution broke out in April 1775, Jones knew which side he was on. He once said that he fought not for money or fame but "in defense of the violated rights of mankind."[3] When the thirteen colonies began assembling a Continental Navy, John Paul Jones was eager to join the revolution. A Scotsman who had heard all his father's complaints about the English, Jones had no love for British rule.

His first commission in the Continental Navy was as a lieutenant on the *Alfred* under Commodore Esek Hopkins, commander of the Continental Navy. On the day of the *Alfred*'s commissioning in February 1776, Jones raised the flag of the thirteen colonies, the Grand Union Flag—the first hoisting of an American ensign over a US naval vessel.

Jones quickly demonstrated his leadership ability and was promoted to captain of the sloop *Providence*. Over the summer of 1776, Jones and his crew captured sixteen British ships as prizes and raided seacoast villages in Nova Scotia. In November, Jones returned to Nova Scotia in command of the *Alfred*. He carried out more raids, captured more ships, and freed three hundred Americans who had been forced to work in British coal mines in Nova Scotia.

When Jones returned to Boston on December 16, 1776, his strong personality got the better of him. He clashed with the equally strong-willed Commodore Hopkins over his eagerness to take the battle to the British. Despite Jones's accomplishments, Hopkins asserted his authority by sidelining Jones for six months. Finally, on June 14, 1777, Hopkins assigned him to the newly constructed USS *Ranger*.

Jones arrived in Portsmouth, New Hampshire, to inspect his new 110-foot sloop—and was shocked to find the *Ranger* woefully unready. There were no sails or rigging on the masts and spars, no ammunition or gunpowder in the holds. The *Ranger*'s sails and armament had been transferred to the frigate *Raleigh*, commanded by Thomas Thompson—a man Jones vehemently disliked. Jones feared that Commodore Hopkins might place him under Thompson's command, a prospect he viewed as a "dishonor worse than death."[4]

In August 1776, the Second Continental Congress sent Benjamin Franklin, Silas Deane, and Arthur Lee to France as commissioners empowered to negotiate a treaty of commerce.[5] Franklin would soon become Jones's most important ally.

Jones set sail for France aboard the *Ranger* on November 1, 1777. He planned to take command of a new frigate, the *L'Indien*, which was under construction in the Netherlands and promised to him by Congress.

Nearing Land's End off the English coast, Jones encountered a British merchant fleet protected by the seventy-four-gun warship *Invincible*. Jones moved the *Ranger* in among the merchant ships—and the *Invincible* didn't notice that the *Ranger* was an enemy warship. Jones used the tense situation to drill his crew while looking for an opportunity to cut a prize ship out of the convoy. No opportunity came. *Invincible* was too well armed for the *Ranger* to attack, so Jones slipped away.

Arriving at the port of Nantes on December 2, Jones learned that the frigate Congress had promised him was no longer available. British officials had pressured the shipbuilders in Amsterdam to sell it to France instead. (At the time, France was not yet officially allied with the United States.) The plan had been for Jones to leave the *Ranger* and take command of the new ship. Instead, he retained command of the *Ranger* and ordered an overhaul of the ship, including relocating the masts, installing new spars, and upgrading the sails.

While the *Ranger* was being refitted, Jones took a carriage to Paris to meet Benjamin Franklin, arriving just before Christmas. The two men bonded like father and son, and Franklin introduced Jones to Parisian society. Jones explained his plan for a naval offensive to terrify the coasts of England and liberate Americans held in English prisons. Franklin became Jones's mentor and ally in matters of political intrigue.

During Jones's stay in Paris, he tried every diplomatic channel to persuade France to supply a vessel for him to command. But his appeals to the French royal court led nowhere.

Meanwhile, Jones became aware that, in the port of Nantes, the *Ranger*'s first lieutenant was angling to replace him as the ship's commander. In Paris, Jones persuaded Franklin and Silas Deane to write new orders to keep Jones in command of the *Ranger* until a new ship was available. The orders broadly directed Jones to "proceed . . . in the manner you shall judge best, for distressing the Enemies of the United States, by Sea, or otherwise, consistent with the Laws of War, and the Terms of your Commission."[6]

The Raids of the *Ranger*

On February 6, 1778, Franklin signed two secret treaties with France: the Franco-American Treaty of Amity and Commerce, recognizing the sovereignty of the United States, and the Treaty of Alliance. On February 13, Jones sailed out of Nantes on the newly refitted *Ranger*. In the Bay of Biscay, he exchanged gun salutes with the French admiral—the first time an American naval vessel and the Stars and Stripes were saluted by a ship of a foreign navy.

In early April, the *Ranger* made for the Irish Sea, where she sank one British ship and captured another. On April 20, the *Ranger* encountered a twenty-gun British sloop of war, the HMS *Drake*, moored at the Irish port of Carrickfergus. Jones was eager to attack the *Drake* in broad daylight, but his New Hampshire crew lacked confidence in their youthful Scottish captain and refused to follow orders. The crew agreed to a night attack, but bad weather scuttled that plan.

Jones turned his attention to the English port of Whitehaven, which he knew well, having sailed from that town in his early years. It would be the first raid of an English seaport in more than a century. Again, Jones's crew was reluctant. Attempting a land battle would take his crew out of their natural element, and the crew came close to mutiny. But Jones quickly restored discipline and divided his crew into two forces that went ashore at midnight on April 22.

One member of Jones's landing party—an Irishman who had signed on purely for the chance to go home—deserted the landing party and ran through Whitehaven, warning the townspeople of an American invasion. Jones's crew managed to render the town's gun batteries unusable and set a fire on the waterfront.

Despite the setback, Jones got his crew back to the *Ranger* without casualties.

The Whitehaven raid sent shock waves through Britain. The British sense of security was shaken, American morale soared, and John Paul Jones became internationally known as a leader of boldness and daring.

His next plan was to capture a prominent English hostage to exchange for Americans held prisoner by Britain. He selected the Earl of Selkirk as his target—an aristocrat whose manor was located on St. Mary's Isle, another place he had known since childhood.

At 11:00 a.m. on April 23, Jones led a landing party of more than a dozen men onto the island. On arrival, he discovered that the earl was not on the island. Jones was prepared to leave the manor undisturbed, but the crew insisted on taking loot. Jones ordered that the looters take the earl's silver dinnerware and nothing else. The lady of the manor later described Jones's sailors as "horrid-looking wretches,"[7] and though the raid was more of a comic misadventure than a military action, it enhanced Jones's reputation as a brigand to be feared.

Jones later returned the dinnerware to the earl with a note of apology.

The following day, Jones returned to Carrickfergus to find the HMS *Drake* leaving port and heading into the North Channel between the Atlantic Ocean and the Irish Sea. The *Ranger* and the *Drake* were evenly matched in size and armament. The *Drake*'s captain was Commander George Burdon, an experienced British officer with a highly trained crew. Jones was a thirty-one-year-old captain with an undisciplined, near-mutinous crew. The only advantage the *Ranger* had was the daring leadership of its captain.

Jones kept the *Ranger*'s stern to the *Drake* so that Commander Burdon was unable to see her gun ports. Burdon sent a junior lieutenant in a boat to board the *Ranger*—and Jones took the lieutenant hostage. Because news of Jones's exploits had already spread far and wide, Burdon soon suspected he was dealing with John Paul Jones. The *Drake* hoisted the British Union Jack, and the *Ranger* raised the Stars and Stripes. Jones brought the *Ranger* across the bow of the opposing ship, unleashing an opening salvo that devastated the *Drake*'s decks.

The two ships pounded each other with cannon fire for about an hour. Finally, Jones sent a marksman up to the fighting top, armed with a musket. The marksman found his target and Commander Burdon fell to the deck, fatally wounded. The *Drake*'s sailing master realized that further resistance was useless. He surrendered—and Jones took the *Drake* as his prize.

It was a stunning victory for the Continental Navy. John Paul Jones had raided the English coast at Whitehaven and defeated the captain and crew of the *Drake*. He returned to France on May 8, 1778.

"Ambitious and Intriguing"

John Paul Jones remained in France as the *Ranger* underwent repairs. He considered the *Ranger* too small and slow. In a letter to one French naval authority, he wrote, "I wish to have no Connection with any ship that does not sale *fast*, for I intend to go in harm's way."[8] That statement speaks volumes about Jones's bold aggressiveness. [Note: the spelling of "sale" for "sail" is in the original.]

He began reading *Les Maximes du Bonhomme Richard*—the French translation of Benjamin Franklin's *Poor Richard's Almanack*. As he read, Jones came across one maxim that would change his life: "If you want your affairs to prosper, go yourself; if not, send someone."[9] That advice struck a responsive chord in him. Jones took it as an omen. Instead of relying on intermediaries, he decided to go himself to the royal court and ask the king for a ship.

Jones went in person to Versailles, and King Louis XVI agreed to give him the *Duc de Duras*, a fourteen-year-old, forty-gun warship that had served as a merchant ship for the French East India Company. It was not a fast ship, but it bristled with cannons.

Jones took possession of the *Duc de Duras* on February 4, 1779. In honor of Franklin's timely advice in *Poor Richard's Almanack*, Jones renamed the ship *Bon Homme Richard* (or, in more correct French, *Bonhomme Richard*).

On May 13, 1779, John Adams attended an elegant dinner in Paris with Jones and other American and French naval officers. That night, Adams recorded his impressions in his journal. He found Captain Jones to be "the most ambitious and intriguing Officer in the American Navy. Jones has Art, and Secrecy, and aspires very high. . . . Excentricities, and Irregularities are to be expected from him—they are in his Character, they are visible in his Eyes. His Voice is soft and still and small, his Eye has keenness, and Wildness and Softness in it."

Jones was, indeed, eccentric and irregular. He was at once keen and wild but with a paradoxical gentleness and dignity that asserted itself amid the thunder and hell of war. Carl Sandburg once called Abraham Lincoln a man of "both steel and velvet," and that description fits Captain Jones as well. Jones had a will of unbending steel—yet he was as gentle as velvet when the situation required.

The Battle of Flamborough Head

On August 14, 1779, Jones, commanding the *Bon Homme Richard*, led a seven-ship squadron out of Île de Groix off the northwest coast of France. Though most of the ships were French and commanded by French captains, they sailed under the American flag—more or less. Several captains chafed at being commanded by a Scotsman, and one challenged Jones to a duel, though Jones refused to take the bait. The squadron sailed north past Ireland (where deserters fled, taking two boats), around the north coast of Scotland, and down the east shore of England. Along the way, the squadron took prize ships and English prisoners.

On the afternoon of September 23, Jones was off the coast of Flamborough Head, East Yorkshire. Accompanied by the brigantine *Vengeance* and the frigates *Alliance* and *Pallas*, Jones encountered a forty-ship merchant convoy. The convoy was escorted by the HMS *Serapis*, a forty-four-gun warship, and a hired armed ship, the *Countess of Scarborough*. Both the *Serapis* and the *Richard* carried crews of about 320 men. Spotting Jones's squadron, Captain Richard Pearson of the *Serapis* moved to protect the merchant vessels.

Signaling with flags and guns, Jones ordered the other three ships under his command to form a line of battle, following in the *Bon Homme Richard*'s wake. Jones wanted to keep the *Serapis* from knowing how many ships were in his squadron, but Captain Pierre Landais of the *Alliance* (the captain who had challenged Jones to a duel) had a plan of his own. Using the *Alliance*'s superior speed and handling, he went around the *Bon Homme Richard* and chased the convoy. The *Countess of Scarborough* abandoned the *Serapis* to block the *Alliance* and defend the convoy. The *Serapis* was alone against the three American ships.

The *Bon Homme Richard* gradually closed with the *Serapis*. Jones ordered boarding weapons be placed in barrels on the deck—swords, pikes, pistols, long guns, and incendiary grenades. Darkness had fallen by the time Captain Pearson of the *Serapis* hailed his pursuer, demanding to know the identity of the ship. Jones answered with a gunshot.

The moon rose majestically in a clear sky over a glassy sea. The *Serapis* grew closer to the *Bon Homme Richard*. Captain Pearson again demanded the identity of Jones's ship. Jones raised the American flag and ordered his gun crew to fire a broadside at the

Serapis—at exactly the moment the *Serapis* fired at the *Bon Homme Richard*. Tragically, two of Jones's aging eighteen-pounders exploded upon firing, killing or maiming several of Jones's own men. The explosions ripped a hole just above the waterline on the starboard side of the *Richard*. The *Serapis*'s guns raked the *Richard*'s decks, shattering timbers and killing men.

The American guns had also found their targets, ripping into deck timbers, rigging, and sailors with devastating effect. Both ships reloaded and exchanged broadsides again. Then again.

"I Have Not Yet Begun to Fight!"

The *Serapis* was more maneuverable than the *Richard*, but Jones managed to get to the windward side of the *Serapis*, taking the wind out of his opponent's sails. Captain Pearson responded by backing his sails and dropping behind the *Richard*. The *Serapis*'s guns were broadside to the *Richard*'s stern. The *Serapis* fired a withering volley into the *Richard*'s cabin windows and poop deck.

Standing away from the battle, Captain Cottineau of the *Pallas* and Captain Ricot of the *Vengeance* helplessly considered their options. Any attempt to intervene might do more harm than good. Both captains watched and waited for an opportunity to help the *Richard*.

Jones knew he couldn't fire the eighteen-pounders of the *Serapis* again without risking more explosions and more damage to his own ship and crew. He had to find a different way to win—and that meant boarding the enemy's ship.

Jones ordered the *Richard* into grappling range of the *Serapis*. Captain Pearson saw what Jones had planned and he tried to maneuver the *Serapis* out of the *Richard*'s reach. Despite the superior maneuverability of the *Serapis*, the *Richard*'s bow crunched into the *Serapis*'s stern.

Pearson and Jones were close enough to see each other's faces by lantern-glow and moonlight. Pearson sneered and asked, "Has your ship struck?" The question was a pun: Had Jones's ship struck Pearson's ship—and had Jones's ship struck its colors in surrender?

With jaunty defiance, Jones called back, "I have not yet begun to fight!"[10]

To Pearson, Jones's words must have sounded like false bravado. The *Richard* was taking on water and becoming unresponsive. Surely the Americans were on the verge of surrender.

Moments later, the *Serapis*'s jib boom—the spar at the end of the bowsprit—became caught in the rigging of the *Richard*'s mizzenmast (the aft-most mast). Jones called to his crew, and all hands began lashing the two ships together, each ship's bow to the other's stern.

Pearson realized that Jones and his crew were about to board the *Serapis*. To prevent this, he dropped anchor. His goal was to suddenly halt his ship while the *Richard*, under full sail, kept sailing—which, he hoped, would tear the two ships free. But Jones and his men had already lashed the two ships tightly together. Instead of separating, the two ships remained bound together, circling slowly like dancers in a minuet.

The *Serapis*'s gun muzzles were pressed up against the *Richard*'s hull, so the British unleashed a broadside at point-blank range, shredding the *Richard*'s gun decks. Jones and his crew armed themselves from the barrels by the gunnels, snatching up swords, pikes, guns, and incendiary grenades. Jones's gunners aimed the nine-pound cannons on the *Richard*'s quarterdeck down at the *Serapis*'s deck, firing grapeshot at the *Serapis*'s crew and bar-shot at her mainmast.

Jones was ready to board the *Serapis* when he saw British marines massing on the stern. He realized his boarding party would have to walk single file along the *Richard*'s bowsprit, like ducks in a shooting gallery. Reluctantly, Jones ordered his men to cut the grappling lines and separate the two ships.

Character Under Fire

As the ships drifted apart, the *Serapis* unleashed another attack on the American ship. The *Bon Homme Richard*'s powder boy, Joseph Brussels—who was probably thirteen or fourteen years old—was fetching gunpowder from the powder magazine belowdecks with a powder horn in hand. The blast from the *Serapis* thundered across the ship, and the horn clattered on the deck. Brussels bent to pick it up—and he saw his severed arm on the deck, his hand still clutching the horn. The ship's surgeon took the boy belowdecks and saved his life by sewing up the stump.

After separating from the *Serapis*, Jones's crew tried to position the *Richard* to fire a broadside from the starboard guns—but their rudder was disabled, and the ship stalled. As the *Richard* wallowed helplessly, the *Serapis* slammed into the American ship like a battering ram. The *Serapis*'s bowsprit entangled itself with the *Richard*'s mizzen sail and rigging.

The collision also struck down the American flag. The British sailors mistakenly thought the Americans had surrendered and started cheering. As one American sailor ran up another flag, his companions fired small arms at the cheering British sailors, dampening the celebration.

Jones seized the moment. He grabbed the *Serapis*'s jib, which had fallen on the deck of the *Richard*, and called to sailing master Samuel Stacey for help. Together, the two men strained to secure the stiff, heavy rope of the *Serapis*'s jib to the *Richard*'s mizzenmast. As they struggled, Stacey began swearing like—well, like a sailor. John Paul Jones, officer and gentleman, rebuked him. "Mr. Stacey, it is no time for swearing now," he said. "You may the next moment be in eternity; but let us do our duty."[11]

Amid the thunder of cannons and the screams of dying men, John Paul Jones maintained his character. He did not want to face his Maker with the stain of foul oaths on his soul—and he urged Mr. Stacey to keep eternity in mind.

After the duel had raged for more than two hours, the *Richard* was losing the battle and had few guns capable of firing. The *Serapis* had blown so many holes in the *Richard*'s hull that many of its cannon shots were whistling through the ship without hitting anything.

At this point, one of Jones's crew, William Hamilton, crawled out on a yardarm (the outer end of the horizontal spar on which the sail is set) with a sack of incendiary grenades. Overlooking the enemy's deck, Hamilton lobbed grenades at the open hatches. With one fortunate throw, he dropped a grenade close to a charge of gunpowder. The explosion scattered flaming debris along the *Serapis*'s gun deck, setting off a chain reaction of deadly explosions.

With his losses mounting, Captain Pearson saw the battle swinging in favor of his enemy. In desperation, he sent a boarding team to assault the *Richard*. The British sailors were met by a determined force of defenders who drove them back onto their own ship.

After another hour of fighting, Captain Landais of the *Alliance* finally decided to lend Jones a hand. He brought the *Alliance* to a point outside the *Serapis*'s cannons' aim and unleashed a barrage of fire. The cannon fire did as much damage to the *Richard* as to the *Serapis*, including a hit below the *Richard*'s waterline. The American men shouted at the *Alliance* to stop firing.

A short time later, the *Alliance* made another pass, firing one broadside then another. As before, the "friendly fire" from the *Alliance*'s guns did as much damage to the *Richard* as to the *Serapis*. Despite the dubious "assistance" from the *Alliance*, Jones fought on.

Finally, a dispirited and reluctant Captain Pearson asked for quarter (a request to be allowed to surrender instead of being killed). Jones agreed. It was not the broadsides from the *Alliance* that convinced Pearson he could not win, but the dogged perseverance of John Paul Jones. Later, when Captain Pearson was court-martialed for surrendering, he testified, "The extraordinary and unheard-of stubbornness of my adversary had so depressed the spirits of my people that, when more than two hundred had been slain or disabled out of three hundred and seventeen all told, I could not urge the remnant to further resistance."[12]

Captain Pearson personally lowered his flag, signaling surrender. Then he climbed over to the deck of the *Bon Homme Richard* and stood face-to-face with John Paul Jones. Vanquished and silent, Pearson proffered his sword to Jones. Years later, Jones wrote an account of that moment for the *Hartford Courant*:

> When Captain Pearson tendered his sword to me he simply bowed and did not speak. Deeming it the part of politeness to say something that might assuage the bitterness of his feelings, I said: "Sir, you have defended your ship with credit to yourself and honor to your service. Allow me, sir, to express the hope that your sovereign may suitably reward you."
>
> When I had said this, Captain Pearson bowed profoundly, but spoke no word. I then requested Mr. Thomas Potter, of Baltimore, one of my midshipmen, to escort Captain Pearson and one of his lieutenants who was with him, to my cabin. During the whole ceremony Captain Pearson was mute. He did not utter one word or audible sound.[13]

Captain Jones and his crew made a valiant attempt to save the *Bon Homme Richard* by pumping the holds while attempting repairs, but the damage was too extensive. On the morning of September 25, two days after the battle, Jones ordered his crew to abandon ship and board the *Serapis*. The *Bon Homme Richard* slipped beneath the waves around eleven in the morning.

Weeks later, Jones learned that King George had knighted Captain Pearson, even though Pearson had lost the sea battle. Jones laughed and said, "He deserves it; if I fall in with him again, I'll make a lord of him!"[14]

In 1780, Louis XVI, King of France, honored Jones with the decoration *l'Institution du Mérite Militaire* and the title of chevalier (knight). Jones wore the title proudly for the rest of his life. When the Continental Congress presented him with a gold medal for valor in 1787, the inscription was addressed to "Chevalier John Paul Jones."

Congress promised him a new ship, the largest ever built in America at that time—a seventy-four-gun ship-of-the-line named *America*. Unfortunately, the war ended before the ship was completed, and Congress gave the ship to France as partial payment of America's war debt.

In that same year, eager to put his leadership skills to good use, Jones entered the service of Empress Catherine II of Russia. As a rear admiral of the Russian Navy, he fought a number of battles against the Ottoman Empire, for which he was awarded the Order of St. Anne, a Russian order of knighthood.

In June 1792, Jones was appointed US Consul to negotiate with the Ottoman Empire for the release of Americans held captive. Before he could complete his mission, he died in bed in Paris on July 18, 1792. The cause of death was kidney disease. He was forty-five years old.

Jones was buried in Paris at the Saint Louis Cemetery, the burial place of the royal family of France. In 1906, his remains were moved to the United States and buried in a crypt at the Naval Academy in Annapolis, Maryland.

★ LEADERSHIP LESSONS ★
from John Paul Jones

One of the most exemplary leaders of the revolution was a Scotsman who spent his teen years at sea, learning leadership skills and developing his character in the vile world of the slave trade. He detested cruelty and oppression, and he loved liberty—and that streak of fierce independence drew him to America like steel to a magnet. Here are some of the lessons of his life.

1. *Great leaders pursue their passion with a single-minded focus.* From his boyhood, John Paul Jones dreamed of being a valiant sea captain, and he pursued this passion throughout his life. He lived, breathed, and dreamed of leadership and the sea. Every decision he made, every challenge he accepted, was focused on achieving that goal.

What is your passion? What did you dream about in your early life? What excites you when you wake up in the morning? What is the last thing you think about at night? It's never too late to pursue that passion with a single-minded focus.

2. *Great leaders communicate their leadership passion to others.* Captain Jones achieved his dream by being bold, assertive, and passionate in his communication with people who could help him reach his goals. When he wanted a faster ship than the *Ranger*, he told French officials that he wanted a fast ship "for I intend to go in harm's way." His strong, persuasive communication style got him the ship that won him fame and glory, the *Bon Homme Richard*.

3. *Great leaders know that leadership can't be demanded—it must be earned.* As the young Scottish-born commander of the *Ranger*, Jones faced resistance to his leadership. When he ordered a daylight attack on the *Drake*, his crew refused to follow his command. When he ordered a raid on Whitehaven, they almost mutinied. But once his plans had succeeded, once he had earned the trust of his crew, they would follow him anywhere.

Your title may be CEO or coach or pastor, but people don't follow a title. They follow leadership they can trust—and trust must be earned. When you enter a new leadership role, be patient with the people you lead. Don't expect them to follow you blindly. Prove you can set achievable goals, formulate plans that work, and lead them to victory. Earn their confidence, and they will follow you into battle.

4. *Great leaders are their own best advocate.* After waiting endlessly for go-betweens to carry his message to King Louis XVI, Jones learned something that changed his mindset: "If you want your affairs to prosper, go yourself." When he took that advice, he got his ship—and he named it after the book that made his dream possible.

Have you been relying on others as go-betweens to your goals? Where has that gotten you? Maybe it's time to go in person to advocate for your dreams. If you want your plans to prosper, be your own best advocate.

5. *Great leaders are made of steel and velvet.* John Paul Jones was mild-mannered and soft-spoken, yet fiercely ambitious and wildly intense in battle. A leader who is all steel and no velvet is a tyrant and a dictator. A leader who is all velvet and no steel is not a leader at all. Great leaders possess those two paradoxical qualities—steel and velvet, strength and gentleness, intensity and a calm steadiness. These are traits that can be studied, practiced, and transformed into leadership habits. Whether you need more steel or more velvet in your leadership style, make an effort to achieve that balance. Learn to lead like John Paul Jones.

6. *Great leaders maintain their character under fire.* When his sailing master swore in frustration, Jones rebuked him and reminded him to do his duty. As these two great ships were locked in a death struggle, Jones kept his eternal soul unstained by sinful speech.

Do your people see you maintaining your composure and character in a crisis? Make sure you are building good character every day so you'll be well prepared when the battle comes.

7. *Great leaders never give up.* Persistence wins. When Captain Pearson taunted Jones with a question of surrender, Jones shouted back, "I have not yet begun to fight!" That defiant reply startled

Pearson and emboldened Jones's crew. Those words have spurred generations of warriors to victory over the years. The *Bon Homme Richard* should have lost the Battle of Flamborough Head—but John Paul Jones won because he refused to give up. Even when his ship was more holes than hull, even when it was sinking beneath his feet, Jones inspired his men to keep fighting—and he found a way to win.

Captain Pearson put it this way at his court-martial:

> The American ship was dominated by a commanding will of the most unalterable resolution, and there could be no doubt that the intention of her commander was, if he could not conquer, to sink alongside. And this desperate resolve of the American Captain was fully shared and fiercely seconded by every one of the ship's company.[15]

Is defeat staring you in the face? Are you being taunted by adversity, by obstacles, by opponents? Remember John Paul Jones and keep fighting. Keep leading. Tell yourself—and tell the world—"I have not yet begun to fight!"

Then find a way to win.

★ 17 ★

Sybil Ludington

The Female Paul Revere

On April 25, 1777, a force of two thousand British soldiers landed at Compo Beach near Fairfield, Connecticut. They were commanded by General William Tryon, the former British governor of New York. The following afternoon, Tryon's troops reached Danbury, Connecticut, where the Continental Army had stashed food, guns, ammunition, and tents. These provisions were guarded by a small force of two hundred American soldiers.

According to journalist Willis Fletcher Johnson, the British troops lost all semblance of military discipline upon entering Danbury. They overwhelmed the American troops, raided the army storehouse, and dragged barrels of dried corn, flour, salted meat, and canvas into the street and torched it. They commandeered gunpowder and ammunition. Opening casks of rum, they went on a drunken rampage, looting and burning the town.

"It was one of the most brutal and disgraceful performances of British arms in all the war," Johnson wrote, "and was unhesitatingly denounced as such by self-respecting British officers. It does not appear that the raid had any other object than the destruction of Danbury."[1]

While the city burned, a Patriot messenger escaped from the chaos on horseback and headed for the home of Colonel Henry Ludington in Fredericksburg, New York. As the messenger rode, the British soldiers sobered up. Having destroyed the town and seized the military provisions, the British headed back to their ships.

Sometime after eight that night—more than four hours after the attack began—the rider from Danbury reached Colonel Ludington's home. After receiving the terrible news, the colonel considered his options. His militia regiment had disbanded for the planting season. His soldiers were scattered on their farms. It was too late to save Danbury—but was there still time to punish the British for what they had done? Colonel Ludington couldn't round up the men himself. He needed to stay and assemble the militiamen when they arrived. So he turned to his daughter Sybil.

She was young, having just turned sixteen, but she could ride a horse and she knew the location of every member of the regiment.

Even though the roads were hazardous in broad daylight—and were twice as dangerous at night—Sybil didn't hesitate. Shunning propriety, she chose to ride in a man's saddle with a halter made of hemp rope. It was raining when she took off along muddy roads with dark woods on either side. Her route may have been as long as forty miles. Whenever she reached a militiaman's home, she rode up to the door, pounded on it with a stick, and gave the word: Form up at Colonel Ludington's house and be ready to fight. What she accomplished that night is nothing less than astounding.

It's no exaggeration to compare the importance of her ride to that of Paul Revere in April 1775, two years earlier. Sybil's ride was every bit as dangerous and two or three times as long as Revere's ride. Her route took her through the villages of Carmel, Mahopac, and Stormville. She rounded up the regiment, and by daybreak, they were all assembled at Colonel Ludington's home. As the regiment started off for Danbury, Sybil fell into bed exhausted.

Like most militias, Ludington's regiment was no spit-and-polish military unit. "They were a motley company," Willis Fletcher Johnson wrote, "some without arms, some half dressed, but all filled with a certain berserk rage."[2] Ludington's regiment joined up with seven hundred Continental Army regulars led by Major General David Wooster, Brigadier General Gold Selleck Silliman, and Brigadier General Benedict Arnold (the attack on Danbury occurred before he showed his traitorous ways). The generals had also received word of the attack at Danbury and were going to confront the British.

On April 27, Ludington's regiment and the army troops encountered the British at the village of Ridgefield, Connecticut. Though outnumbered and low on ammunition, the Americans took positions behind trees, buildings, and fences, harassing and killing the redcoats with sharpshooter fire. General Wooster was wounded in the fighting (he died five days later) and General Arnold had his horse shot from underneath him. The British forced the Patriots to retreat in a running battle along the streets of Ridgefield. But the British were harried by snipers and suffered significant casualties all the way back to Compo Beach.

Though the battle was considered a British victory, British forces paid a high price in dead and wounded. The Americans were cheered at having pursued the redcoats all the way to their ships. George Washington later visited Sybil at her home and personally thanked her.

Grateful Americans should remember the courage of Sybil Ludington—the sixteen-year-old leader on horseback who sounded the alarm and rallied the regiment.

★ LEADERSHIP LESSONS ★
from Sybil Ludington

What is leadership? It's the willingness, ability, and initiative to rally people to a common purpose combined with the courage and confidence to make tough decisions and stand alone. By that definition, sixteen-year-old Sybil Ludington was a leader. She decided quickly, acted without hesitation, courageously and confidently rode alone, and rallied the people of Colonel Ludington's regiment to the battle.

1. *Great leaders act decisively, courageously, and without hesitation.* Imagine how young Sybil must have felt when the rider from Danbury arrived. She was probably getting ready for bed when she heard a pounding at the door of her home. In moments, her world was turned upside down. Her father offered her a dangerous assignment. She didn't hesitate. She accepted the challenge and rode into the night.

2. *Great leaders rally their people to a cause.* The fate of a battle hung on her willingness and ability to rally her father's troops that night. She completed her mission. She rallied the troops. She made a difference. She helped pay the British back for their unprovoked attack. The town of Danbury couldn't be saved, but it could be avenged—and young Sybil Ludington was a leader and an avenger.

What is the cause that stirs your blood and motivates you to action? Who are your troops? Have you rallied them to action? Have you summoned them to the battle? When you know your cause, when you have recruited your troops, when you have rallied them to action, then you are truly a leader.

3. *Great leaders defy their fears and act with courage and confidence.* There were no headlights on Sybil's horse and no streetlights on the roads she took. She had nothing but the moon and stars to light her path. It was *dark*. It was *scary*. Racing down rain-slickened roads with dark woods on either side meant danger for a girl out alone at night. The rain, the darkness, the exhaustion,

the worry, the urgency, the weight of responsibility all must have pressed on her mind and emotions as she rode.

But Sybil Ludington had the courage and confidence to ride alone into danger. She had the boldness to summon the troops from their homes and assemble them at her father's house. She ignored the fear, loneliness, and self-doubt that must have crowded her thoughts as she rode that night. And she accomplished her mission.

Sybil Ludington is not just a role model for young leaders or female leaders—though she is certainly all of that. She's a role model for *all* leaders in every arena, in every era of history, of every age and gender. She is an example for every ordinary person who wishes to achieve extraordinary results in a time of crisis and adversity.

You're not too young. You're not too old. Are you ready to saddle up and ride? Are you ready to plunge into the darkness and accept the risks? Then you, like Sybil, are ready to lead.

☆ 18 ☆

Baron von Steuben

The Flamboyant Warrior

On September 11, 1777, British forces under General William Howe and American forces led by General George Washington met near the town of Chadds Ford, Pennsylvania. For eleven hours, they fought the Battle of Brandywine Creek—the longest single-day battle of the Revolutionary War. The British Army routed Washington's troops, forcing the Americans to retreat to the northeast, leaving Philadelphia, the then-capital of the United States, vulnerable. The British captured the American capital on September 26 and would occupy the city for nine months.

On October 4, the forces of General Howe and General Washington clashed again, this time at Germantown, Pennsylvania, six miles northwest of the center of Philadelphia. Washington attacked with four converging columns of troops, hoping to surprise Howe's forces, in the same way he had surprised and vanquished the Hessians at Trenton the previous Christmas. A heavy fog confused the advancing Americans, resulting in casualties from friendly fire. That night, the Americans made repeated attacks against well-fortified British troops, suffering enormous casualties. Finally, Washington withdrew his troops from the battlefield.

The American defeat would have been disastrously worse if General Howe had sent his forces after the retreating Americans. Instead, Howe let the Americans go. Washington and his remaining twelve thousand troops withdrew to Valley Forge for the winter of 1777 to 1778. There, they hoped to regroup and emerge stronger and ready to fight.

But the Continental Army was low on resources, poorly fed, short on blankets, and exhausted from long battles and even longer marches of retreat. One in three continental soldiers had shoes. Many were dying of infections, disease, or exposure. Hundreds deserted. Most had lost hope. Washington knew he was losing the war.

Most of the founding fathers were graduates of great American colleges, such as Harvard or King's College (later called Columbia University). But Washington had no formal higher education, and he candidly admitted to a friend, "I am conscious of a defective education."[1] Despite his tactical brilliance in his later years, he suffered in his early years from a lack of formal military instruction. He had learned military tactics through on-the-job training in the French and Indian War. And he had learned well, growing from an inexperienced and error-prone young leader to a distinguished and highly regarded commander in the Virginia Militia.

But there were still important gaps in Washington's knowledge, even when he was commander in chief of the Continental Army. Washington designed the layout of the army camp at Valley Forge. Every road, every barrack, every cook tent, mess tent, and supply tent—all were mapped out by Washington himself. Yet his men were suffering from a series of maladies and exposure. Instead of growing stronger at Valley Forge, his forces were eroding—and that was due, in large part, to Washington's lack of formal military training.

In an anguished letter to Henry Laurens, who had succeeded John Hancock as president of the Continental Congress, Washington wrote from Valley Forge on December 23, 1777.

> I am now convinced beyond a doubt, that unless some great and capital change suddenly takes place in that line this Army must inevitably be reduced to one or other of these three things. Starve— dissolve—or disperse, in order to obtain subsistence in the best manner they can. Rest assured, Sir, this is not an exaggerated picture, and that I have abundant reason to support what I say.[2]

The "great and capital change" Washington hoped for was money and material provision for his troops. It was a forlorn hope. There was no more money for Congress to provide.

Yet help was on the way, and it was coming in the form of a flamboyant and eccentric Prussian military officer named Friedrich Wilhelm Ludolf Gerhard Augustin von Steuben. Days before Washington wrote that letter to Laurens, Baron von Steuben had arrived in America and was already on his way to Valley Forge. He would be the "great and capital change" the Continental Army needed.

Sleigh Bells and Silk

Friedrich von Steuben was born the son of a military engineer. He joined the Prussian army at age seventeen and served with such competence and distinction that he was soon promoted to the general staff of Frederick the Great. He studied the military arts in King Frederick's elite school of war, which taught the tactics and strategies of the most advanced and feared army in the world.

Von Steuben's rise in the ranks came to an abrupt halt in 1763 when the thirty-three-year-old Captain von Steuben was abruptly discharged. The reason for his discharge: an accusation of homosexual behavior.

Following his discharge, von Steuben accepted a position as chamberlain to Fürst Josef Friedrich Wilhelm, a minor prince at the court of Hohenzollern-Hechingen in Swabia. Because the prince was deeply in debt, the position paid very little, but it did come with a title: *freiherr*, or baron. Calling himself Baron von Steuben, Friedrich adopted the style and position of an aristocrat.

Seeking to better his financial condition, von Steuben sought military employment in a foreign army. He came to the attention of the French minister of war, who passed his name along to Benjamin Franklin in Paris. Franklin viewed von Steuben's résumé with favor and recommended him to General Washington in a letter. Due to a mistranslation, Franklin said that von Steuben had achieved the rank of lieutenant general in the king of Prussia's service—quite a few steps above von Steuben's actual rank of captain. Franklin advanced von Steuben's travel funds for his passage to America.

Before leaving for the United States, Baron von Steuben acquired several French companions—aide-de-camp Louis de Pontière, military secretary Pierre Etienne Du Ponceau, and two others. Von Steuben and his entourage left Marseilles on September 26, 1777, aboard the frigate *Flamand*, and they arrived in Portsmouth, New Hampshire, on December 1, 1777. Von Steuben made the mistake of outfitting himself and his companions in red uniforms, and they were nearly arrested in Portsmouth as British soldiers.

On February 5, 1778, von Steuben arrived in York, Pennsylvania, to meet with the Continental Congress, which was exiled from Philadelphia due to the British occupation. Von Steuben reluctantly agreed to accept a deferred payment for his services, payable only after the successful completion of the Revolutionary War.

On February 23, General Washington received word that Baron von Steuben was on his way to Valley Forge from York. The general saddled up and rode out of Valley Forge, accompanied by his staff, to meet von Steuben on the road. His first impression of his new military advisor must have come as a shock.

Baron von Steuben traveled in a grand style, riding along the snow-clad road in a lavishly appointed sleigh with twenty-four jingling bells. The sleigh was pulled by beautiful, black Percheron draft horses. Von Steuben was decked out in a fur-trimmed silk robe. On his lap was a miniature greyhound named Azor, who went everywhere with him. His entourage also rode in the sleigh with him.

One of Washington's soldiers recorded his first impression of von Steuben: "Never before or since have I had such an impression of the ancient fabled God of War, as when I looked on the baron: he seemed to me a perfect personification of Mars. The trappings of his horse, the enormous holsters of his pistols, his large size, and his strikingly martial aspect, all seemed to favour the idea."[3]

Latrines and Other Innovations

Arriving at Valley Forge, von Steuben was horrified by conditions in the camp. His first official act was to reorganize the camp to improve basic hygiene. He moved all the kitchen tents to one end of the camp and all the latrines to the other, with latrines on a hillside so that waste material would flow away from the camp. This change reduced the level of disease that had ravaged the camp.

Next, von Steuben introduced modern boot camp drill techniques that were standard procedure in European armies. He wrote the drills in German, and his secretary, Pierre Du Ponceau, translated them into French; then Washington's secretary translated them into English. Colonel Alexander Hamilton and General Nathanael Greene also assisted von Steuben in preparing the drill manual. Copies of von Steuben's drill manual, entitled *Regulations for the Order and Discipline of the Troops of the United States*, were printed and distributed throughout the Continental Army. Many of its precepts are still employed by the United States military today.

Baron von Steuben showed the ragtag American soldiers a faster and more efficient technique for firing and reloading their weapons. The Americans practiced this technique until it became automatic. Von Steuben also drilled the Americans in marching, bayonet technique, and marksmanship. The better trained and disciplined the soldiers were, the less likely they would be to freeze up or run away in the heat of battle.

Though von Steuben was demanding, he was also good-humored, and he quickly became fluent in American profanity (he had already been fluent in the swear words of various European languages). Von Steuben's multilingual expletives, along with his excellent instruction, endeared him to the troops.

Soldiers who excelled under von Steuben's personal instruction were sent out to train other regiments in the "Prussian Exercise." General Washington was amazed at the change in his troops and his camp. On May 5, at his request, Congress appointed von Steuben inspector general of the Continental Army, with the rank and pay of a major general.

Baron von Steuben would walk through the camp, talking to the officers and men, inspecting their tents, and checking their weapons and equipment. He also established record-keeping protocols to reduce losses due to incompetence or theft.

He chose men from various regiments to form an elite honor guard to accompany General Washington and drill the rest of the troops in military decorum. Von Steuben spoke only German (save for the many expletives he picked up), and all his commands to the troops were conveyed through interpreters. His exacting Prussian speech and mannerisms, his elaborate uniform, and his eccentric personality gave him a mystique that impressed and inspired the troops.

Before von Steuben arrived, American soldiers were issued bayonets but were not instructed in their use. Most soldiers used their bayonets for skewering meat over a cook fire or for digging in the dirt. Von Steuben introduced Prussian techniques of bayonet charges, and the bayonet quickly became an essential instrument of warfare for the Continental Army.

On July 16, 1779, American troops under the command of Brigadier General "Mad Anthony" Wayne attacked a British emplacement at Stony Point, New York, about thirty miles north of New York City. The attack took place under cover of darkness. The Americans were armed with unloaded muskets with bayonets to maintain stealth. The attack was overwhelmingly successful, depriving the British of control of the Hudson River highlands overlooking the Kings Ferry crossing. Much of the credit goes to Baron von Steuben's bayonet training.

In the final years of the war, von Steuben served as General Washington's chief of staff, and they remained friends after the war. Von Steuben even attended President Washington's first inauguration in New York City in 1789.

At the end of the war, Congress was slow in paying von Steuben his promised compensation. Fortunately, he'd made many influential friends during his service, and they helped him obtain valuable tracts of land in New Jersey and upstate New York, plus an annual pension of $2,400—the equivalent of more than $70,000 today. Due to his extravagant spending, von Steuben never developed his properties and remained debt-ridden until his death on November 28, 1794. He died in a log cabin on his estate in Oneida County, New York, and was buried in a shady grove on that property. The nearby town of Steuben is named for him.

★ LEADERSHIP LESSONS ★
from Baron von Steuben

Like John Hancock, Baron von Steuben was known for his flamboyant personal style, and this sense of style contributed greatly to his leadership success. His Prussian manner and eccentric personality inspired a sense of awe among the troops. Though von Steuben's flashiness made him an intriguing leader, his competence and mastery of the art of war were even bigger factors in his success. His formal training under Frederick the Great gave him an understanding of every aspect of the military arts, from camp hygiene to bayonet warfare. The way he lived his life teaches us some vitally important leadership lessons.

1. *Great leaders impose discipline on their organization.* Discipline is the process of training a collection of individuals to fly in formation, obey the rules, and focus on the objective. It's the practice of transforming a gaggle of untrained, uncoordinated people into a roster of intensely focused team players. That's what Baron von Steuben accomplished with his boot camp at Valley Forge. If you have recruited the right kind of people to your organization, they will respect you for focusing their energy and talent on an important goal.

2. *Great leaders master the details.* Because of his Prussian military background, von Steuben recognized the importance of sanitation, cleanliness, and good nutrition to the health and effectiveness of an army. He knew that he could not drill and discipline an army of chronically sick, malnourished soldiers. So he completely reorganized the camp at Valley Forge to create a safe, clean environment for his drills and exercises. Von Steuben mastered the nonmilitary details that would prepare American soldiers to fight more effectively on the battlefield.

3. *Great leaders multiply their own effectiveness by training and mentoring others.* Von Steuben trained soldiers to become leaders and trainers of the "Prussian Exercise." He chose some to become the best of the best—an elite honor guard—who would drill other troops in the Prussian approach to discipline and decorum. Who are you training? Who are you mentoring? Who are you training as the "best of the best" so they can spread your leadership values and principles throughout your organization?

4. *Great leaders codify the traditions, values, rules, and goals of the organization in writing.* Von Steuben oversaw the creation of a standardized manual for the entire Continental Army, the *Regulations for the Order and Discipline of the Troops of the United States.* Every team or organization needs a written reference manual to ensure that everyone is on the same page. Written rules and regulations prevent misunderstandings and provide a ready reference for clarifying practices and procedures. A good manual should be written in everyday language, not jargon, and should promote orderly functioning without being overly restrictive.

5. *Great leaders seek to earn respect—not popularity.* Von Steuben was a tough, demanding leader who didn't care if the troops liked him. Yet, in the process of earning the respect and obedience of his soldiers, he also earned their genuine admiration. The troops knew that von Steuben cared about their lives and well-being—and he cared about winning just as much as they did. Though he was demanding and strict, the soldiers trusted and admired him because he was turning them into warriors and victors.

If you are a leader like von Steuben—an experienced and well-trained expert who is able to train others—make your leadership skills available to solve problems and generate success. A leader like you will always be in demand.

If you're like Washington and you're aware of some gaps in your knowledge, find a Baron von Steuben who can supply what you lack. Find a qualified, capable leader who can help you and your team become even more successful.

Then go out and win some leadership battles.

★ 19 ★

Nathanael Greene

The Fighting Quaker

When asked to name the most underrated general in American history, defense analyst Robert Killebrew of the Center for a New American Security chose Nathanael Greene. Killebrew called Greene the "second-best American general in the [Revolutionary] war (after Washington)," adding that Greene "would have assumed command if [Washington] had been disabled." Greene's leadership accomplishments are all the more amazing, Killebrew notes, when you realize that General Greene was a "Quaker who learned war from textbooks."[1]

An underrated general indeed. Few Americans are familiar with Nathanael Greene's name, much less his exploits and his contribution to the Revolutionary War.

Greene walked with a limp as the result of a childhood injury. That limp prevented him from being selected as an officer in the Rhode Island militia, so even his peers underestimated him. He also suffered from chronic asthma and impaired vision in his right eye, the result of a smallpox inoculation. Yet General Washington considered Nathanael Greene his most brilliant and reliable officer—an assessment confirmed by the pivotal role Greene played in winning the Southern campaign of the war.

Who was this lesser known yet vitally important leader in the Revolutionary War? Who was Nathanael Greene?

Greene was born to a devout and wealthy Quaker family in Warwick, Rhode Island, in 1742. His father purchased a mill in Coventry, Rhode Island, for Nathanael to operate. Nathanael took a leadership role in Coventry, including helping to establish the first public school in that community. Greene was elected to the legislature in 1770 and was an early supporter of the cause of independence.

Like so many great leaders, Nathanael was a voracious reader from an early age. As a young man, he began acquiring an extensive library. One book that profoundly influenced him was John Locke's *Essay on Human Understanding*, which advocated Enlightenment principles of rational inquiry and evidence-based knowledge. Though his faith in God never wavered, he began to question some of the tenets of his Quaker upbringing. Also on his shelves were many books on military science, which he studied intently.

Greene's passion for military knowledge strained his relationship with his family and his strict pacifist church. Though he was a devout Quaker throughout his life, Greene struggled to reconcile the church's pacifist teachings with his own belief in the cause of liberty. After he attended a military parade in 1774, church leaders expelled him from the Quaker fellowship.

That same year, Nathanael Greene married Catharine Littlefield, and they went on to have six children. Catharine was an independent-minded woman who shared Nathanael's interest in politics and the military. After the start of the Revolutionary War, she often visited her husband at the army camp.

Greene helped establish a Rhode Island militia, the Kentish Guards, as a first step in preparing for a revolution against Great

Britain. Though he was one of the organizers of the group and its best tactician, he was denied an officer's commission because of his limp. So he served as a private instead.

In April 1775, after the Battles of Lexington and Concord ignited the Revolutionary War, the legislature commissioned Greene as a general in the army of Rhode Island. Later that same year, the Continental Congress commissioned Greene as a general in the newly created Continental Army, where he served alongside the army's commander in chief, General George Washington.

Like Henry Knox, Nathanael Greene was a self-taught soldier. The foundation of his military education came from books. But Greene quickly added battlefield experience to his book education. He honed his leadership skills in the Siege of Boston, the New York and New Jersey campaign, and the Philadelphia campaign.

Washington appointed Greene quartermaster general of the Continental Army in 1778, during the bleak winter at Valley Forge. It was not an assignment Greene wanted. Instead of leading men into battle, he was running an army camp. The job involved bookkeeping and administration, but no tactical skills. It was a thankless job—but in his Quaker humility, Greene was willing to do whatever Washington asked of him.

In February 1779, the arrival of Baron von Steuben brought a new level of energy and discipline to Valley Forge. Nathanael Greene, working closely with General Washington's aide-de-camp, Alexander Hamilton, assisted von Steuben in drafting a training manual for the Continental Army. Greene learned a great deal about military training by watching von Steuben transform a camp full of beaten, dispirited men into a well-trained, highly motivated fighting force.

The Horatio Gates Disaster

Washington's chief rival in the Continental Army was General Horatio Gates, who favored defensive rather than offensive action.

Gates's primary leadership skill was taking credit for the victorious actions of others. He took credit for the American victory in the Battles of Saratoga in 1777, though the tactics were planned and executed by his field commanders. In many cases, victory was the result of field commanders *ignoring* Gates's orders.

Along with General Thomas Conway, Gates was a member of the infamous Conway Cabal, a group of military leaders who conspired to discredit Washington. When the Conway Cabal was exposed in 1778, Gates apologized to Washington and accepted an assignment as commander of the eastern section of the army.

By 1780, the war was going badly in the South. The Second Continental Congress, believing Gates to be a military genius, sent him to take command of the demoralized continental forces in North Carolina.

Gates, commanding a joint force of continental soldiers and poorly trained Virginian and North Carolinian militia, squared off against the British forces of General Charles Cornwallis at Camden, South Carolina. The date was August 16, 1780. When 800 British infantry advanced with fixed bayonets against 2,500 American militiamen, the militia threw down their fully loaded weapons, turned, and ran. One of Gates's officers, General Edward Stevens, later described the chaotic retreat in a letter to then-governor of Virginia Thomas Jefferson: "Picture it as bad as you possibly can and it will not be as bad as it really is."[2]

The British captured more than a thousand Americans. Gates fled on horseback as soon as he saw the panicked retreat. By nightfall, he was sixty miles away in Charlotte, North Carolina. He later persuaded influential friends to help him avoid a court-martial for cowardice.

After the Horatio Gates disaster, Congress realized its mistake in choosing Gates over Washington to command the Southern war effort. Congress restored Washington's authority over the Continental Army in the South. Washington chose his trusted general from Rhode Island, Nathanael Greene, to oversee the Southern battlefront.

Greene now faced a sobering challenge. Cornwallis was the most brilliant tactician of all the British commanders—and he led forces that were far better trained and better disciplined than the Continental Army and the militias. Greene knew he could not defeat Cornwallis on an open battlefield, as General Gates had attempted. Greene needed to fight an entirely new kind of war.

Historian James A. Warren, former visiting scholar in the American Studies department at Brown University, has called Nathanael Green "the Revolution's unconventional mastermind" and "the most brilliant American strategist you've never heard of."[3]

Guerilla Warriors

General Greene employed a previously unknown approach to war that we now call "guerrilla warfare" or "asymmetrical warfare." It's an approach in which small, fast-moving groups of combatants employ sabotage, ambushes, hit-and-run raids, stealth, surprise, and strategic retreats to wear down a larger, less mobile, and less flexible traditional army. The goal of guerilla warfare is not to defeat the enemy on the battlefield but to deplete the enemy's strength over time. Guerilla forces typically take advantage of terrain—mountains, swamps, forests—that pose problems for large armies.

Where did Greene get the idea for employing guerilla tactics against General Cornwallis? Such tactics had never been used in the history of European warfare. The only writer who advocated guerilla tactics was the ancient Chinese military strategist Sun Tzu, author of *The Art of War*, written in the fifth century BC.

Had Greene read *The Art of War*? It's possible. The first Western translation of the classic East Asian text was a 1772 French translation by a Jesuit priest, Jean Joseph Marie Amiot. Perhaps

Greene was influenced by *The Art of War*. But then again, Greene might have simply sized up the forces of the enemy and realized that only an imaginative and unconventional approach could win.

In December 1780, Nathanael Greene arrived in Charlotte, North Carolina, to take command of the Southern forces. By that time, British troops controlled strategically important sections of Georgia and South Carolina. General Cornwallis's six-thousand-man army was strengthened by well-equipped cavalry and artillery units plus Loyalist militias—American military units that supported the British Army.

General Greene's key allies and subordinates in the Southern campaign included his second-in-command, Baron von Steuben; Cavalry Commander Henry "Light-Horse Harry" Lee (the father of future Confederate general Robert E. Lee); the Marquis de Lafayette; Brigadier General Daniel Morgan (an expert in sniper warfare); and Francis Marion (aka the "Swamp Fox").

It's worth noting that Francis Marion's approach to warfare was a perfect fit for Nathanael Greene's guerilla tactics. Marion led a loose-knit militia called Marion's Men. They were self-sufficient, provided their own provisions and arms, and served without pay. It was Marion's foe, Colonel Banastre Tarleton, who nicknamed him the "Swamp Fox"—a *nom de guerre* that elevated Marion to the status of living legend throughout the South.

Marion's Men would appear like ghosts, strike with speed and precision, then fade into the forests and swamps. Marion terrorized the Loyalists and exasperated the British. General Cornwallis complained about Marion's Robin Hood–like habit of plundering British supply wagons and distributing the goods among the locals, so that "there was scarcely an inhabitant . . . that was not in arms against us."[4] The US Army claims Francis Marion as the founder of US Army Special Forces (the Green Berets).

Nathanael Greene's first decision upon arriving in North Carolina was to divide his meager forces. After the defeat at Camden,

South Carolina, the Americans were demoralized, ill-fed, and ill-equipped. In Greene's estimation, these soldiers were in no condition to undertake a military operation of any kind. He decided to take the main force of one thousand soldiers southeast. He assigned Daniel Morgan to lead a smaller force southwest.

Daniel Morgan's specialty was the long rifle. The difference between a musket and a long rifle is the bore, the hollow space inside the barrel. Musket barrels are smooth-bored; rifle barrels have spiral grooves that spin the bullet during firing. A musket is accurate up to eighty yards, but a long rifle can be accurate up to three hundred yards. At the start of the Revolutionary War, Daniel Morgan recruited a company of ninety-six skilled marksmen nicknamed Morgan's Riflemen. Morgan trained them as long-range snipers. Because of the rifle's added range, his men killed many British officers who thought they were safely out of range. When British officers fell, their troops often fled in leaderless panic.

Nathanael Greene met Daniel Morgan for the first time on December 3, 1780, in Charlotte. When Greene gave him six hundred men to lead, he ordered Morgan to avoid direct contact with the enemy—the men needed rest.

So Daniel Morgan led his men through the backcountry to the southwest. He knew he was being pursued by Lieutenant Colonel Banastre Tarleton, whom Americans called "the Butcher" or "Bloody Ban" (Tarleton's tactics included terrorizing citizens and pillaging towns). As they traveled, Morgan talked to soldiers who had fought Colonel Tarleton's British Legion. They described Tarleton's tactics on the battlefield—and Morgan conceived a plan. He decided to disobey Greene's order and provoke a confrontation with Tarleton. The place he chose for that confrontation was a little town called Cowpens, South Carolina.

Morgan knew that Tarleton was contemptuous of American militias. He would not expect a sophisticated trap from a bunch of backwoods Americans. Morgan would place his marksmen up front and Tarleton would mistake them for the usual motley militia. He'd place the militia behind the marksmen and the army regulars behind the militia. The marksmen and militia would inflict damage on the redcoats, then withdraw, luring the British to charge right into a trap.

On the morning of January 17, 1781, Tarleton and his troops walked into that trap—and Morgan snapped it shut, surrounding one thousand British troops and cavalry. The Battle of Cowpens went exactly according to plan—Tarleton's troops were trapped in a shooting gallery. While Morgan's forces suffered only twenty dead and sixty-nine wounded, Tarleton's forces were effectively destroyed, suffering 30 percent casualties and 55 percent captured or missing. Tarleton managed to escape along with two hundred troops. Though Morgan had disobeyed General Greene's orders, his victory over "the Butcher" was a huge morale-lifting victory—and Nathanael Greene forgave him for not following orders.

An infuriated Cornwallis set out in pursuit of Daniel Morgan's forces, but Nathanael Greene linked up with Morgan, then retreated toward North Carolina. It was a strategic retreat on Greene's part. It was designed to lure Cornwallis away from his supply lines—and it was effective.

While General Greene's main force continued the retreat, Greene sent a smaller contingent under Colonel Otho Williams to harass British forces with guerrilla tactics. These were tactics Cornwallis had never seen before and couldn't understand. Were the Americans cowards? Why didn't they stand on an open battlefield and fight like civilized men?

Cornwallis didn't realize that Greene was looking for a battlefield that would give his troops an advantage. On February 22, Greene selected his battlefield and led his troops across the Dan River into North Carolina. There he continued to vex Cornwallis with guerilla warfare.

The Savior of the South

By early March 1781, Greene had received reinforcements from Virginia and North Carolina, increasing his army to about four thousand. On March 14, Greene's army encamped at Guilford Courthouse, North Carolina (named Greensboro in Nathanael Greene's honor in 1808). There Greene's forces prepared for Cornwallis's attack.

Greene set up three defensive lines, one manned by North Carolina militiamen, a second manned by Virginia militiamen, and the third consisting of Continental Army regulars. Retreat was part of the plan. On the afternoon of March 15, Cornwallis ordered an all-out assault against the Americans. As the British charged the first line, the North Carolina militiamen fired volleys at the British then turned and fled. The British thought the Americans were fleeing in panic, as they had under Horatio Gates's command, but everything was proceeding according to Greene's plan.

Next, the British encountered the second line, and the Virginia militia put up a stiffer resistance for a while—then they also fled the battlefield. Cornwallis ordered an assault against the third line of Continental Army regulars—but the British were surprised by the fury of the American resistance and fell back. Cornwallis reformed his troops and launched another assault, this time on the left flank of the third defensive line—but this assault was forced back by "Light-Horse Harry" Lee's cavalry.

Watching his forces being devastated by these uncouth Americans, a frustrated Cornwallis ordered his artillery to fire into the melee. British grapeshot shredded British and American soldiers indiscriminately. Greene saw that the Continental Army's left flank was collapsing, so he ordered a retreat.

The Battle of Guilford Courthouse was over. The Americans had technically lost. But the British had suffered such high casualties, and American losses were so light, that history considers General Nathanael Greene the victor in that encounter. He had won by losing. He had advanced the American cause by retreating from the battlefield.

Greene and Cornwallis were fighting completely different battles. Cornwallis was trying to take real estate. Greene was fighting to keep his losses to a minimum and the enemy's losses at a maximum. Not only did the Battles of Cowpens and Guilford Courthouse seriously deplete British forces but the British soon found it next to impossible to recruit Loyalists to supplement the British Army. These battles demoralized the British and contributed greatly to Cornwallis's surrender in the Siege of Yorktown, Virginia, in October 1781.

During the war, General Cornwallis wrote this assessment of Nathanael Greene: "[Greene is] as dangerous as Washington. He is vigilant, enterprising, and full of resources—there is but little hope of gaining an advantage over him. I never feel secure when encamped in his neighbourhood."[5]

And historian Terry Golway wrote,

> His grasp of military strategy, his competence, his organizational skills, and his persistence in defeat led Congress to promote him quickly from brigadier to major general. Washington's appreciation for Greene's talents was such that on at least two occasions, fellow officers and politicians described Greene as . . . the man Washington had designated to succeed him if he were killed or captured.[6]

Nathanael Greene resigned his commission in the Continental Army in late 1783. The Fighting Quaker, aka "The Savior of the South," limped home to a hero's welcome in Rhode Island. The legislatures of North Carolina, South Carolina, and Georgia awarded him grants of land to thank him for his service. Facing mounting debts, Greene moved to the South and took up residence at the Mulberry Grove Plantation outside of Savannah. He fell ill in June 1786 and died at the age of forty-three.

★ LEADERSHIP LESSONS ★
from Nathanael Greene

Nathanael Greene is unquestionably one of the most unusual and instructive leadership role models to emerge from the Revolutionary War. Here are some of the lessons of his leadership life.

1. *Great leaders study the art of leadership*. Read books on leadership and biographies of great leaders. Nathanael Greene's library shelves bulged with books on history, philosophy, biography, and military science. After he had absorbed all the leadership wisdom he could from books, he was mentored by one of the greatest leaders in American history, George Washington. As Greene worked closely with General Washington and Baron von Steuben, he was taking a master class in leadership.

When Washington appointed Greene quartermaster general of the army, Greene was inwardly disappointed—but the experience deepened his appreciation for the importance of logistics and supply lines to a successful war effort. His stint as quartermaster general may have influenced his decision to lure General Cornwallis away from his supply lines to weaken and stress Cornwallis's troops. Greene was a great leader because he studied the art of leadership.

2. *Great leaders are resilient and flexible*. Leaders easily fall prey to rigid thinking. Some leaders assume that if a certain approach has worked in the past, it will work in every situation. But conditions change and leaders must be nimble, flexible, and willing to try unconventional tactics. Charles Cornwallis was a brilliant strategist when it came to traditional, conventional warfare, but he could not adjust to the innovative schemes of Nathanael Greene. A fast-changing world needs agile thinkers and pioneering leaders.

3. *Great leaders don't let others define victory for them*. At the Battle of Guilford Courthouse, Nathanael Greene won by losing. He advanced by retreating. Cornwallis won the real estate, but he paid an unacceptably high price. Throughout the Southern

campaign, Greene would retreat and Cornwallis would give chase. To Cornwallis's astonishment, the army that retreated won the war. In your own leadership arena, don't be afraid to lose a battle here and yield ground there. Define victory on your own terms.

4. *Great leaders recruit the best and build teams of excellence.* General Greene's list of subordinates in the Southern campaign reads like a who's who of Revolutionary War leadership: Baron von Steuben, "Light-Horse Harry" Lee, the Marquis de Lafayette, Daniel Morgan, and more. One of the most important functions of leadership is assembling great teams. General Greene started with demoralized, malnourished, defeated troops, and within months he and his leadership team transformed them into an unconquerable fighting force. As you build your teams, seek out people with talent, skill, character, enthusiasm, and a proven track record.

5. *Great leaders innovate and keep their competition guessing.* Nathanael Greene used tactics and strategies that General Cornwallis had never seen before and couldn't grasp. In a competitive leadership arena, you must continually innovate and keep your competition off balance. If your competitors expect you to stand and fight, you might want to turn tail and run. If they expect you to mass your forces in one place, you might want to divide and take off in two directions. Whatever you do, make sure it's unexpected.

6. *Great leaders pay attention to details but always keep the big picture in view.* Don't get so obsessed with winning the battle that you lose the war. Be aware of the operational, personnel, and tactical details—but make sure you understand how they all fit into the overall strategy. Nathanael Greene saw the big picture. While the British were focused on winning the battle, Greene was busy winning the war. If defeat and retreat are necessary to win the war, so be it.

Greene expressed his new concept of warfare in this simple formulation: "We fight, get beat, rise, and fight again."[7]

★ 20 ★

Marquis de Lafayette

The Aristocratic Warrior

When he first arrived in the United States, the Marquis de Lafayette had no battle experience. In fact, when Lafayette first met General George Washington the night of July 31, 1777, he was a starstruck teenager, just nineteen years old—and Washington at first saw Lafayette not as a fellow military leader but as a headache. In time, however, Lafayette would become one of Washington's most trusted generals and a close friend, and he would earn the title "The Hero of Two Worlds."

The Marquis de Lafayette was born in Chavaniac in south central France on September 6, 1757. His full name was Marie Joseph Paul Yves Roch Gilbert du Motier, Marquis de Lafayette, and he was born of noble military lineage. One of his ancestors, Gilbert de Lafayette III, served in Joan of Arc's army at the Siege of Orléans in 1429. According to legend, another of Lafayette's ancestors returned from the Sixth Crusade with a holy relic, the crown of thorns of Jesus. Lafayette's own father, Colonel Michel Louis

Christophe Roch Gilbert, was slain by an English cannon in the Battle of Minden in 1759, during the Seven Years' War.

Lafayette lost his father when he was two years old and his mother when he was thirteen. He was raised thereafter by his paternal grandmother. In 1771, the thirteen-year-old Lafayette was commissioned a *sous-lieutenant* in the Musketeers. His duties were purely ceremonial, such as marching in parades or performing precision drills for King Louis XVI. In 1774, he was commissioned a lieutenant in the Noailles Dragoons, a mounted infantry.

A year later, while Lafayette was training with his unit at Metz in northeast France, several of his comrades spoke excitedly of the Revolutionary War in America. The notion of an entire people rising up against English tyranny ignited his imagination. Lafayette had found a cause worth fighting for.

The Marquis's aristocratic family was well connected with the court of King Louis XVI, and in 1776, Lafayette asked the king's blessing to go to America and fight for the glory of France. The king pointed out that France was not officially supporting the American cause, and he ordered Lafayette to remain home. But Lafayette was determined to go to America, even if it meant disobeying the king.

Lafayette introduced himself to the American diplomat Silas Deane, who was in Paris negotiating with the French government for assistance. Deane was impressed with Lafayette's earnestness and enthusiasm. Despite Lafayette's youth and lack of battlefield experience, Deane eagerly recruited him for the Continental Army and promised him the rank and authority of a major general. Deane undoubtedly expected the rank to be purely ceremonial. He was primarily interested in Lafayette's wealth, family name, and connections.

The Marquis de Lafayette paid his own way to America and agreed to serve in the Continental Army without pay. He arrived in South Carolina on June 13, 1777, and traveled to Philadelphia to

meet with the Continental Congress. He carried a letter of introduction from Silas Deane, praising his military prowess. Congress
commissioned Lafayette as a major general in the Continental
Army on July 31.

On the night Lafayette was commissioned, General George
Washington was in Chester, Pennsylvania, just down the road from
Philadelphia. He was the guest of honor at a dinner at City Tavern,
where military officers and members of Congress often gathered.
When Lafayette learned that Washington was just down the street,
he went to get his first look at the famed American general.

Lafayette never forgot his first impression of "that great man,"
as he called Washington in his memoirs.[1] At six-foot-two, Washington stood much taller than most of the officers and townspeople in the tavern. (Lafayette, at five-foot-nine, was also taller
than the average man of that era.) It was hero worship at first
sight. Lafayette recalled that "the majesty of his figure and his size
made it impossible" to mistake him for anyone other than George
Washington.[2] The general symbolized everything Lafayette wished
to become—a man of dignity, honor, and battlefield distinction.

The Battle of Brandywine

Having grown up without a father, Lafayette idolized Washington
as a father figure—the man he hoped to make proud someday.
The night they were introduced, Washington welcomed Lafayette
warmly and invited him to travel with him for an inspection of
the Delaware River fortifications.

Later, when Washington learned that young Lafayette had been
assigned to his command—and with a rank of major general,
no less!—he was horrified. Though he was unfailingly cordial to
the worshipful young Lafayette, Washington wrote to Congress
asking what he was supposed to do with this nineteen-year-old
from France. Did Congress expect him to give Lafayette command

of an American division? Would this teenager lead Americans into battle?

Lafayette followed Washington around, spending every available moment at his hero's side. It was clear to Washington that Lafayette took his rank seriously and fully expected to command American troops, even though his military experience consisted of only two summers of training with the Dragoons. Washington tried to stall Lafayette, but a letter from Paris, signed by both Silas Deane and Benjamin Franklin, urged him and Congress to give Lafayette a minor battlefield assignment to boast of. A battlefield opportunity would arrive soon.

In August and September 1777, seventeen thousand British and Hessian troops under the command of General William Howe marched toward Philadelphia. Washington believed that Howe's forces would cross the Brandywine River at Chadds Ford, so he positioned his main force at that location. Then he assigned Lafayette to a division led by Major General John Sullivan and sent Sullivan's division more than a mile north of Chadds Ford. His goal was to keep the Marquis de Lafayette away from the thick of the battle.

But Washington didn't know that only half of General Howe's forces were at Chadds Ford, under the command of Hessian General Wilhelm von Knyphausen. General Howe was personally leading a second column to the north. Instead of keeping young Lafayette out of harm's way, he sent him to face General Howe's main force.

Sullivan's troops were caught by surprise, but they boldly engaged the enemy. Lafayette was on the front lines as musket balls zipped past his head. One musket ball hit Lafayette in the left leg, passing cleanly through his calf. Lafayette continued fighting, but he soon grew weak from loss of blood and was helped to his horse by an aide. Reluctantly, he left the battlefield—but he had won the admiration of the Americans.

Though the Battle of Brandywine was a bitter loss for the Americans, leading to the British capture of Philadelphia, it was a defining moment for Lafayette. Washington placed the young Frenchman under the care of his own personal surgeon. In Washington's account of the Battle of Brandywine, he cited two wounded officers by name, General Woodford and the Marquis de Lafayette. That account was widely circulated throughout the thirteen colonies, and Lafayette became a household name among Americans.

More importantly, the Brandywine experience welded Washington and Lafayette together as lifelong comrades and friends.

A Conspiracy against Washington

In a skirmish that became known as the Battle of Gloucester, Lafayette led a regiment of three hundred Patriots, mostly militia, to a British encampment near Gloucester, New Jersey. The encampment was manned by some four hundred Hessian *jägers* (light infantry). Under cover of darkness, Lafayette led a surprise attack, catching the Hessians off guard. Disorganized and panicked, the Hessians retreated while Lafayette and his soldiers gave chase.

From the main British encampment, General Charles Cornwallis sent highly trained British Grenadiers to provide cover for the retreating Hessians. Lafayette's regiment returned fire for a while, then withdrew and returned to General Greene's main force. Lafayette's regiment suffered one killed and five wounded, but the British suffered roughly thirty killed and thirty wounded.

Because of his success at the Battle of Gloucester, Lafayette's stock rose rapidly with General Washington, General Greene, and the troops at Valley Forge.

Lafayette remained with Washington at Valley Forge throughout the grim winter of 1777 to 1778. Despite the wretched conditions at the camp (prior to Baron von Steuben's reorganization efforts), Lafayette made many important friends at Valley Forge, including von Steuben, Greene, and Alexander Hamilton.

As his English improved, Lafayette began to understand the politics of America more clearly. He realized he had naively thought that all Americans believed in the Whig political philosophy—a belief in representative democracy and tolerance of dissent. He was shocked to discover that vast numbers of Americans were Tories, monarchists, and Loyalists who supported King George III, the Anglican Church, and Mother England. Steeped in the military traditions of his aristocratic family, Lafayette was bewildered by the pacifist neutrality of the Quakers.

In a letter to Washington, he expressed his growing awareness of the divisions within the American population: "When I was in Europe I thought that here almost every man was a lover of liberty and would rather die free than live slave. You can conceive my astonishment when I saw that Toryism was as openly professed as Whigism itself."[3] While shedding his illusions, Lafayette remained eager to fight and ready to sacrifice for the cause of liberty. He identified the cause of American independence with the cause of human liberty.

Meanwhile, General Horatio Gates conspired with a few members of Congress and officers of the army in the so-called Conway Cabal. Gates arranged to have Congress create a Board of War with Gates himself as president. Through this power play, General Gates—Washington's military subordinate—managed to make himself Washington's civilian superior, a bizarre conflict of interest. Gates was angling to replace Washington as commander in chief of the Continental Army.

Members of the Conway Cabal, including Gates, viewed Lafayette as an obstacle to their goal of ousting Washington. They saw Lafayette as young, impressionable, and ambitious, and they believed they could lure him into their intrigues against General Washington by giving him the military responsibilities he craved. The members of the cabal planned an invasion of Quebec, which

England had wrested from France in the Seven Years' War. The invasion would be led by General Thomas Conway, with a minor leadership role given to Lafayette. Members of the cabal believed Lafayette would leap at the opportunity to strike a blow against England for the honor of France.

Lafayette understood what the conspirators were trying to do, and he wanted to refuse the appointment, but Washington urged him to accept it. Lafayette dutifully agreed to help prepare the invasion, which was to be staged from Albany, New York. When Lafayette went to Albany, he found the troops to be ill-trained and too few to carry out an invasion. He called off the plan and wrote to Washington, informing him of the situation.

Upon his return to Valley Forge, Lafayette wrote Congress and denounced the Board of War's plan to invade Quebec. Congress agreed with Lafayette's assessment—and the Conway Cabal began to unravel. In November 1778, Gates was forced to resign from the Board of War, apologize to Washington, and accept reassignment to the eastern section of the army. Thanks to Lafayette, the conspiracy against General Washington came to an end.

Monmouth Courthouse and Rhode Island

In March 1778, France formally recognized the United States as a sovereign nation. Great Britain, worried about potential French intervention in the American Revolution, pulled out of Philadelphia to concentrate its forces around New York City. When the British made camp at Monmouth Courthouse in central New Jersey, General Washington appointed General Charles Lee to lead an assault at Monmouth. Lee, aided by the Marquis de Lafayette, launched the attack on June 28, but he issued confusing orders to the troops, which resulted in chaos.

Lafayette saw the American attack collapsing and sent a dispatch to General Washington, urging him to come and personally take command of the battle. Washington came, found the army in disarray, and relieved Lee of command. Then he rallied the Americans for another assault, forcing the British to withdraw.

In July, the French fleet arrived at Delaware Bay under the command of Admiral Charles Henri Hector d'Estaing. Washington hoped to attack Newport, Rhode Island, with the help of Admiral d'Estaing. He sent Lafayette and Nathanael Greene to Rhode Island with a three-thousand-man force. Lafayette proposed a plan to Admiral d'Estaing that involved a joint French-American force with Lafayette in command. The admiral refused, preferring to attack the British fleet on the open sea. A storm wrecked Admiral d'Estaing's plans and damaged both the British and French fleets.

After the storm, Admiral d'Estaing moved his ships to Boston for repairs. News of the French fleet's abandonment of Newport had reached Boston—and the city was in an uproar. John Hancock and the Marquis de Lafayette went to Boston to calm the citizens. Then Lafayette returned to Rhode Island to organize an orderly retreat of American forces to Boston.

For his gallantry, Congress awarded Lafayette a citation of valor.

The Road to Yorktown

In October 1778, Lafayette asked permission to return to France on temporary leave. General Washington and the Continental Congress granted him leave, and Lafayette set sail in January 1779.

Because Lafayette had disobeyed King Louis XVI in going to America, the king had him arrested upon his arrival in February. Lafayette served eight days of house arrest in a luxury hotel, then was released, still in the good graces of King Louis XVI. The arrest had been a mere face-saving gesture—the king was justly proud of Lafayette's exploits in America. Lafayette had brought glory and honor to France and had won fame on both sides of the Atlantic.

Soon after Lafayette's release from house arrest, William Temple Franklin (standing in for his ailing grandfather, Benjamin Franklin) presented Lafayette with a ceremonial sword, a gift from a grateful Continental Congress. While in France, Lafayette urged the king to provide more aid to America, and he purchased supplies for American troops at his own expense.

In March 1780, fourteen months after he returned to France, Lafayette left aboard the frigate *Hermione*, arriving back in Boston on April 27. Though he returned to a hero's welcome, Lafayette was dismayed to learn that the war effort was faltering. The American attempt to recapture Savannah in October 1779 had failed.

Washington had wintered in Morristown, New Jersey, during the worst winter of the eighteenth century—worse, in fact, than the winter at Valley Forge. Washington's underclothed, underpaid, malnourished troops barely survived that disastrous winter. But Lafayette's arrival at the Morristown camp on May 10, 1780, was a happy reunion for both he and Washington. The American troops were encouraged to learn that a large French force was on the way, commanded by General Jean-Baptiste de Rochambeau.

In early 1781, Washington placed Lafayette in command of the Virginia continental forces, with orders to join up with troops led by Baron von Steuben. Their goal was to defeat the British forces commanded by Benedict Arnold, who had defected to the British in September 1780. Lafayette was ordered to capture Benedict Arnold and summarily hang him.

In August, Lafayette went to Yorktown, Virginia, where British forces under Cornwallis were encamped. He set up artillery emplacements on Malvern Hill. From that location, his troops kept General Cornwallis pinned down with his back to the York River.

On September 5, 1781, the French fleet of Admiral François de Grasse fought the English fleet in the Battle of the Chesapeake, near Yorktown. The French prevailed and established a blockade, sealing off Chesapeake Bay and the York River.

Soon after the Battle of the Chesapeake, seventeen thousand American and French troops, led by General George Washington and General Jean-Baptiste Rochambeau, arrived and surrounded British-occupied Yorktown. Cornwallis and his army were trapped in Yorktown without access to supplies and ammunition.

On October 14, two small American forces, one led by Lafayette and the other by Alexander Hamilton, charged two of the ten redoubts (defensive fortifications) that surrounded Yorktown. They cleared the British defenders from those two redoubts, leaving Yorktown vulnerable to attack. Cornwallis launched a last-ditch counterattack, but his demoralized troops were easily beaten back.

The British general was out of options. There was no escape from Yorktown except by capitulation. On October 17, Cornwallis requested a cease-fire. After two days of negotiation, Cornwallis surrendered his army of eight thousand troops to Washington. He signed Washington's Articles of Capitulation in Moore House at Temple Farm on October 19, 1781.

Cornwallis knew that his surrender at Yorktown meant the war was over. Great Britain did not have the resources to rebuild its army and fight again. Though the British continued to hold several American cities, the Siege of Yorktown was the last major land battle of the Revolutionary War. Almost two years later, on September 3, 1783, the British government signed the Treaty of Paris and the war was officially over.

The Hero of Two Worlds

On December 21, 1781, Lafayette left Boston aboard the frigate *Alliance*. As the ship put out to sea, Lafayette wrote a touching letter to Washington, which included these words of friendship:

> Adieu, my dear General; I know your heart so well that I am sure that no distance can alter your attachment to me. With the same candor, I assure you that my love, my respect, my gratitude for

you, are above expression; that, at the moment of leaving you, I felt more than ever the strength of those friendly ties that forever bind me to you.[4]

The Marquis returned to France as a conquering hero and was awarded the rank of major general in the French army. The American Congress also made him an honorary United States citizen—the only foreigner so honored until Congress similarly honored Sir Winston Churchill in 1963.

An incident that occurred in 1783 speaks volumes about Lafayette's character and his serving heart. During that year, the wheat harvest failed across much of France, but Lafayette's estate at Chavaniac managed to reap a great harvest. Lafayette knew that the market price of wheat had risen sharply and the peasants in nearby villages could not afford the inflated cost. When the manager of Lafayette's farm told him, "This is the time to sell," Lafayette replied, "No, this is the time to *give*."[5]

A few years after Lafayette's return to France, he developed a strong friendship with Thomas Jefferson. Lafayette and Jefferson had barely known each other during the Revolutionary War, despite being well-acquainted with each other's reputations.

In 1784, Congress appointed Thomas Jefferson minister plenipotentiary to France (the title refers to the head of a diplomatic mission, below the rank of ambassador). Soon after Jefferson's arrival in Paris, Lafayette told him to consider his house as a second home, and he introduced Jefferson to many of the most influential people in Parisian society.

Five years later, Lafayette began drafting France's Declaration of the Rights of Man and of the Citizen. Lafayette asked Jefferson to help him write it and Jefferson eagerly agreed. The two included a clause that called for the end of slavery.

In 1824, President James Monroe and Congress invited Lafayette to tour the United States and celebrate the nation's fiftieth anniversary on July 4, 1826. Lafayette arrived in New York on

August 15, 1824, accompanied by his son, Georges Washington Louis Gilbert de La Fayette. He was greeted by Revolutionary War veterans who had fought at his side. Lafayette was astonished to find the road to Boston lined with cheering Americans who saw him as a figure out of legend. Then he went to Philadelphia, where he was also honored with cheers and speeches.

Wherever he went, he saw new buildings under construction and amazing economic vitality. The thirteen states had grown to twenty-four—and Lafayette visited each one. He had originally planned to spend four months in America, but he extended his stay to sixteen months. He was especially honored to visit Fayetteville, North Carolina, the first American city named after him. He visited Mount Vernon in Virginia and knelt at the grave of his old friend George Washington. He also visited Yorktown on October 19, 1824—the fiftieth anniversary of the surrender of Cornwallis.

Finally, he visited Monticello, the home of his old friend Thomas Jefferson. Huge crowds followed Lafayette wherever he went—and the crowd at Monticello was no exception. About four hundred people stood in reverent silence as an aging Lafayette stepped down from his carriage. The door of Monticello opened, and an aging Thomas Jefferson emerged from the domed house.

The two men walked toward each other and embraced.

"Ah, Jefferson!"

"Ah, Lafayette!"

Both men had tears on their faces—tears of joy to see each other and to see what America had become in its first fifty years. Then, with arms around each other, they walked inside for a long talk.[6]

Having played a key role in both the American Revolution and the French Revolution of 1789, the Marquis de Lafayette richly deserved the title *Le Héros des Deux Mondes*, "The Hero of the Two Worlds." When King Charles X was overthrown in the July Revolution of 1830, the people wanted Lafayette to become dictator of

France. He refused, though he did agree to serve as commander of the National Guard.

On May 20, 1834, after a battle with pneumonia, he passed from life into legend. America mourned. Black bunting draped both houses of Congress for thirty days—the same honor previously bestowed on Lafayette's hero, George Washington.

★ LEADERSHIP LESSONS ★
from the Marquis de Lafayette

George Washington welcomed a number of foreign-born military leaders to the revolution, including cavalry officer Casimir Pulaski, combat engineer Tadeusz Kościuszko of Poland, and Bavarian-born division commander Baron Johann de Kalb, who died (as he said with his dying breath) "fighting for the rights of man." But of all the international heroes at Washington's side, none was more celebrated and beloved than the Marquis de Lafayette. Here are some of the leadership lessons that stand out in his illustrious life.

1. *Great leaders are idealists.* Lafayette believed in the cause of liberty for all humanity, and he threw himself into that cause, body and soul. He took great personal risks for that cause. He was wounded in battle and bled for it. He preached that cause to the world through the Declaration of the Rights of Man and of the Citizen, which he wrote with the help of Thomas Jefferson.

When Lafayette met Washington for the first time, he was brimming with energy and enthusiasm for the American cause. His motives were probably mixed. This nineteen-year-old French aristocrat undoubtedly hated the British, who had deprived him of his father when he was two years old. Yet there is no question that a belief in the Jeffersonian ideals of "life, liberty and the pursuit of happiness" was deeply ingrained in Lafayette. He fought for those ideals in both the American and French Revolutions.

Great leaders believe in great ideas. They preach their ideas and sacrifice for them, fight for them, and even die for them. Great leaders invest their lives in causes that are greater than themselves.

2. *Great leaders are realists*. Don't let your idealism blind you to reality. In time, Lafayette realized that America was a divided land (much as it is today). He had naively entertained an idealized view of all Americans as freedom-minded champions of democracy and dissent and was shocked and dismayed by the many Loyalists in the land.

Lafayette was able to shed his illusions while remaining true to his ideals of freedom. Though not all Americans were willing to sacrifice for their own freedom, Lafayette remained committed to the cause. Though the divisions within America dismayed him, Lafayette never lost his zeal. He remained faithful to his beliefs to the end of his life.

3. *Great leaders seek out great mentors*. Lafayette sought to be mentored by his hero, George Washington, and, over time, they became friends for life. From Washington, Lafayette learned to temper his eagerness for battle, care for the needs of his troops, inspire loyalty by demonstrating genuine love for the troops, and invest time in planning and preparation. When Washington first met nineteen-year-old Lafayette, he found an eager, aggressive, but impetuous young man full of unrealized potential. Within a short time, Washington and other officers, such as Nathanael Greene, were mentoring Lafayette and transforming him into a mature and seasoned leader.

4. *Great leaders focus on character and courage*. At first glance, Washington saw Lafayette as an overly ambitious youth who was given too big a title too soon. Major general indeed! But Lafayette soon proved that there was more in him than met the eye. He was only nineteen and had very little training, yet he was steeped in the military traditions of his family—and especially the tradition of unflinching courage on the battlefield. When it mattered most,

his courage showed. It flowed red from his wound. It showed in his will to keep fighting and leading even as he was weakening from loss of blood.

A leader who is fearless in battle inspires fearlessness in his troops. Courage is one of the most important traits every leader must have. Lafayette had courage in abundance. And his abundant courage made him a leadership legend.

How far will your courage take you?

★ 21 ★

Mary Hays, Anna Marie Lane, Deborah Sampson, and Others

Revolutionary Women in Combat

American women have demonstrated leadership in the defense of freedom ever since the founding of the United States of America. Some fought as soldiers, disguised as men. Some were spies and message couriers. Some risked the dangers and horrors of war to take pitchers of water to thirsty soldiers. As a result, women who served in supportive roles on the battlefield were nicknamed "Molly Pitcher."

Many historians think the original "Molly Pitcher" was Mary Ludwig Hays, who fought in the Battle of Monmouth in June 1778. Others think Margaret Corbin, who fought at Fort Washington,

New York, in November 1776 was the inspiration for the name. It's important to remember the role these early women in combat played in securing the blessings of liberty for us today. Here are the stories of some of the courageous women who led during the Revolutionary War.

Mary Ludwig Hays

Born in Trenton, New Jersey, in October 1744, Mary Ludwig was thirty years old when the American Revolutionary War broke out. In early 1777, two years after the war began, she married William Hays, a patriotic activist and an artilleryman in Captain Francis Proctor's Fourth Artillery of the Continental Army.

During the harsh and dismal winter of 1777, Mary Hays joined her husband at General Washington's winter camp at Valley Forge in Pennsylvania. Washington's wife, Martha, organized a group of women, mostly wives of soldiers, to launder uniforms and blankets and care for sick soldiers.[1] Mary was one of those women.

While Mary's husband trained as an artilleryman under Baron von Steuben, she and other soldiers' wives carried water to the troops in the field. Water was important not only to slake the soldiers' thirst but also for the maintenance of artillery pieces. After firing, each gun barrel had to be swabbed out with a wet sheepskin mop to remove spent powder and hot embers. To wet the mop, a water bucket next to the cannon had to be continually replenished.[2] Mary and the other soldiers' wives were the water carriers—the "Molly Pitchers"—for the artillerymen.

Mary Hays accompanied her husband to the battlefield near Monmouth Courthouse in central New Jersey. There, on June 28, 1778, a large American force—roughly a third of the Continental Army—attacked British forces commanded by General Henry Clinton. The American forces were commanded by General Charles Lee. General Lafayette also took part in the engagement.

The battle began at about eight in the morning, and by ten thirty, General Lee's plan of attack was collapsing as Proctor's Fourth Artillery dueled with the cannons of the Royal Artillery. Because of a heat wave in the region on the day of the battle, many soldiers on both sides were falling unconscious from heatstroke. One of those who fell—either from wounds or from heat exhaustion—was Mary's husband, William. When William was taken off the battlefield to be treated, Mary took his place and proceeded to swab and load the gun, just as she had seen her husband do so many times before.

Private Joseph Plumb Martin—whose memoir of the war is considered a prime source of information by Revolutionary War historians—witnessed Mary Hays standing at the breech of her husband's cannon, ramrod in hand, when a British cannonball whooshed between her legs, ripping away the lower part of her petticoat. She reportedly looked at the torn garment "with apparent unconcern" and calmly observed "that it was lucky it did not pass a little higher." Then she continued reloading the cannon.[3]

Fighting ceased as darkness fell. The Americans expected the battle to resume in the morning, but the British forces retreated during the night, leaving the result of the battle inconclusive. Mary's husband survived and continued serving as an artilleryman, and Mary returned to serving as a "Molly Pitcher."

According to some accounts, General Washington personally commended Mary Hays for her bravery on the battlefield.[4] Years later, the Commonwealth of Pennsylvania awarded Mary an annual pension of forty dollars in gratitude for her service. She died in 1832 at the age of eighty-seven.[5]

Anna Marie Lane

The first woman documented as having served in the American Army was Anna Marie Lane of Virginia. Disguised as a man, she went with her husband, John Lane, to enlist in the Continental Army. The husband-and-wife team fought side by side in numerous battles between 1776 and 1781. She was probably in her early twenties at the beginning of the American Revolutionary War.

Countless American women served the cause of independence, assisting the war effort as nurses, cooks, and laundry workers. But Anna wanted to serve on the front lines. Soldiers of the colonial era rarely bathed, and they slept in their uniforms, so it might not have been difficult for Anna to keep her gender a secret. There was no enlistment physical to pass. If a soldier was able to load and fire a musket, he—or, in Anna's case, she—could serve.

John and Anna Lane fought in battles in New York, New Jersey, Pennsylvania, and Georgia. The most crucial battle Anna fought in was the Battle of Germantown, near Philadelphia, on October 3, 1777. During that battle, Anna was wounded. Though details are sketchy, there are indications she may have refused medical treatment to prevent doctors from discovering her secret. The wound caused her to have difficulties walking for the rest of her life.

Despite her injury, Anna continued serving and fighting alongside her husband until the land war ended in 1781. John and Anna Lane settled in Virginia after the war, and she volunteered in a military hospital, tending to soldiers. In 1808, the state of Virginia awarded Anna a pension and recognized her for receiving wounds in battle and for rendering extraordinary service to the nation while wearing the uniform of a soldier. She died on June 13, 1810.

Deborah Sampson

She was born Deborah Sampson in Plympton, Massachusetts, in 1760. In the Continental Army, however, she was known as "Robert Shirtliff." Deborah was orphaned at an early age and lived for a while with a widow who taught her to read. The widow died when Deborah was just ten, so the young girl went to work as an indentured servant for a family in Middleborough. She would remain an indentured servant—in essence, a slave—until she was emancipated by law at age eighteen.

Though she was not mistreated as a servant, Deborah was not allowed to attend school (the master of the house didn't believe in education for women). Eager to learn, Deborah asked the boys of the family to share their schoolwork with her. She was so diligent in educating herself that, by age nineteen, she was able to make a living as a schoolteacher. She also worked as a weaver, a maid, and a carpenter.

The Revolutionary War broke out when Deborah was fifteen years old. The war was in its sixth year when Deborah Sampson put on men's clothes and enlisted in the Continental Army under the name "Timothy Thayer." At five-foot-nine, Deborah Sampson was taller than most women of that time and on par with most men. She was well-suited to disguise herself as the opposite gender.

Unfortunately, a local citizen recognized her when she was signing her enlistment papers and told the company commander that "Timothy" was a woman. Her enlistment was revoked—and the Baptist church she belonged to disciplined her for her deception, barring her from fellowship until she confessed and asked forgiveness. There is no record that she ever did so.

On May 20, 1782, Deborah Sampson went to a different Massachusetts town and enlisted again, this time under the name "Robert Shirtliff" (or "Shurtleff"—historical records use both spellings). She served with the Fourth Massachusetts Regiment, Light Infantry Company, an elite unit consisting of fifty or sixty men who were specially trained as marksmen. She fought in New York State and received a battle wound to the forehead in June 1782, as well as two musket wounds to the thigh on July 3, 1782, while fighting near Tarrytown. She performed surgery on herself and managed to remove one of the musket balls with a knife and sewing needle.

The second musket ball had penetrated too deep, and she carried it in her leg for the rest of her life.

Deborah Sampson also served as an orderly to General John Patterson in Philadelphia from June to September 1783. During that time, she fell sick and was treated by Dr. Barnabas Binney. He discovered her secret but decided not to tell the authorities that "Robert Shirtliff" was a woman—at least, not yet. He took her to his house, and his wife and daughters helped nurse her back to health.

When she had recovered enough to return to duty, Dr. Binney gave her a note to deliver to General Patterson. Deborah Sampson delivered the note, which informed the general of Sampson's gender. General Patterson treated her kindly and gave her expense money for her journey home to Massachusetts. She was honorably discharged on October 25, 1783.[6]

In 1802, Deborah Sampson began traveling and giving lectures about her service as a woman in the Continental Army. After her talk, she would put on her army uniform and demonstrate a drill routine.

But just two years later, she was in debt and facing poverty. She sometimes borrowed money from her friend Paul Revere, the Boston Patriot and silversmith. Revere believed she deserved a pension, so he petitioned Congress to award her an army pension in view of her good character and excellent service record. Congress approved the request in 1805 and awarded her additional back pay in 1809.

Deborah Sampson died of yellow fever at age sixty-six on April 29, 1827.

The Guardian of the Bridge and Other Heroines

When the soldiers from Pepperell, Massachusetts, marched off to war, their wives stepped up and defended the town. The woman the wives chose to lead them was Prudence "Pru" Cummings Wright. They armed themselves with clubs, cutlery, pitchforks, and anything else that could serve as a weapon. They took turns making regular patrols around the town.

Born in 1740, Pru was a Patriot and was married to militiaman David Wright (they had eleven children together). She was thirty-five years old when the Revolutionary War began. Much to Pru's dismay, two of her brothers, Thomas and Samuel, were Loyalists who actively aided the British.

In April 1775, soon after the Battles of Lexington and Concord, Pru was visiting her mother in Hollis, New Hampshire, six miles north of Pepperell. Also in her mother's home that day were Pru's brother Thomas and a Loyalist friend and fellow conspirator, Captain Leonard Whiting of Hollis. Pru eavesdropped as her brother and Captain Whiting discussed a plan to send a message to the British in Boston, revealing the location of a gunpowder cache that was hidden by the Patriot militia.

Prudence hurried back to Pepperell and summoned the other women. They hatched a plan to stop the two Loyalist conspirators at Jewett's Bridge. Gathering their clubs and pitchforks, the women headed for the bridge. They shielded their lantern and waited in silence.

After a while, the women heard the approach of two riders on horseback—Pru's brother Thomas and Captain Whiting. Pru stepped forward, unshielded the lantern, and shined the glare in the eyes of the two men. She told them to halt and dismount. Then the other women came out of the darkness and surrounded the men.

Pru's brother was momentarily dazzled by the lantern light—but he recognized the voice of his sister. He knew her patriotic convictions and he also knew she would deal with him as if he were any Loyalist stranger. He wheeled his horse about and fled.

Captain Whiting believed he had nothing to fear from these women, so he spurred his horse on toward the bridge—but the women dragged him from his horse and searched him. After finding the treasonous documents hidden in his boots, they pulled him to his feet and marched him off to Solomon Roger's tavern. They held him prisoner that night and turned him over to the militia in the morning.[7]

Pru's leadership during the Revolutionary War earned her the title "Guardian of the Bridge." She died in 1823 at age eighty-three. A marker near her grave is inscribed: "In Memory of the Captain of the Bridge Guard."[8]

Another heroine of the war was Margaret Cochran Corbin, who went into harm's way alongside her husband, serving as a nurse and cook. Her husband, John Corbin, was an artilleryman at Fort Washington in upper Manhattan. On November 16, 1776, John was one of six hundred American soldiers holding the fort against four thousand Hessian troops. Margaret had accompanied John out of fear that something would happen to him if she wasn't watching his back.

The fort was defended by two cannons. John Corbin was on one of the gun crews, and Margaret was standing nearby when John was felled by an enemy bullet. The thing she had always feared had finally happened. Her beloved John was dead—but there was no time for grieving. She stepped up and took his place, loading and firing the cannon until she, too, was hit—wounded in the arm, chest, and jaw.

The British won the Battle of Fort Washington, taking any survivors as prisoners and completing the British conquest of Manhattan Island. Because of her wounds, Margaret Corbin was released. On July 6, 1779, Congress's Board of War granted Margaret a military pension.

Then there was Sally St. Clair from South Carolina. Like Anna Marie Lane and Deborah Sampson, Sally St. Clair disguised herself as a man to join the Continental Army. She was a woman of mixed African and French descent. Little is known about her, though legends claim that she joined the army to be close to her lover, an army sergeant. What we know for sure is that she served for a while in the militia of Francis Marion, the Swamp Fox, and she fought bravely in the Siege of Savannah in 1782. Her gender was not discovered until she was found dead on the battlefield of that siege.[9]

Sally was memorialized by the nineteenth-century poet George Pope Morris in "Sally St. Clair: A Song of Marion's Men." Morris probably romanticized and fictionalized Sally's death. In his poem, he portrayed Sally as so well-disguised that even her lover didn't recognize her:

> In the ranks of Marion's band,
> Through morass and wooded land,
> Over beach of yellow sand,
>   Mountain, plain and valley;
> A southern maid, in all her pride,
> March'd gayly at her lover's side,
>   In such disguise
>   That e'en his eyes
>   Did not discover Sally.[10]

According to legend, Sally stepped in front of a lance aimed at her beloved. True or not, these legends speak to the way her leadership and sacrifice gripped the American imagination.

Finally, there is the story of Kate Barry, the heroine of the Battle of Cowpens. Catherine Barry was a skilled horsewoman who was well-acquainted with the backwoods trails and shortcuts around her plantation in South Carolina. She served as a scout for the Continental Army.

As British troops were moving into place for the Battle of Cowpens on January 17, 1781, Kate rode swiftly, summoning the local militia to come to the aid of General Daniel Morgan. Because of her boldness, swiftness, and knowledge of the terrain, she helped Morgan launch a surprise attack against Lieutenant Colonel

Banastre Tarleton. Tarleton's forces were effectively wiped out—a turning point in the Patriots' reconquest of South Carolina.

☆ LEADERSHIP LESSONS ☆
from Revolutionary Women in Combat

One of the least discussed aspects of the Revolutionary War is the role of women in the struggle for liberty. The women who fought for American independence inspire us all, regardless of our gender, and there are many lessons we can draw from their lives.

1. *Great leaders remain calm in the thick of battle.* In times of conflict, confusion, and opposition, remember Mary Hays standing by her husband's cannon, ramrod in hand, as an enemy cannonball whooshed between her legs. "Lucky it didn't pass a little higher," she said, then calmly continued reloading. If you can keep your head in the heat of battle, you are truly a leader.

2. *Great leaders never give up.* Though Deborah Sampson was found out the first time she tried to enlist in the army, she tried again under a different name. She refused to let a little thing like gender get in her way. She was determined to fight on the battlefield—but first she had to fight a battle against gender stereotypes. Because she believed in herself and refused to give up, she made a valuable contribution to the cause of freedom.

3. *Great leaders use what they have and do what they can—and that's how they make a difference.* The wives of Pepperell, Massachusetts, saw their husbands march off to war, then they stepped up to defend their town and their new nation. They selected a leader—Prudence Cummings Wright—and armed themselves for battle with clubs, cutlery, and pitchforks. They used what they had, did what they could, and made a difference on behalf of freedom.

4. *Great leaders put principle above favoritism.* When Prudence Cummings Wright learned that her Loyalist brother was carrying

messages to the British, she acted on principle instead of favoritism toward a family member. She and the other wives of Pepperell stopped the men at Jewett's Bridge and prevented them from getting word to the British. As a leader, show no favoritism or nepotism. Don't use your leadership position to gain an unfair advantage. Instead, maintain your principles and integrity.

5. *Great leaders keep leading, despite personal loss and suffering.* Margaret Cochran Corbin stood alongside her husband as an enemy bullet killed him. In that moment, her entire life changed, and she lost the person who meant more to her than life itself. Yet she didn't stop to grieve. She stepped into the gap where her husband had stood, and she carried on his work.

Leaders like Margaret Cochran Corbin are selfless. They do whatever needs to be done to achieve their objective. When one soldier falls, leaders stand in the gap and finish the job. When danger arises, they summon the troops and meet the threat head-on. They don't accept the limitations that culture may place on them because of racial or gender stereotypes. Like Kate Barry, they use their knowledge and skills. They mount up and ride. They summon the troops. They fight. They sacrifice. Sometimes, like Sally St. Clair, they die. But as long as they have breath in their bodies, they rally the troops, they inspire, and they lead.

★ 22 ★

Alexander Hamilton

The Father of American Prosperity

We don't know the date or even the year that Alexander Hamilton was born. He emerged from obscurity in the British West Indies to become one of the most famous and influential of all the founding fathers.

Hamilton was one of General George Washington's most reliable commanders. After the Revolutionary War, he played a key role in the adoption and interpretation of the United States Constitution. He championed the concept of a strong federal government and founded America's financial system. He also founded a popular newspaper, the *New York Post*.

Though Alexander Hamilton never visited Europe, he understood European history, culture, and politics better than any other American of his time. He was fluent in French, and he subscribed to periodicals from France and England. He also read countless books on European history.

Hamilton became well-acquainted with the longtime French diplomat Talleyrand (Charles Maurice de Talleyrand-Périgord), who was impressed with the depth of Hamilton's understanding of European affairs. Talleyrand once told American academician George Ticknor that Hamilton was one of the most brilliant men of his time. When Ticknor contradicted Talleyrand's praise of Hamilton, Talleyrand replied, "*Mais, monsieur, Hamilton avait deviné l'Europe*. [But, sir, Hamilton had foretold Europe.]"[1] In other words, Hamilton's understanding of European cultural and political trends was so insightful that he predicted European events before they happened.

His many accomplishments notwithstanding, Alexander Hamilton would have been amazed to gaze more than two centuries into the future and find that his life would inspire a 2015 Broadway musical incorporating such noncolonial-era music genres as hip-hop, pop, rhythm and blues, and soul.

Emerging from Obscurity

Hamilton was born out of wedlock in Charlestown on the tiny island of Nevis, which is part of the Leeward Islands of the West Indies. Though we do not know the exact date of his birth, historians believe he was born sometime between 1755 and 1757. His father, James Hamilton, was a roguish merchant from Scotland. At the time of Alexander's birth, his mother, Rachel Faucette Lavien, was married to, but estranged from, a plantation owner named Johann Michael Lavien. Rachel had left her husband because he had squandered her family fortune and publicly accused her of adultery. The accusation led to her imprisonment for several months in a ten-by-thirteen-foot cell with a single, small window.

James Hamilton abandoned Rachel Lavien and her two sons, James Jr. and Alexander, in 1765. It's possible that he left them to prevent Rachel from being charged with bigamy by her estranged husband. James continued to write to his family, and he signed his letters to Alexander, "Your very Affectionate Father."[2]

Three years after James left the family, Rachel died due to a tropical fever. Fortunately, Thomas Stevens, a prosperous merchant on Nevis, provided a foster home, a library of books, and an education for young Alexander. But nothing could fill the hole in his heart left by the loss of his mother.

As a boy, Alexander Hamilton was an avid reader, and his reading inspired his desire to see the world beyond his little island. Reading also inspired Hamilton's interest in writing. In 1772, the teenage Hamilton wrote a letter to his father that contained an exciting account of a hurricane. James Hamilton showed the letter to Hugh Knox, a minister and journalist. Knox published the hurricane essay in the *Royal Danish-American Gazette*. The people of the Nevis island community were so impressed by the teen's writing that they collected contributions to send him to college in America.

Hamilton arrived in Boston in October 1772, then he proceeded to New York City. He spent a year at Elizabethtown Academy Preparatory School in New Jersey, where he lived with William Livingston, a leading lawyer and Patriot intellectual who later became governor of the state. Hamilton enrolled at King's College in New York City in the fall of 1773.

While in college, Hamilton wrote essays in support of the revolutionary cause. Though he advocated American independence and opposed the Loyalists, he condemned mob violence as a matter of conscience. On May 10, 1775—a month after the start of the Revolutionary War—he saved Myles Cooper, a Loyalist Anglican priest and president of King's College, from a howling mob by talking to the mob and distracting them long enough for Cooper to get away.

Soon after the start of the Revolutionary War, Hamilton and other students from King's College joined a New York volunteer militia. Hamilton drilled with the militia in the morning before classes. He studied military tactics and history from books and was quickly promoted within the militia. He led a successful raid, capturing British cannons at the battery in lower Manhattan while under fire from a British ship. As a result of those captured cannons, Hamilton's militia company became an artillery company.

His studies were interrupted by a shattering event on August 22, 1776—the Battle of Long Island. The thunder of artillery could be heard all over New York City. Five days later, a massive force of 32,000 British troops, 30 warships, and 170 transports forced General Washington's retreat at Kip's Bay and began the seven-year British occupation of New York City. King's College was forced to close—and Hamilton became a full-time soldier in the revolution.

During the early years of the revolution, Hamilton became acquainted with a number of influential Patriot leaders. These included Nathanael Greene, John Jay (an abolitionist founding father and the future first chief justice of the Supreme Court), and Sons of Liberty leader Alexander McDougall.

Hamilton organized a sixty-man military company, the New York Provincial Company of Artillery, to defend New York against the British Army. He led the company with distinction in the Battles of White Plains, Trenton, and Princeton, and other major military engagements. His achievements were noticed by a number of ranking officers in the Continental Army, who offered him positions on their staffs. He refused all offers but one—aide-de-camp to the commander in chief of the Continental Army, General George Washington.

A Broken Relationship

Hamilton served as Washington's top aide for four years, drafting orders and letters at Washington's direction. He took part in high-level discussions of sensitive issues, including intelligence and diplomacy. He gained an intimate understanding of Washington's thought processes and use of authority, and the four years he spent at Washington's side were a master class in leadership. Hamilton's fluency in French was especially helpful when the Marquis de Lafayette and other French officers joined the American cause.

In 1780, Hamilton married Elizabeth Schuyler, whom he called Eliza. Her love and devotion sustained him through the turbulent years of the revolution and beyond.

On February 15, 1781, an unfortunate misunderstanding over a petty matter fractured the close relationship between Washington and Hamilton. Washington was under stress because of mutinies among Pennsylvanian and New Jerseyan troops during the harsh winter. Hamilton, too, was in a sour mood, feeling that Washington had been unfair to him for months, passing him over for promotion.

On that day, Washington was ascending the stairs of the New Windsor farmhouse that served as his winter headquarters on the Hudson in New York. At the same time Hamilton was coming down the stairs. As they passed, Washington said he wished to speak to him. Hamilton nodded and continued down the stairs to deliver a letter, then he paused briefly for a word with Lafayette. Finally, he went back up the stairs to find Washington waiting at the top, fuming with impatience.

"Colonel Hamilton," Washington said angrily, "you have kept me waiting at the head of the stairs these ten minutes. I must tell you, sir, you treat me with disrespect."

Hamilton replied, "I am not conscious of it, sir, but since you have thought it necessary to tell me so, we part."

"Very well, sir, if it be your choice."

Hamilton later claimed that the "ten minutes" wait that Washington claimed did not last more than two minutes.

Washington later thought better of his rebuke and sent an aide to tell Hamilton he regretted his angry words. He urged Hamilton to allow him to make amends, but the twenty-six-year-old

Alexander Hamilton was still angry. He replied, "I certainly would not refuse an interview if he desired it, yet I should be happy [if] he would permit me to decline it."

With sadness, Washington honored the request, and Hamilton was no longer part of the general's staff. Hamilton biographer Ron Chernow summed up the episode this way:

> The rupture with Washington highlights Hamilton's egotism, outsize pride, and quick temper and is perhaps the first of many curious lapses of judgment and timing that detracted from an otherwise stellar career. Washington had generously offered to make amends, but the hypersensitive young man was determined to teach the commander-in-chief a stern lesson in the midst of the American Revolution. Hamilton exhibited the recklessness of youth and a disquieting touch of *folie de grandeur*. On the other hand, Hamilton believed that he had been asked to sacrifice his military ambitions for too long and that he had waited patiently for four years to make his mark. . . .
>
> Fortunately, Washington and Hamilton recognized that each had a vital role to play in the war and that this was too important to be threatened by petty annoyances. Despite their often conflicted feelings for each other, Washington remained unwaveringly loyal toward Hamilton, whom he saw as exceptionally able and intelligent, if sometimes errant; one senses a buried affection toward the younger man that he could seldom manifest openly.[3]

Why would Alexander Hamilton willingly ruin his relationship with this great leader over such a trivial matter? Why would he spurn Washington's generous offer to reconcile? At first glance, this seems like sheer immaturity on Hamilton's part, but I think there's more to this incident than meets the eye. It's important to understand the wounds Hamilton suffered in his childhood and how those experiences shaped the ambitions of his early adulthood.

Because of the abandonment and loss he suffered early in life, Hamilton probably grew up with insecurities and a sense that personal relationships are tenuous and impermanent. Perhaps he saw Washington—viewed by so many as a father figure—as an *abandoning* father like his biological father, a father who frustrated his son's ambition to overcome the past.

Hamilton desperately wanted to get back to the battlefield, where he had first distinguished himself. He had demonstrated courage and tactical ingenuity in war, and he expected his association with Washington to lead to greater exploits and glory. Instead, Washington had kept him in a dead-end desk job. Washington undoubtedly considered him indispensable in that job—but Hamilton worried that he was ruining his chances of bettering himself after the war.

Historian Michael E. Newton, author of *Alexander Hamilton: The Formative Years*, explains Hamilton's ambition to prove himself on the battlefield: "In Hamilton's day, showing courage on the field of battle was one of just a few ways for an unknown person to win fame. Hamilton had a genius and was hard-working but did not come from an illustrious family like most of the Founding Fathers. He knew that winning glory in battle would make him famous and help him further his career."[4]

Hamilton and Lafayette at Yorktown

Though Hamilton took his leave of General Washington in February 1781, he remained committed to his goal of obtaining a battlefield command. In early July, he played a daring gambit. He wrote to Washington expressing his desire for a command—and he included his commission document in his letter. In essence, he was issuing an ultimatum: Give me a field command or I'm resigning my commission.

Many leaders in Washington's position would have bristled at Hamilton's impudence—but Washington probably admired Hamilton's boldness. So he sent an aide to Hamilton with a message.

Hamilton later recalled that Washington "pressed me to retain my commission, with an assurance that he would endeavor by all means to give me a command."[5]

During most of the summer of 1781, Washington had been focused on liberating New York City. But sometime in August, two pieces of information changed his thinking and turned his attention toward Yorktown, Virginia. First, he learned that the French fleet under Admiral François de Grasse was sailing from the West Indies to Chesapeake Bay. Second, Major General Lafayette reported that General Cornwallis had entrenched his forces in Yorktown—which was surrounded on three sides by water.

Washington understood Cornwallis's thinking: Yorktown was an impregnable fortress, nearly surrounded by a vast moat. But Washington realized that Cornwallis had unwittingly trapped himself and left his army vulnerable to a siege. With the French fleet on one side and American forces on the other, the British Army would be cornered.

So Washington sent two thousand American soldiers along with four thousand French soldiers under General Jean-Baptiste de Rochambeau. Admiral de Grasse brought three thousand troops from the West Indies. Lafayette commanded another force of seven thousand American troops. Alexander Hamilton was also sent in command of a light infantry battalion made up of companies from New York and Connecticut.

When Hamilton arrived at Williamsburg, the staging site for the Yorktown operation, he rejoined his good friend the Marquis de Lafayette. Hamilton and Lafayette enjoyed a special bond of friendship due in part to Hamilton's understanding of French culture and his mastery of the French language. Hamilton was one of the few Americans Lafayette could converse with easily and at length. For the Yorktown siege, Hamilton's light infantry battalion would serve under the divisional command of Lafayette.

Hamilton and his men arrived at the outskirts of Yorktown on September 29. There Cornwallis had erected a series of ten defensive strongholds called redoubts. Eyeing the ninth and tenth redoubts, Hamilton pondered possible plans of attack.

On October 8, American and French cannons began bombarding Yorktown from land and sea. The thunder of the guns was terrifying. Death rained down on the town with relentless fury and horror. At the same time, the soldiers and civilians in Yorktown were being ravaged by starvation and smallpox. Out of compassion for the enemy as much as his own troops, Washington wanted to shorten the siege and keep casualties on both sides to a minimum.

The key to Washington's plan was the ninth and tenth redoubts—and the key to seizing those redoubts involved stealth and surprise. The assault would take place by night. Lafayette would lead the attack on the ninth redoubt and Hamilton's battalion would attack the tenth.

On the night of October 14, Lafayette and Hamilton each assembled a team of about three hundred men. They fixed bayonets but left their muskets unloaded. Military planners had chosen the moonless night so that the attackers would not only be silent but invisible to the enemy.

At the appointed time, Hamilton and his men sprang from their trenches and sprinted toward the tenth redoubt, a quarter of a mile away. A line of "sappers"—soldiers responsible for breaching fortifications—ran at the front of the charge to penetrate the barrier of sharpened stakes, opening a lane for the infantrymen to enter. Hamilton's men poured through the breach and approached the redoubt wall. One soldier would kneel at the wall and another would jump up on his shoulder and leap onto the parapet. Hamilton himself was one of the first over the parapet and inside the redoubt.

Once inside, Hamilton's men surprised the British defenders, bayoneting any soldier who put up a fight. Hamilton made sure that every British soldier who stopped resisting was spared and treated humanely. He believed that war should be conducted according to rules of honor, similar to the rituals of dueling.

The capture of the redoubt was accomplished in the space of less than ten minutes with few American casualties. Hamilton had finally achieved the battlefield victory he sought, and the mission he led could hardly have gone better.

Lafayette's capture of the ninth redoubt was also successful, though his troops met with stiffer resistance and suffered more casualties.

Alexander Hamilton wrote a report on the assault on the tenth redoubt that was published in newspapers across the country. His account was exceptionally humble. He praised his troops but made no mention of his own heroism that night. If not for his friend the Marquis de Lafayette, Alexander Hamilton might have missed his chance to become a founding father. Lafayette's widely published report was full of praise for Alexander Hamilton's courage and leadership at Yorktown.

A Leader of Vision

After his triumph at Yorktown, Alexander Hamilton resigned his commission and returned to the state of New York. His wife, Eliza, gave birth to a son, Philip, on January 22, 1782, the first of eight Hamilton children.

The American victory at Yorktown unofficially ended the Revolutionary War, though the fight wouldn't officially end until the Treaty of Paris was signed on September 3, 1783. In the meantime, Hamilton decided to finish his formal education since his studies had been interrupted by the British occupation of New York City in 1776. He purchased law books, studied diligently on his own, and passed the New York bar exam in October 1782.

Just one month later, Hamilton began serving in the Congress of the Confederation as a representative from New York. It didn't take long for Hamilton to realize how weak and powerless Congress was.

Due largely to his fame as a war hero, Hamilton was selected as a delegate to the federal convention in Philadelphia in 1787. He developed the plan for a strong federal government, which he explained in a six-hour speech to the convention. One of Hamilton's ideas was that the chief executive of the United States should be made president for life. Many delegates were aghast at this notion and accused Hamilton of wanting to set up a monarchy.

Two other delegates to the convention, James Madison and John Jay, took the lead in drafting a new document—the Constitution of the United States of America. In 1787 and 1788, Madison, Jay, and Hamilton published a series of eighty-five essays explaining and defending the new Constitution while advocating for a stronger federal government. Hamilton wrote more than half of these essays, which became known as *The Federalist Papers*.

In 1789, George Washington was elected president of the United States, and he appointed Hamilton as the nation's first secretary of the Treasury. Hamilton took office in September 1789 and left office at the end of January 1795. During those five years, Hamilton defined much of the structure of the government, from the functioning of the cabinet to the creation of the United States Mint to the establishment of the Revenue Cutter Service (forerunner of the United States Coast Guard).

Hamilton also designed most of the features of the economic system, which have long been the backbone of American prosperity. The financial cost of fighting for independence had plunged the newborn nation into debt. Hamilton structured America's debt into national, state, and foreign categories and devised a separate payment strategy for each. As the architect of American prosperity, he planned for a government that would live within its means.

After stepping down from his position at the Treasury in 1795, Alexander Hamilton resumed his private law practice in New York. When George Washington was nearing the end of his second term as president, he asked Hamilton to help him write his farewell address.

Tragedy struck the Hamilton family in 1801. It began with a July 4 speech given by a New York lawyer named George Eacker. In his speech, Eacker declared that Alexander Hamilton was a monarchist who would gladly overthrow the presidency of Thomas Jefferson. Months later, Hamilton's eldest son, Philip, learned of Eacker's remarks and, along with a friend named Stephen Price, heckled Eacker as he was attending a play. Eacker insulted Price and young Hamilton, and they challenged him to a duel.

The three men met on the dueling field in Weehawken, New Jersey, on November 22. Eacker and Price squared off, each fired twice, but all shots missed. The next day Eacker and Philip Hamilton faced each other on the same dueling field. Alexander Hamilton had told Philip about the French dueling tradition of the *delope*, in which the deloping duelist would fire and deliberately miss, wasting his first shot in the hope that honor would be satisfied, the conflict would be ended, and no one would be hurt.

When Eacker and Philip faced each other, Philip deloped. Eacker did not. His bullet entered Philip's right hip, passed through his body, and lodged in his left arm. Philip fell, mortally wounded. He died fourteen hours later at his aunt's home in Manhattan, with his grief-stricken parents at his side. Alexander and Eliza Hamilton never recovered from their loss.

In 1804, a long and bitter rivalry between Alexander Hamilton and the sitting vice president, Aaron Burr, culminated in a duel. It had become clear that President Thomas Jefferson planned to drop Burr from the ticket when he ran for reelection. So in response,

Burr ran for governor of New York, and Hamilton vigorously campaigned for Burr's opponent, Morgan Lewis.

During the campaign, the *Albany Register* published a letter claiming that Hamilton had insulted Burr as a dangerous man who could not be trusted with the reins of government. Burr lost the election and blamed Hamilton. He demanded that Hamilton disavow the remarks, but Hamilton sidestepped Burr's demand, saying he didn't recall making them.

Finally, Burr issued a formal challenge (a request to duel) to Hamilton, and the two men met at dawn on the morning of July 11, 1804. They chose the same Weehawken dueling ground where Hamilton's son Philip had been fatally wounded just three years before.

The two men squared off. Hamilton fired first. Honoring the tradition of the delope, which he had taught his son, Hamilton aimed his pistol at a tree above and beyond Aaron Burr. He deliberately wasted his shot. Burr, who was unacquainted with the same tradition, took deadly aim at Hamilton and fired. The bullet entered Hamilton's lower abdomen above the right hip, lodging in his lumbar vertebra. Hamilton fell to the ground.

Burr approached his fallen opponent, speechless and apparently full of regret. Initially unconscious, Hamilton came to and warned the people who bent over him that a pistol on the ground was cocked and loaded and could hurt someone.

Hamilton's friends took him to the home of William Bayard Jr., a prominent New York banker and Hamilton's close friend. He was attended by the same doctor who had cared for Hamilton's son Philip in his final hours. As Hamilton was dying, he summoned the strength to say, "This is a mortal wound, doctor."[6]

He received communion from Episcopal Bishop Benjamin Moore and was visited by his wife, Eliza, and their children. He died the day after being wounded, July 12, 1804. Aaron Burr was charged with murder in both New York and New Jersey but never stood trial.

★ LEADERSHIP LESSONS ★
from Alexander Hamilton

Some aspects of Alexander Hamilton's life serve as a leadership example while others serve as a warning. Here are some of the lessons from his life.

1. *Great leaders don't let humble beginnings hold them back.* Alexander Hamilton was deeply conscious of—and probably insecure about—his humble origins. He was born out of wedlock, raised on a tiny island in the West Indies, and essentially orphaned as a young boy. Yet he was determined to overcome the disadvantages of his past and build a better future for himself. A voracious reader, he learned to be an incisive thinker and writer as well. It was his writing ability that brought him to the attention of the people who paid his way to college. His military exploits—in part the result of his study of military history and military science—brought him to the attention of General Washington. The rest is history—American leadership history.

2. *Great leaders are writers.* Leadership involves written communication—communication that informs, persuades, inspires, and motivates. Hamilton was a gifted writer, and he wrote most of Washington's correspondence and written orders. He later wrote most of *The Federalist Papers.* You may not be a gifted writer like Hamilton, but you can do as George Washington did: find a "Hamilton" who can capture your thoughts and turn them into brilliant prose. Hamilton knew Washington well, and the general relied on him to act as his alter ego. Later, as president, Washington turned to Hamilton again for help in writing his farewell speech. Great leaders are great communicators.

3. *Great leaders learn to forgive.* Impetuous and ambitious, Hamilton saw Washington as a stern and remote father figure and an obstacle to achieving his goals. His resentment toward Washington boiled over in an argument with Washington on the stairs. Hamilton was bitter and unforgiving when Washington first

tried to reconcile. But the headstrong young Hamilton eventually learned to forgive his mentor.

Later, President Washington recruited Hamilton for a crucial post in his administration. Still a young man in his thirties when he joined the Washington administration, Hamilton had room to learn and grow while working at the side of one of the greatest leaders of all time. He let go of his former resentment and became one of the most influential and effective founding fathers as secretary of the Treasury of the United States.

Effective leaders learn to let go of grudges. Conflicts and disagreements come with the territory. Both subordinates and superiors will disappoint from time to time, but forgiveness is the lubricant that keeps successful organizations running smoothly. To be a great leader, learn to forgive.

4. *Great leaders say NO to temptation.* In the summer of 1791, while Alexander Hamilton was secretary of the Treasury, twenty-three-year-old Maria Reynolds came to his home in Philadelphia, claiming her husband had abandoned her and asking Hamilton for travel money. Hamilton took the money to her boardinghouse, and she invited him in. They began an affair that lasted about a year. As it turned out, Maria's husband, James Reynolds, hadn't abandoned her but had conspired with Maria to seduce and blackmail Hamilton. In 1797, Hamilton publicly admitted the affair so that the blackmail would stop. He nearly destroyed his career—and his marriage (Eliza eventually forgave him).

Good moral character is essential to the life of every leader. Alexander Hamilton paid a high price for yielding to temptation and cheating on his wife. Learn from Alexander Hamilton's folly. Flee from temptation. Maintain strong boundaries around your relationships. Never compromise your integrity. Say NO to temptation and you'll never put your leadership reputation in jeopardy.

5. *Great leaders set clear goals.* Hamilton knew what he wanted: a field command. When he felt that General Washington stood in

the way of his goals, he took action. He wrote to Washington and brazenly *demanded* a field command. While I don't recommend Hamilton's approach, I admire his intense focus on his goals. I believe Washington saw a desirable command quality underlying Hamilton's impudence—an intense ambition to achieve distinction on the battlefield. Washington tolerated Hamilton's rudeness, though another leader might not have been as understanding.

6. *Great leaders make connections with influential people.* Alexander Hamilton cultivated the art of making friends and influencing people. His alliances with people like Washington, Madison, Lafayette, Jefferson, Jay, and Greene opened doors for him at key points in his career. Though he came close to destroying his relationship with Washington over a petty misunderstanding, their friendship endured and enabled Hamilton to become one of the most influential leaders in American history—and, yes, in the history of Broadway musicals.

★ 23 ★

James Madison

The Father of the Constitution

James Madison authored many of the wise provisions of the Constitution that still shape the American system of government to this day. He had a reputation for being reserved and quietly dignified at all times—except when giving a speech. Small and wiry at five-foot-four and 122 pounds and known as "Little Jamie" to his friends, Madison was a compact mass of oratorical energy when addressing an audience.

One day during the 1787 Constitutional Convention at Independence Hall, Madison asked a friend to sit behind him as he gave a speech. If he became overly excited, his friend was instructed to tug on Madison's coattails. So Madison rose and gave one of the most impassioned speeches of his career. He shouted, he harangued, he overflowed with enthusiasm and energy. Finally, wrung out like a dishrag, he sat down as the applause of the other delegates thundered throughout the hall.

Then Madison turned to his friend and said, "Why didn't you tug on my coat?"

His friend replied, "I would as soon have laid a finger on the lightning."[1]

This electrifying speaker was born on March 16, 1751, in Port Conway, Virginia. He and his eleven siblings were raised on the family plantation, Montpelier. He attended the College of New Jersey, which is now known as Princeton University. He studied Latin, Greek, Enlightenment philosophy, and theology, and he became skilled in debate and speech. Madison was tutored by College of New Jersey president John Witherspoon, a Scottish Presbyterian minister and a founding father of the United States. Witherspoon had a profound effect on the ideas and beliefs of young James Madison, who completed the college's three-year degree in two years, graduating in 1771.

Madison was keenly interested in the conflict over oppressive taxation between Britain and the American colonies. As the thirteen colonies prepared for war, Madison joined the Orange County, Virginia, militia and received an appointment as a colonel. Because of his small stature, Madison realized that his future lay in politics, not in the military. In 1776, he attended the Virginia Constitutional Convention to help organize a new and independent government for Virginia, free of British rule. Once Virginia had adopted its Constitution, Madison became a representative of his county to the Virginia House of Delegates. During this time, he became a close friend and ally of the governor of Virginia, Thomas Jefferson.

The Father of the Constitution

After more than a year and a half of debate, the Second Continental Congress approved the first constitutional document of the United States on November 15, 1777. That document, the

Articles of Confederation, was ratified by all thirteen states on March 1, 1781.

The state of Virginia selected Madison as a delegate to the Continental Congress in 1780, after the Articles of Confederation had been hammered out but before they were ratified. Madison was deeply concerned about the weak central government the document created. Under the Articles of Confederation, the United States had no power to pay its debts or maintain a standing army. Those powers were retained by the individual state legislatures. The states operated like sovereign nations under a loose alliance, comparable to the United Nations. Madison believed the United States needed to be truly *united* under a strong federal umbrella.

He helped organize the Constitutional Convention of 1787 with the goal of producing a new Constitution and a stronger federal government. Madison was convinced that he could get greater attendance and participation at the convention if George Washington attended. He persuaded Washington to come, and the general's celebrity status resulted in a packed house, just as Madison expected.

After an intense study of the governments of other nations, Madison coauthored the Virginia Plan as a basis for the new Constitution. Though Madison was the principal author, he humbly called it the Randolph Plan, after Virginia's governor, Edmund Randolph. This plan introduced the concept of a bicameral (two-house) legislative branch—a Senate with equal representation among the states and a House of Representatives with proportional representation. Madison's Virginia Plan laid the foundation for the United States Constitution. He believed there should be a system of checks and balances among the coequal branches of the government. That concept, introduced by Madison, is the key to the genius of the American system of government.

Once the new Constitution was approved by Congress, it had to be ratified by at least nine states to be adopted. Many independent-minded states were wary of giving the central government too much power. After all, the nation had just fought an eight-year Revolutionary War to throw off the oppressive yoke of a very powerful central government in Great Britain. Those, like Madison, who supported the new Constitution called themselves Federalists, while opponents called themselves anti-Federalists.

Madison became one of the leading advocates for the ratification of the new Constitution. He collaborated with Alexander Hamilton and John Jay to write *The Federalist Papers*, some of the most influential essays on political thought in American history. These eighty-five essays were penned anonymously and published under the title *The Federalist* from 1787 to 1788. They are widely considered among the founding documents of the United States, alongside the Declaration of Independence and the Constitution.

Delegates of the Constitutional Convention signed the United States Constitution in September 1787. It was ratified in 1788, and the new United States government was open for business in 1789.

One of the Virginia delegates to the Constitutional Convention, George Mason, was not happy with the Constitution that James Madison had helped draft. Mason felt the new Constitution was dangerously incomplete, and he refused to sign it. The Constitution needed to be amended, he said, with a Bill of Rights. Otherwise, the people's rights might be trampled by the strong central government.

Madison opposed the idea of a Bill of Rights. He believed that the Constitution, as written, placed adequate limits on the power of the central government. Article I limited the powers of Congress. Article II limited the powers of the president. Madison believed that a Bill of Rights might do more harm than good. By listing certain guaranteed rights, such as freedom of speech, religion, press, and so on, the document might be seen as giving the central government permission to trample any rights *not* explicitly listed.

Fortunately, Thomas Jefferson was able to persuade Madison of the necessity of a Bill of Rights. Writing from Paris on December 20, 1787, Jefferson told Madison, "A bill of rights is what the people are entitled to against any government on earth, general or particular, and what no government should refuse, or rest on inference."[2]

Jefferson converted Madison from an opponent of the Bill of Rights to an advocate. Madison not only ceased his opposition to the Bill of Rights but he agreed to draft them. Drawing inspiration from George Mason's Virginia Declaration of Rights (1776), the Declaration of Independence (1776), the Magna Carta (1215), and the English Bill of Rights (1689), Madison drafted the new document and introduced the ten amendments to Congress on June 8, 1789. The states ratified them on December 15, 1791.

The Bill of Rights gave the weight of constitutional law to the Jeffersonian ideals enshrined in the Declaration of Independence. These ten amendments assert that every human being is entitled to certain natural rights and that the government should have no power to abridge or deny those rights. One of the most important innovations of the Bill of Rights is preventing the rights of a minority (such as a religious or political minority) from being trampled by the majority.

The First Amendment prohibits the establishment of a state religion, guarantees the free exercise of religion, guarantees freedom of speech and the press, and guarantees the right to assemble peaceably and petition the government for the redress of grievances. The Second Amendment protects the individual right to keep and bear arms. The rest of the amendments defend such important rights as the protection against unreasonable searches and seizures, the rights of the accused in criminal procedures, the right to a trial by an impartial jury, and so forth.

Madison's conversion from opponent to advocate for the Bill of Rights was a turning point in the effort to adopt the Constitution.

The Ninth and Tenth Amendments were especially vital in securing support for the Constitution from the anti-Federalists. If Madison had not written the first ten amendments, we might not have the Constitution, the freedom, and the rights we are blessed with today.

President Madison and the War of 1812

In 1792, James Madison and Thomas Jefferson founded the Democratic-Republican Party—America's first opposition political party.

Two years later, in 1794, forty-three-year-old Madison married twenty-six-year-old Dolley Payne Todd after a brief courtship. The contrast in their personalities was striking. Madison was reserved; Dolley was outgoing. She loved to host receptions and dinner parties, which enabled Madison to widen his circle of influential friends and acquaintances. A devout Quaker widow, Dolley transformed Madison's life and made him truly happy.

After Jefferson became president in 1801, Madison served as secretary of state. He played a key role in America's purchase of the Louisiana Territory from France in 1803.

Jefferson served two terms as America's third president, and Madison succeeded him in 1809, becoming America's fourth president. During his presidency, a hostile Great Britain resumed the practice of halting American merchant ships and "impressing" American sailors into the British Navy. Madison responded with a proclamation of war against Great Britain in 1812. America entered the War of 1812 ill-prepared and with an underfunded, undermanned military. The war was unpopular, especially in New England. Opponents of the war called it "Mr. Madison's War."

America suffered a series of setbacks and defeats in the War of 1812, the worst being the burning of Washington, DC, on August 24, 1814. After defeating the Americans at the Battle of

Bladensburg in Maryland, British forces set fire to the White House (or Presidential Mansion, as it was then called), the Capitol, the War Department building, the Treasury, and other structures. As the British were on their way to burn the White House, Dolley Madison directed the removal and preservation of many priceless artifacts, including the famous Gilbert Stuart painting of George Washington.

Madison ran for reelection in the midst of the War of 1812, defeating the anti-war Federalist candidate DeWitt Clinton. Though Madison was widely criticized for his handling of the war, he negotiated peace with Britain through the Treaty of Ghent, which was signed in December 1814. The United States also achieved a major military victory in the Battle of New Orleans in January 1815—after the Treaty of Ghent was signed but before word of the signing reached America. This victory restored popular support for Madison as a wartime leader.

Madison left Washington, DC, in 1817 and retired to Montpelier with Dolley. He died of heart failure at home on June 28, 1836, at age eighty-five. University of Virginia historian J. C. A. Stagg observed that Madison "was on the winning side of every important issue facing the young nation from 1776 to 1816."[3] He left a legacy of leadership as one of the most influential founding fathers of the United States.

★ LEADERSHIP LESSONS ★
from James Madison

Madison was not a hero of the Revolutionary War, but as the Father of the Constitution, he ensured that the war would produce a nation of free people whose human rights would be respected and protected. The United States government, with its limited and delineated powers, its three wisely constructed branches, and its system of checks and balances, sprang almost entirely from the keen mind of James Madison. Here are some of the leadership lessons we can draw from his life.

1. *Great leaders don't care who gets the credit.* Madison referred to his plan for the Constitution as the Randolph Plan. Though most of the ideas in the plan were Madison's, he gave credit to Virginia's governor, Edmund Randolph. Sharing the credit broadens support for a leader's ideas. President Ronald Reagan kept a plaque on his Oval Office desk that read, "There's no limit to what a man can do or where he can go if he doesn't mind who gets the credit."[4] We owe the basic structure of the United States government to a man who lived by that principle, James Madison.

2. *Great leaders achieve results through alliances with others.* Madison built personal alliances that helped him achieve his leadership goals. Madison's alliance with George Washington enabled him to draw many people to the Constitutional Convention—people who might not have come if Washington hadn't been there. And Madison's longtime friendship with Thomas Jefferson eventually led to Madison being named secretary of state, and later president. Leaders need influential allies to help them reach their goals.

3. *Great leaders are enthusiastic, persuasive communicators.* As a public speaker, Madison was the fiery opposite of the quiet, reserved man he was in private. He was excited about ideas, and he communicated that excitement to his audiences. When Madison got carried away as a speaker, his friend was afraid to tug on his coattails—"I would as soon have laid a finger on the lightning." Great public speakers are like lightning—crackling with energy, brilliant with illumination, and explosively powerful. Madison was that kind of speaker.

He was also a powerful, persuasive communicator through the written word. Along with Alexander Hamilton and John Jay, Madison was a major contributor to *The Federalist Papers*. Those essays on government helped move public opinion in favor of the US Constitution and a strong federal government, and they continue to inspire and instruct us in the role of good government today.

4. *Great leaders cling to core principles but keep an open mind regarding strategies and tactics.* Madison believed that the Constitution was perfect as drafted, and he rejected the suggestion that it be amended with a Bill of Rights. But he listened to the arguments of George Mason and Thomas Jefferson—and he changed his mind. He still believed that the principles of the Constitution were sound and adequate. But Jefferson convinced him that the American people were entitled to have certain rights explicitly listed and protected by the Constitution. Merely inferring those rights was not enough; they needed to be spelled out. Madison changed his mind—and became the author of the document he originally opposed.

Great leaders know how to be tenacious without being stubborn, principled without being hidebound, mentally tough yet open-minded. Great leaders don't hesitate to support what they once opposed when they are presented with persuasive new arguments. If Madison hadn't listened to George Mason and Thomas Jefferson, the Constitution might never have been ratified, and it would not be the wise and enduring document it is today.

The next time you hear or read about the Constitution or the Bill of Rights, remember James Madison. Remember the leader who listened, the leader who changed his mind, the leader who invented the United States government.

★ 24 ★

George Washington
The Father of His Country

The first biography of George Washington was *The Life of Washington* by Parson Mason Locke Weems. It was first published in 1800, a year after Washington's death, and it went through many printings. It's a curious mixture of historical fact and sheer invention. For the fifth edition in 1809, Weems originated the famous story of young George cutting down the cherry tree, in which George tells his father, "I cannot tell a lie. I did it with my little hatchet."

Parson Weems's book was intended as an inspirational tribute to the sterling character of America's first president. It was also intended to give young people a role model to emulate. The problem with false stories about Washington's good character is that they make it hard to distinguish the truth from fables. If the cherry tree story is made up, how are we to believe all the other stories about Washington's character?

The truth is that George Washington, while not perfect by any means, was a leader of extraordinarily strong character. His example is worth studying.

Washington was born in Virginia on February 22, 1732. He grew up on Ferry Farm near Fredericksburg and later acquired Mount Vernon, a plantation on the Potomac River, as an inheritance when his older half brother died.

By the time Washington was sixteen, he had painstakingly copied, with a quill pen and ink, a document called *110 Rules of Civility & Decent Behavior in Company and Conversation*. These 110 life rules were originally composed in 1595 by French Jesuits. I've reproduced a few examples of these rules with the antique spelling and capitalization intact, followed by my twenty-first-century translations.

"Let your Discourse with Men of Business be Short and Comprehensive." (Be concise.)

"Use no Reproachful Language against any one neither Curse nor Revile." (Be respectful and don't swear.)

"In all Causes of Passion admit Reason to Govern." (Keep your cool in times of conflict.)

"Be not Curious to Know the Affairs of Others." (Mind your own business.)

"Speak not Evil of the absent for it is unjust." (Don't slander people behind their backs.)[1]

From his earliest years, George Washington trained himself to be a man of character. His sterling character became the foundation of his leadership. True, he could be quick-tempered and impatient. At times he stubbornly stuck with a battle plan that wasn't working. But whatever his flaws, he never stopped focusing on moral and spiritual self-improvement.

His courage was unyielding—he never flinched in the face of danger. His perseverance was unstoppable, and his humility was unrivaled. And above all else, he was unswervingly loyal to his troops.

Battle-Tested Character

On May 28, 1754, twenty-one-year-old Lieutenant Colonel Washington led a Virginia colonial militia unit and a band of Iroquois warriors into a region of Pennsylvania that was claimed by both Britain and France. In that location, where the city of Pittsburgh stands today, British construction workers had been building a fort. The workers were driven off by French-Canadian soldiers under the command of Joseph Coulon de Villiers de Jumonville.

Washington had orders to kill or capture the French soldiers so the British fort could be built. He led a force of about forty British colonists against Jumonville's thirty-five French-Canadians. During the attack, Jumonville was killed (there are conflicting accounts as to how he died). The battle lasted less than fifteen minutes, and Washington's forces won handily.

When word of the attack reached the French, Jumonville's brother, Captain Louis Coulon de Villiers, attacked Washington's garrison at Fort Necessity. Washington surrendered on July 3, 1754, and Captain de Villiers prepared a surrender document, written in French, and demanded that Washington sign it. Though Washington could not read French, he signed—and later learned that the document called Jumonville's death an "assassination."

(Washington never would have admitted to carrying out an "assassination" if he had been able to read the document. He learned a lesson that day: Never sign your name to a document when you don't know what it says.)

The incident became known as the Battle of Jumonville Glen. Afterward, Washington wrote to his brother John, "I heard the bullets whistle, and, believe me, there is something charming in the sound."[2] The battle contributed to the start of the Seven Years' War.

The 1754 publication of *The Journal of Major George Washington*, written when Washington was twenty-one years old, brought him to the attention of the American public and British government officials. It led to Washington's assignment in 1755 as an aide-de-camp to British General Edward Braddock, commander in chief of the thirteen colonies.

On July 9, 1755, Washington accompanied General Braddock on a military expedition into the Ohio Valley. The goal was to capture Fort Duquesne and expel the French. Braddock's 2,100 British regulars were ambushed by a smaller force of French soldiers and Indian warriors. Braddock rallied his troops again and again until he was shot in the chest. Without regard to his own safety, Washington rounded up his troops so they could retreat safely.

General Braddock was taken from the field of battle. As he was dying, he gave Washington the ceremonial sash he wore with his uniform. Washington kept the sash for the rest of his life and wore it both as commander in chief of the Continental Army and as president. The sash is still on display at Mount Vernon.

Washington later commanded a thousand soldiers in the Virginia Regiment. He and his soldiers fought twenty battles in a ten-month period, losing a third of their troops.

Despite his many military successes, Washington stepped down from military life in 1758, never imagining the military and political career that lay ahead of him. The following year, he married a twenty-eight-year-old widow, Martha Dandridge Custis, and they lived on his Mount Vernon estate. His early exploits taught him valuable lessons in leadership, military discipline, and battlefield tactics— lessons that would serve him well in a time of revolutionary crisis.

Retreat, Escape, but Never Surrender

On December 16, 1773, the Sons of Liberty staged the Boston Tea Party, triggering a chain reaction that led to the Battles of

Lexington and Concord on April 19, 1775—and the start of the Revolutionary War. Two months after the war began, Congress created the Continental Army, and John Adams nominated Washington as commander in chief.

Washington humbly responded, "I this day declare with the utmost sincerity, I do not think myself equal to the command I am honored with." He agreed to accept the position because of the unanimous support of the Congress. Refusing any compensation, Washington went to work, forming the various state militias into a cohesive and disciplined Continental Army.[3]

Though Washington had gained fame for his military exploits in the French and Indian War, he was more widely known as a man of character. Historian David McCullough wrote, "He was chosen because they knew him; they knew the kind of man he was; they knew his character, his integrity. . . . He was a man people would follow. And as events would prove, he was a man whom some—a few—would follow through hell."[4]

Even the British press respected the character of George Washington. Historian Troy O. Bickham of Missouri State University observed:

> Throughout the American Revolution, the press in Britain portrayed the commander of the rebel army as a model of citizen virtue and an ideal military leader. Most press reports supported the effort to crush the rebellion and considered the Continental Congress a den of self-serving scoundrels but heaped praise on George Washington. . . . The general personified the dilemma that faced many Britons during the conflict: he was a quintessential English-American gentleman, despite being the enemy. He represented much of what the British Atlantic community thought admirable while commanding an army in a cause that many Britons believed would ruin the empire.[5]

The opening phase of the American Revolutionary War was the eleven-month-long Siege of Boston that lasted from April 19, 1775, to March 17, 1776. In those days, Boston was a peninsular city with the mouth of the Charles River on the west and Boston Harbor on the east. The militias of New England kept the British pinned down in Boston while awaiting the arrival of General Washington, the commander in chief of the newly formed Continental Army.

In June 1775, the British attacked the American militias on Bunker Hill and Breed's Hill. The artillery emplacements of Henry Knox took a heavy toll on the British regulars. Though the Americans were ultimately forced to retreat, the British paid a high price for those two hills.

Meanwhile, Washington was headed to Boston. Everywhere he went, crowds cheered him as a living symbol of freedom. He arrived at the outskirts of the city on July 2, 1775—two weeks after the American defeats at Bunker Hill and Breed's Hill. He set up headquarters in nearby Cambridge. His first inspection of the troops revealed an ill-prepared, undisciplined collection of would-be warriors. He began drilling his soldiers and urging his men to summon their character for the fight ahead.

In November, Washington sent twenty-five-year-old Henry Knox to the recently captured Fort Ticonderoga in upstate New York to transport its big guns to Boston. Washington knew it would take heavy artillery to break the stalemate at Boston. Knox returned with the cannons in January 1776. In March, British commanders looked up at Dorchester Heights in the south—and stared down the throats of a deadly gun battery. British General Howe hurriedly moved his troops and ships to Halifax, Nova Scotia.

The Siege of Boston was over.

After that initial victory, Washington suffered a series of devastating defeats. In fact, over the course of the Revolutionary War, he would lose more battles than he'd win. Though he often lost and often retreated, Washington surrendered only once in his career—in the Battle of Jumonville Glen. After that defeat, he never wanted to taste the bitterness of surrender again.

When a battle went badly, Washington always had an escape plan so his men could retreat, regroup, then return and fight another day. We see Washington's genius for strategic retreat in the Battle of Long Island—his first major battle after the Siege of Boston.

The Battle of Long Island was fought on August 27, 1776, in western Long Island (present-day Brooklyn, New York). It was the first major battle after the Declaration of Independence was signed. Following the Siege of Boston, Washington moved the Continental Army to New York, hoping to deny the port of New York to the Royal Navy. Washington's army set up defenses, then waited for the inevitable British assault.

General William Howe's forces arrived in July and August, growing into a force of more than thirty-two thousand troops, who were based on Staten Island. Washington moved his main force to Manhattan, and on August 22, the British attacked, inflicting heavy casualties on the Americans and forcing them to withdraw to their fortifications in Brooklyn Heights. The British prepared for a long siege—but Washington, knowing New York was lost, prepared to evacuate.

A heavy rain drenched the countryside on the afternoon of August 28. Washington ordered his cannons to bombard the British troops as night fell. Then he sent a dispatch to General William Heath at Kings Bridge, asking for every boat he could scrounge.

On the afternoon of August 29, Washington posted the Pennsylvania regiments as a rearguard to hold the line while the main force withdrew to the boats. The evacuation proceeded under a heavy downpour. To prevent the British from detecting their movements, soldiers maintained strict silence and even muffled the wheels of the wagons. The rearguard also maintained numerous campfires to make it appear that thousands of troops still camped on the heights.

Washington had planned to complete the evacuation by daybreak, but the movement of nine thousand troops, together with artillery and supplies, took longer than expected. He knew that if the British caught them evacuating, there would be many casualties.

Then, as if by a divine miracle, a fog rolled in, concealing the American evacuation from the enemy. When British patrols began searching the heights, they found them deserted.

Down on the fog-shrouded shore, the last American soldier stepped onto the final boat to leave New York. That last soldier's name was George Washington. He had safely extracted his troops—all nine thousand of them. Not one American life was lost.

Much of the credit for the miraculous American withdrawal from New York goes to Washington for his strategic brilliance in outmaneuvering the British that night. But not all the credit can go to Washington. If that unexpected fog hadn't rolled in at just the right time, the Americans would have been completely vulnerable to a British attack and unable to effectively fight back.

I can imagine God watching this scene, sending storm clouds here, summoning a fog bank there, making sure this grand experiment in freedom, the United States of America, didn't end on the western shore of Long Island. America's future was balanced on a razor's edge that night. God had a plan in history for the United States, and he had his hand of protection on General Washington and his troops that night.

A String of Losses

After the escape from the Battle of Long Island came the Battle of Brandywine in Pennsylvania on September 11, 1777. Washington's troops again clashed with the British forces of General Howe. It was here that the newly arrived Marquis de Lafayette was wounded while rallying American troops near Chadds Ford. The fighting raged for eleven hours. More soldiers fought in the Battle of Brandywine than in any other battle of the Revolutionary

War. The British Army forced Washington's troops to withdraw toward Philadelphia.

Five days later, General Howe's redcoats prepared to attack Washington's troops, who were encamped twenty miles west of Philadelphia. Washington learned of Howe's plan and prepared an ambush. Before the battle could begin, a torrential storm swept through the region, soaking the gunpowder of both armies. Washington's troops retreated farther toward Philadelphia, while the British remained at Chadds Ford. The rained-out battle is known as the Battle of the Clouds.[6]

As Washington retreated toward Philadelphia, the American capital, he left Brigadier General "Mad Anthony" Wayne's Pennsylvania Division at Chester to slow the British advance. On the night of September 20, British forces surprised Wayne's troops at their encampment near Paoli Tavern. The Americans rallied quickly and suffered few casualties—but those who tried to surrender were granted no mercy.

Colonel Adam Hubley later recalled hearing British troops shouting, "No quarters!" and added, "The greatest Cruelty was shewn on the side of the Enemy. I with my own Eyes, see them, cut & hack some of our poor Men to pieces after they had fallen in their hands and scarcely shew the least Mercy to any, they got very few prisoners from us."[7] The engagement became known as the Paoli Massacre.

Though Washington tried to roadblock General Howe's advance toward Philadelphia, Washington was outflanked and Howe entered the city unopposed. British forces were jubilant on September 26 as they seized the American capital. According to eighteenth-century European tradition, the army that seized the enemy's capital won the war. But the Continental Congress had already cleared out of Philadelphia and established a new capital at Lancaster (and later moved again to York). The British were not used to fighting an enemy that could just pack up its government and move down the road.

When General Howe realized that the war was far from over, he camped nine thousand troops in Germantown, five miles north of occupied Philadelphia. Washington reconnoitered the Germantown camp and saw an opportunity. The British general had divided his forces, and the camp at Germantown was poorly defended. A surprise attack might catch them napping and produce a sorely needed American victory.

Unfortunately, Washington overestimated the capability of his ill-trained troops. He drew up a complicated battle plan that divided his forces into four columns, all attacking from different directions. To be successful, the attack required precise timing. But when the fight began on October 4, the four columns arrived at staggered times. One column ignored orders and fired at the British camp without advancing. Two of the columns—one led by Mad Anthony Wayne, the other by Nathanael Greene—encountered each other in a thick fog and mistook each other for the enemy. Both sides exchanged fire, then retreated.

British forces formed up and launched a counterassault that drove the rebels from the battlefield. The Americans suffered roughly a thousand casualties, twice the number they inflicted on the redcoats. It was a disaster—and a lesson to Washington. The complexity of his battle plan had contributed to the defeat. After the loss at Germantown, his plans would be simpler and easier to execute.

But would Washington keep his job as commander in chief? He had lost New York, he had lost Philadelphia, and he had lost a string of battles from Brandywine to Germantown. In all of 1777, the Continental Army tasted victory only once, at the Battles of Saratoga, which took place on September 19 and October 7. Though General Washington had crafted the overall strategy for the Saratoga campaign, most of the credit for the decisive victory at Saratoga had gone—rightly or wrongly—to General Horatio Gates.

As winter set in, the Revolutionary War ground to a standstill. Washington led his army of eleven thousand men to Valley Forge, north of Philadelphia, to await the springtime and better fighting weather. The war effort was in crisis, and Washington faced the supreme test of his leadership ability and his character.

The Character of a Christian

In the dismal winter at Valley Forge, Washington's army lost a dozen men per day to disease, hunger, and desertion. Washington sent repeated messages to Congress, pleading for food, clothing, and blankets for his troops. Congress told him to send his troops out to steal from nearby farmers because many traded beef and corn for British gold. They suggested that by stealing from farmers, the army would eat well and deprive the enemy of provisions.

But Washington refused to steal. The very notion was an affront to his moral principles, which he based on the Bible. Besides, stealing from farmers would cause the new American government to be hated by its own citizens. Not only did Washington refuse to steal but he also warned his soldiers that anyone caught stealing would be hanged.

Though Washington's men often went hungry at Valley Forge, his principles inspired them. Historian Burton W. Folsom Jr. of Hillsdale College explains:

> The starving army was impressed by Washington's integrity. His men trained hard that winter, leaving bloody footprints in the snow. The next summer brought a smaller but tougher fighting unit that stood up to the seasoned British army for the first time at the Battle of Monmouth. With that victory, Washington took a giant step in ousting the British and winning independence for his country.
>
> During Washington's presidency, his character would be tested often but it served him and the nation well.[8]

On February 23, 1778, Washington welcomed Baron von Steuben to Valley Forge. Von Steuben reorganized the camp, improving sanitation and hygiene and introducing European precision drill techniques. It was a sign of Washington's humble character that he welcomed von Steuben's reforms at Valley Forge. Many leaders feel threatened by subordinates who demonstrate skills and knowledge they themselves lack. But Washington was humbly grateful for the reforms von Steuben instituted at his camp. He was so impressed by von Steuben's "Prussian Exercise" that he immediately stopped all other training so that his entire army could be drilled in the new techniques. Great leaders like Washington care more about the people they lead than about their own egos.

During the winter, Washington made the rounds of the camp, talking to his soldiers and giving them a word of encouragement. On one occasion, Washington happened upon a soldier named John Brantley. The soldier had a jug of wine, and he and his friends were cheerfully consuming it together. When Brantley looked up and saw Washington in front of him, he drunkenly said, "Come drink some wine with a soldier!"

"You have no time for drinking wine," the general said, turning away.

Brantley called out a curse upon Washington's "proud soul," and added, "You're above drinking with soldiers."

Washington stopped and turned. "I will drink with you," he said. He took the jug from Brantley's hands, downed a swig, then offered it back.

Brantley waved the jug away, saying, "Give it to your servants," meaning Washington's aides, who stood nearby. So Washington passed the jug to his aides.

Seeing that the commander in chief of the Continental Army was not too proud to drink with his men, Brantley vowed to Washington that he would "spend the last drop of my heart's blood for you."[9] By taking that drink, Washington had inspired Brantley's loyalty.

Washington's character was rooted in his Christian faith. He told his men: "While we are zealously performing the duties of good citizens and soldiers, we certainly ought not to be inattentive to the higher duties of religion. To the distinguished character of Patriot, it should be our highest Glory to laud the more distinguished Character of Christian."[10]

The Cincinnatus of the West

Washington led the Continental Army for eight years, from victory at Boston to retreat at Long Island, from the successful Delaware crossing to the disasters at Brandywine and Germantown, from the desperate winter at Valley Forge to the final battle at Yorktown. In all that time, he never left his troops. Washington never returned home to his beloved Mount Vernon, except for a brief visit just before the Battle of Yorktown.

At the Siege of Yorktown, Washington gathered a stellar collection of leaders. His brilliant artillery engineer, Henry Knox, directed the bombardment of the city. Alexander Hamilton and the Marquis de Lafayette led the coordinated assault on two redoubts. Forces led by Baron von Steuben and Mad Anthony Wayne maintained the pressure on the city's perimeter.

General Charles Cornwallis surrendered on October 19, 1781— and the Revolutionary War unofficially came to a close.

A short time after Washington's victory at Yorktown, Benjamin Franklin, United States minister to France, attended a state dinner in Paris. During the dinner, the French foreign minister rose to propose a toast: "His Majesty, Louis the Sixteenth, who, like the moon, fills the earth with a soft benevolent glow."

The British ambassador then stood, raised his glass, and said, "George the Third, who, like the sun at noonday, spreads his light and illumines the world."

Next, Franklin rose and said, "I cannot give you the sun or the moon, but I give you George Washington, General of the armies of the United States, who, like Joshua of old, commanded both the sun and the moon to stand still, and both obeyed."[11]

In March 1783, an incident occurred that threatened the stability of the newly independent nation. A conspiracy reared its head, possibly involving members of the Congress. Someone circulated an anonymous letter in the army camp at Newburgh, New York. Washington's soldiers had not been paid in many months, and the anonymous letter urged the soldiers to take action against Congress—perhaps in the form of a coup d'état. Many soldiers in Washington's camp were close to rebellion.

On March 15, a group of mutinous officers met to form a plan of action. Soon after the meeting was called to order, General Washington unexpectedly entered the room. The room went deathly still. The general looked around at the sullen faces of soldiers who had endured much but had not been paid in a very long time. Washington went to the front of the room and delivered a brief speech from his heart, asking the men to be patient. He urged them to oppose anyone who "wickedly attempts to open the floodgates of civil discord and deluge our rising empire in blood."[12]

Washington drew a letter from his pocket, written by a member of Congress to the army officers. Then he took a pair of reading glasses from his pocket and put them on. His men had never seen him wearing glasses before. "Gentlemen," he said, "you will permit me to put on my spectacles, for I have not only grown gray but almost blind in the service of my country."[13]

As he read the letter, soldiers choked back tears, realizing all that Washington had sacrificed for the revolution.

Minutes earlier, Washington had walked into a room full of conspirators ready to revolt. The moment he began to read, the conspiracy collapsed. Washington's character reaffirmed their confidence in Congress and their loyalty to the United States of America. Soon afterward, Congress began issuing the back pay and pensions the soldiers had been promised.

Washington passed up the chance to become king of the United States. In October 1781, he set up headquarters in a house on the

Hudson to await news from the peace conference in Paris. He kept the Continental Army in a state of readiness—just in case.

In May 1782, Colonel Lewis Nicola wrote to Washington telling him that a democratic government would be unstable and that Washington should consider leading a British-style constitutional monarchy. Under Nicola's plan, Washington would become "King George I" and Nicola and his comrades would back him as king.

Washington replied with a "mixture of great surprise and astonishment" at the notion that he might become America's first king. He added, "You could not have found a person to whom your schemes are more disagreeable." Washington implored Nicola to "banish these thoughts from your Mind, and never communicate, as from yourself, or anyone else, a sentiment of the like Nature."[14]

If not for Washington's character and humility, the American Revolution might have produced a very different result—and the American people might be living today under a king, or worse, a dictator.

After commanding the Continental Army for more than eight years, Washington bade his officers farewell at Fraunces Tavern in New York on December 4, 1783. Two days before Christmas, he resigned his commission as commander in chief, refuting the predictions of his critics that he would never relinquish command. He then returned home to Mount Vernon, intending to live out his days as a gentleman farmer.

But his plans of early retirement were again disrupted. In 1789, Washington was elected the first president of the United States. He took the oath of office on the balcony of Federal Hall in New York. Most of the customs we associate with the presidency bear the imprint of George Washington's character. Congress gave him wide latitude in creating the duties, functions, and traditions of the presidency. He carefully avoided the trappings of royalty, insisting on a simple, unpretentious title: "Mr. President."

Washington's personal integrity echoes across the years, setting a standard that Americans still measure their leaders against. As constitutional scholar Thomas Sowell wrote, "Presidents of the United States lacking character and integrity have inflicted lasting damage on the office they held and on the nation. . . . The nation as a whole is stronger when it can trust its President."[15]

Presidential historians compare Washington to a Roman leader named Cincinnatus, who lived five centuries before Christ. Cincinnatus won many battles as a general in the Roman army, then he retired to live humbly as a farmer. When Rome was invaded by a neighboring tribe, the people begged Cincinnatus to rule as a supreme dictator.

Cincinnatus ascended the throne and called his generals together. Through a series of battles over the next two weeks, the Roman army prevailed over the invaders. Once the crisis was over, Cincinnatus abdicated the throne and returned to his farm—the only Roman dictator to willingly relinquish power.[16]

George Washington served two terms as president, then—like Cincinnatus—he relinquished his powerful role and returned to his farm at Mount Vernon. In his farewell address to the nation on September 19, 1796, he said that American liberty and prosperity rested on a foundation of faith and moral character. "Of all the dispositions and habits which lead to political prosperity," he said, "religion and morality are indispensable supports. In vain would that man claim the tribute of patriotism, who should labor to subvert these great pillars of human happiness, these firmest props of the duties of man and citizens."[17]

King George III of England was astounded to hear that Washington had relinquished power. He said that if Washington walked away from the presidency, he would be "the greatest character of the age." After Washington's death in 1799, the poet Lord Byron eulogized him as "the Cincinnatus of the West."

The French emperor Napoleon was baffled by Washington's decision. Napoleon craved power and waged endless wars of conquest to expand his domain. Shortly before his death in exile, Napoleon reflected bitterly, "They wanted me to be another Washington."[18]

Washington's One Great Flaw

Honesty requires us to acknowledge a flaw in this great leader: George Washington was a slave owner. He was born into a world where human slavery was considered normal, but over time, his views on slavery evolved. By 1786, three years before Washington was elected president, the practice of slavery troubled him deeply. On April 12, 1786, in a letter to financier Robert Morris, Washington wrote:

> There is not a man living who wishes more sincerely than I do to see a plan adopted for the abolition of [slavery]; but there is only one proper and effectual mode by which it can be accomplished, and that is by Legislative authority; and this, as far as my suffrage will go, shall never be wanting.[19]

And on September 9, 1786, he wrote to John Francis Mercer, "I never mean to possess another slave by purchase; it being among my first wishes to see some plan adopted by which slavery in this country may be abolished by slow, sure, and imperceptible degrees."[20]

We have to ask ourselves the question: Does slave ownership disqualify Washington as a person of character? Historian Stephen Ambrose points out that, of the nine US presidents who owned slaves, only George Washington set his free. Ambrose writes:

> History abounds with ironies. These men, the Founding Fathers and Brothers, established a system of government that, after much struggle, and the terrible violence of the Civil War, and the civil rights movement led by black Americans, did lead to legal freedom for all Americans and movement toward equality. . . .

Slavery and discrimination darken our hearts and cloud our minds in the most extraordinary ways, including a blanket judgment today against Americans who were slave owners in the eighteenth and nineteenth centuries. That the masters should be judged as lacking in the scope of their minds and hearts is fair, indeed must be insisted upon, but that doesn't mean we should judge the whole of them only by this part. [21]

Ambrose insists that we assess this man as a whole human being:

Washington's character was rock solid. He was constant. At the center of events for twenty-four years, he never lied, fudged, or cheated. He shared his army's privations. . . . They respected him, even loved him. Washington came to stand for the new nation and its republican virtues, which was why he became our first President by unanimous choice.[22]

It would be easy to say, "If I had lived in that era, I would have fought slavery and opposed discrimination in all its forms." Perhaps you would have—but perhaps not. Our views are shaped by the mood of our times. It's heartening to realize that, by 1786, Washington's conscience was troubled over the injustice of slavery. Had he lived longer, perhaps his strong sense of morality and ethics would have propelled him to take up the cause of abolition.

A Leader Faces Death

Historian Peter R. Henriques observes that George Washington "always confronted the prospect of his own death with remarkable equanimity and composure."[23] In September 1799, Washington learned that his brother Charles had died. In a letter to Charles's son-in-law, Washington wrote, "When the summons comes I shall endeavour to obey it with a good grace."[24] He didn't imagine that the summons of death would arrive in less than three months.

On December 12, 1799, Washington rode around Mount Vernon, inspecting his plantation in freezing rain. The next morning, he awoke with a sore throat—probably acute epiglottitis caused by a bacterial infection. Henriques wrote:

> The truly frightening aspect of acute epiglottitis is the obstruction of the larynx that makes both breathing and swallowing extremely difficult. The first thing an infant masters is to breathe and the second is to swallow. To have these two absolutely basic functions dramatically impaired is very frightening to anyone, no matter how brave and courageous he or she might be. Like any mortal, Washington had to face the terror of air hunger, of smothering and gasping for each breath. . . . Essentially, Washington slowly and painfully suffocated to death over many hours.[25]

The medical treatment Washington received only intensified his sufferings. Four times he was bled by leeches at a cost of five pints of blood. He received medicines that induced diarrhea, vomiting, and blistering of his skin. At one point in his sufferings, he said, "I die hard."

Yet, as Henriques concludes, the way Washington endured the dying process "reveals a great deal about the man and his character." In his final hours, Washington reassured his anxious doctor, "Don't be afraid." And when a servant named Tobias Lear tried to move Washington and make him comfortable, Washington apologized for burdening him. Washington's last words, as recorded in Tobias Lear's journal, were, "'Tis well."[26] Death came for him an hour or two before midnight, December 14, 1799, as Martha sat at the foot of his bed.

On December 26, 1799, more than four thousand mourners gathered for George Washington's memorial service. Congressman Henry "Light-Horse Harry" Lee of Virginia, who had served with Washington in the revolution, delivered the eulogy at Philadelphia's German Lutheran Church. After tracing Washington's illustrious career as a leader, Lee softly spoke the words that would forever define Washington's character: "To the memory of the Man, first in war, first in peace, and first in the hearts of his countrymen."[27]

★ LEADERSHIP LESSONS ★
from George Washington

The life of George Washington reminds us that our character determines our leadership destiny. The character we are building, day by day through the choices we make, will shape the way we live, the way we lead, and the way we die. Here are some of the leadership lessons we find in the life of George Washington.

1. *Great leaders know it's never too early or too late to improve their character*. In his youth, Washington wrote down 110 life principles that guided his choices from his early life until his last breath. Good character is the daily accumulation of good moral choices. Every time we choose honesty over deception, hard work over laziness, courage over cowardice, boldness over timidity, we make our character stronger. Whether you are young or old, commit yourself now to building good character, because every choice counts.

2. *Great leaders remain humble*. Washington told Congress, "I do not think myself equal to the command I am honored with." I don't believe that was false humility—it was sincere. Washington knew there were gaps in his knowledge. That's why he humbly stood aside and allowed Baron von Steuben to take charge of instruction and drilling at Valley Forge. He never let his leadership position go to his head, and he maintained his humility through the end of his life.

3. *Great leaders listen carefully to their conscience—and obey what it tells them*. Washington hoped slavery would be abolished by legislation. He said he would never purchase another slave.

That's good—but he didn't go far enough. He was listening to his conscience—but he didn't fully obey it.

At the end of the Revolutionary War, Washington had a vast deposit of moral and political capital he could have spent to liberate the slaves. People were in awe of his character and accomplishments and were ready to follow wherever he led. Suppose that, at the height of his popularity, he had said, "I'm going to free all my slaves, and I encourage my countrymen to do the same." Had he made such a statement, many slave owners would have rebelled—but many others might have joined him. Washington might have been acclaimed as both the Father of His Country and the Great Emancipator.

If your conscience whispers to you, listen carefully—then act decisively. That's your character urging you to demonstrate moral leadership.

4. *Great leaders take time to reflect on life and leadership goals.* Three months before his death, Washington wrote, "When the summons comes I shall endeavour to obey it with a good grace." Washington spent time reflecting on the most important questions in life: Am I in a right relationship with God? Am I setting a good example of godly character to the people around me? How am I influencing others? How will I face my own death?

He faced these questions with courage, character, and faith in God. When his time came to leave this life, he was ready.

Are you ready? Are you living to influence others? Have you made peace with God and with your own mortality? The greatest leaders of all—those who lead as Washington led—are those who demonstrate great character, great moral strength, and great faith. They are the ones who, at the end of their leadership journey, can say, "'Tis well."

Epilogue

Wanted—Leaders for Today's Crisis

When I was a boy, I was fascinated with heroes. I was a sports fanatic, so most of my heroes were baseball players. But I was also enthralled by the tale of Paul Revere's midnight ride, the epic sea battles of John Paul Jones, and the daring exploits of Francis Marion. What kid doesn't love stories about cannons thundering, muskets cracking, and swords clashing?

At that age, I measured myself against my heroes. I imagined myself in those times and wondered if I could face danger as they did—with courage and character.

My family would sometimes make the hour-long journey from Wilmington, Delaware, to Philadelphia, Pennsylvania. We visited Independence Hall, where the Declaration of Independence and the Constitution were debated and adopted. We went to Valley Forge, where Washington's troops endured a miserable winter. Mom and Dad taught me to value my freedom and love my country.

But it wasn't until I became an adult that I truly became a student of history and wanted to know everything I could about Revolutionary War times. I read dozens of biographies and historical accounts of those early American heroes—and I found myself wanting to go out and see the places where their exploits took place.

My car became my time machine. I drove across the years to the battlefield at Brandywine Creek. Growing up in Wilmington, I spent my entire boyhood a mere twelve miles from that battle-field. I lived *that* close to the field where Washington fought (and lost) the longest single-day battle of the revolution. It had taken me all those years to travel twelve miles, but I had finally made it. Gazing across that field, I imagined General John Sullivan's badly outnumbered division squaring off against rank after rank of Brit-ish lobsterbacks, the cannons thundering, the musket balls zipping by, nineteen-year-old Lafayette with his sword raised, rallying the troops, then falling, wounded in the leg.

I had studied the battle again and again in books, but when I stood on that field and saw those events playing out in my mind's eye, I was transported to September 11, 1777. After those moments spent surveying the battlefield, I could never look at history the same way.

Before, when I had only read about Revolutionary War heroes, they had been like characters in a novel. But when I stood on the same ground where Patriots fought and bled and died, they became real flesh-and-blood human beings to me. They became people I could identify with, learn from, and *know*.

History All around Me

I continued visiting battlefields at every opportunity. I had that same "time machine" experience again and again. I went to the battlefield at Germantown, north of Philadelphia. There, on Oc-tober 4, 1777, Washington suffered a harsh defeat. I stood on the field where, in a dense fog, Mad Anthony Wayne's division collided with Nathanael Greene's division and they mistakenly fired on each other. I toured the Benjamin Chew Mansion, where Washington made a tragic decision to launch repeated assaults against the British, suffering heavy casualties and learning a bitter lesson.

On trips to Boston with my teams or to run the Boston Marathon, I toured the Old North Church, Breed's Hill and Bunker Hill, Lexington and Concord, and many other Massachusetts sites that are sacred to the memory of the war.

While attending a camp in upstate New York, I visited the battlefield at Saratoga, the site of a huge victory for American forces. I went to New York City and hired a guide who took me to all the historic sites of the Battle of Long Island, where a divinely appointed fog miraculously covered Washington's escape.

I went to Trenton, New Jersey, and looked out upon the Delaware River, imagining those waters choked with ice as Washington made the treacherous crossing. Also in New Jersey, I visited the site of the Battle of Princeton—a small victory for the Americans over General Cornwallis, but a huge boost for American morale.

In North Carolina, I toured the battlefields at Moores Creek and the Guilford Courthouse. Though they were practically within shouting distance of Wake Forest University, where I spent my college career, I didn't visit those sites until much later in my life.

In South Carolina, I toured Cowpens, Kings Mountain, Camden, Eutaw Springs, and Musgrove Mill, battlefields clustered around Spartanburg, where I had worked as a minor league baseball executive, completely unaware of the rich Revolutionary War history all around me.

I once had a speaking engagement in eastern Virginia. Part of the deal was that, after my speech, my hosts would give me a tour of the battlefield sites around the famed Yorktown.

I had grown up largely unaware that I was surrounded by a great legacy of courage, freedom, and leadership. Now that you've read the stories in this book, I urge you to step into a time machine of your own. Walk the blood-soaked fields where it all happened.

Listen to the voices of Patriots speaking from the past, calling you into the future, urging you to confront the crises of your own time.

Those Patriot leaders did the groundwork. Now it's up to you and me to keep building on the foundation of liberty and independence they laid before us.

The Miracle of America

The more I have studied these stories and visited these hallowed sites, the more I realize that the United States of America is an absolute miracle. The Continental Army was chronically short on manpower, short on food, short on clothing, short on weaponry and ammunition. This band of patriotic shopkeepers and farmers took up arms against the well-supplied, well-trained, well-disciplined military forces of the British Empire.

The newly formed government of the United States was ill-structured, divided, cash-poor, and largely powerless. No one knew how to finance the war. With Loyalists around the countryside aiding the British enemy, the Americans could never be sure who was for them or against them.

Yet whenever the fledgling nation was in critical need of leadership, men and women of character stepped up. When America needed a decisive, inspiring military strategist, George Washington rose to the challenge. When he needed an artillery genius to break the stalemate in Boston, Henry Knox emerged from his bookshop and volunteered. He dragged 119,000 pounds of artillery over the Berkshire Mountains to Dorchester Heights and sent the British forces scurrying to Nova Scotia.

When America was losing the war in the South, Nathanael Greene, Daniel Morgan, and Francis Marion harassed the redcoats with a totally new approach to warfare. When America was short on native-born military talent, leaders came to our shores from all over the world—Baron von Steuben from Prussia, John Paul

Jones from Scotland, the Marquis de Lafayette and Jean-Baptiste de Rochambeau from France, and Casimir Pulaski and Tadeusz Kościuszko from Poland. When the war effort ran short of manpower, patriotic women supplied an abundance of womanpower, doing everything from carrying water to shouldering muskets and firing cannons.

Again and again, when the cause seemed lost, leaders stepped up at just the right time. But what if they hadn't? There's a long list of seemingly *indispensable* leaders—George Washington, Henry Knox, Benjamin Franklin, Thomas Paine, Alexander Hamilton, and on and on. If you subtract just one of those leaders from the equation, it's likely that America would have lost its fight for independence.

The United States had absolutely no business winning the Revolutionary War. The closer you look, the more improbable the story becomes. Again and again, if you are alert to the signs, you see an invisible, divine hand shaping events, moving leaders into position, guiding ideas and actions, and changing the world.

To me, America is a miracle of God. It's not a perfect nation. Revolutionary heroes and leaders were far from perfect people. Some demonstrated serious moral defects. Some showed incredibly poor judgment at times. Some owned slaves.

Just as a fish in water doesn't know it is wet, today we are unaware of the many horrors and obscenities we tolerate without thinking. Just as we look down on the slave owners of the seventeenth through nineteenth centuries, later generations may look down on us and ask why we bought devices made by forced labor, why we tolerated abortion and infanticide, why we allowed the exploitation of undocumented immigrants, why we ignored our broken and abusive foster care system, why we didn't care for our environment, and why we passed a crushing burden of federal debt along to our children and grandchildren.

We have every reason to detest the eras of slavery and segregation in America. But we have no basis for feeling self-righteous.

America was born in a crisis, and America is still in crisis today. We need leaders who will step up and lead.

Needed: Moral Leadership

America desperately needs moral leadership. We need men and women who are willing to take a stand for their principles, regardless of the price. We need people who will stand up for life, for liberty, and for the freedom to speak and worship and pursue happiness. We need people who will courageously stand up against the mob, the book burners, the church burners, and the statue wreckers. Unfortunately, we see all-too-little moral leadership these days—and an abundance of moral cowardice.

When I was growing up in Wilmington, I watched my parents, Jim and Ellen Williams, start a nonprofit organization to benefit kids in Delaware with Down syndrome and other mental disabilities. I saw them recruit sports figures, politicians, journalists, doctors, and the governor of the state to their cause. They spoke at meetings, gave media interviews, and ran up a phone bill as big as their mortgage payment. They did it because they cared and because they were leaders. I don't remember my parents ever preaching leadership to me. They just led—and I absorbed their example by osmosis.

Dad teamed up with Bob Carpenter, owner of the Philadelphia Phillies, to start a tradition called the Delaware All-Star High School Football Game—also known as the Blue-Gold Game—to raise funds for the Delaware Foundation Reaching Citizens with Cognitive Disabilities. The motto of the Blue-Gold Game was "We Play So That They May Learn." Dad also helped found the Opportunity Center, a training program for people with Down syndrome, cerebral palsy, autism, and similar challenges.

During my sophomore year in high school, we held a Blue-Gold Game with all-star high school football players from the North and the South. Two of the best players representing the North were African American men from Wilmington's Howard High School. The all-star players practiced at a prep school outside of Wilmington and stayed in the dormitories on campus. The headmaster of the prep school, unfortunately, exemplified moral cowardice rather than moral leadership. He told Dad that players from the South might be prejudiced, so he would not allow the two Black athletes to stay in the dormitories.

Dad was furious. He argued with the headmaster and tried to convince him to show some backbone instead of catering to bigotry—but the headmaster wouldn't budge. So we hosted the two Black players, Joe and Alvin, at our home. I hadn't been exposed to racial prejudice before, so this was a learning experience for me. I learned about the stupidity of segregation—and about the urgent need for moral leadership.

The bitterly divided times in which we currently live remind me of a speech Abraham Lincoln gave when he was a twenty-eight-year-old Illinois lawyer. Speaking at the Young Men's Lyceum of Springfield, Illinois, on January 27, 1838, he warned of the threat of racism, extremism, lawlessness, and mob violence. In his speech "The Perpetuation of Our Political Institutions," Lincoln said:

> At what point shall we expect the approach of danger? By what means shall we fortify against it? Shall we expect some transatlantic military giant, to step the Ocean, and crush us at a blow? Never! All the armies of Europe, Asia and Africa combined . . . could not by force, take a drink from the Ohio, or make a track on the Blue Ridge, in a trial of a thousand years.
>
> At what point then is the approach of danger to be expected? I answer, if it ever reach us, it must spring up amongst us. It cannot come from abroad. If destruction be our lot, we must ourselves be its author and finisher. As a nation of freemen, we must live through all time, or die by suicide.[1]

The social unrest, hatred, and division that worried Lincoln in 1838 would erupt into a full-blown Civil War in 1861—a war he would preside over. Today, we see equally deep divisions in American culture—and Lincoln's words seem prophetic. The threat has sprung up among us. America seems on the verge of dying by suicide.

America Needs You and Me

Where does this internal threat come from? People from all over the world still see America as a land of hope and opportunity, a land of liberty and the American dream. Yet many who were born here have been taught to hate their home country.

I only recently learned where much of this hatred comes from: You and I have been unknowingly subsidizing this self-destructive hate. As American citizens, we have been dutifully paying our taxes and entrusting our children to the public schools. There they have been indoctrinated by a widely used textbook called *A People's History of the United States*, written by a Marxist history professor named Howard Zinn.

Introduced in 1980, Zinn's book has been frequently updated and remains in print to this day. Zinn wrote the book with the specific purpose of tearing down America's founding fathers and filtering American history through the lens of an oppressor-versus-victim narrative—with America as the oppressor. Zinn makes his intentions clear in the first chapter of *A People's History of the United States*:

> The pretense is that there really is such a thing as "the United States," subject to occasional conflicts and quarrels, but fundamentally a community of people with common interests. . . .
>
> My viewpoint, in telling the history of the United States, is different. . . . Nations are not communities and never have been. The history of any country, presented as the history of a family, conceals

fierce conflicts of interest (sometimes exploding, most often repressed) between conquerors and conquered, masters and slaves, capitalists and workers, dominators and dominated in race and sex.[2]

Zinn's venomous narrative redefines America and its founding principles as a massive system of injustice and oppression. The book recasts America's founders—Washington, Jefferson, Madison, Hamilton—as villains. Princeton historian Sean Wilentz described Zinn's version of history this way: "What he did was take all of the guys in white hats and put them in black hats, and vice versa. . . . Abraham Lincoln freed the slaves. You wouldn't know that from Howard Zinn."[3]

For more than forty years, American parents and taxpayers were unaware that class after class of high school history students were being indoctrinated by this Marxist portrayal of American history. If you've ever wondered why radical anti-American bias has poisoned our universities, our media, and our political institutions, the answer is most likely Howard Zinn. As social commentator Roger Kimball stated, "Zinn's book has probably done more to poison the minds of high school students than any other work of history."[4]

Historian Mary Grabar, author of *Debunking Howard Zinn: Exposing the Fake History That Turned a Generation against America*, put it bluntly: "Zinn's *People's History of the United States* is probably the biggest con job in American history writing ever."[5] Grabar added that Zinn's Marxist narrative is at the heart of an even more radical assault on America's founding, the 1619 Project.

Published by the *New York Times Magazine* in 2019, the 1619 Project claims that America's founding took place not in 1776 but in 1619, when the first African slaves arrived on American shores. The 1619 Project asserts that the *real* motive behind the Declaration of Independence and the United States Constitution was not liberty but the perpetuation of slavery. It's a false claim, easily disproved (I've disproved it in this book).

The writers of the 1619 Project hid the words of Jefferson, who wrote, "The spirit of the master is abating, that of the slave rising from the dust." They covered up Jefferson's attempt to insert an antislavery clause into the Declaration of Independence. They ignored the words of Washington, who wrote, "There is not a man living who wishes more sincerely than I do to see a plan adopted for the abolition of [slavery]."

As Mary Grabar concludes,

> *A People's History* and the 1619 Project not only teach a false history but also make students cynical about their country, about historical truth, and about the possibility of reasoned debate. History must be reclaimed from its new aristocracy of ideological scholars, who see the past only as a battlefield of ideological, ethnic, racial, and sexual conflict. This approach, which Howard Zinn did much to advance, has been distressingly successful in misleading young people in the United States.[6]

Slavery and racism are shameful chapters in American history, but slavery predated the founding of America by thousands of years. It has existed throughout human history, and it is still practiced today in many nations. Unique among all nations, America fought a bloody civil war to abolish slavery.

In high schools and colleges across America, students are being taught the lie that the United States is an oppressive and racist society, founded on the institution of slavery. In these pages, I have told you the truth about America's founding, including some uncomfortable truths. I don't want my children and grandchildren to grow up with any illusions about America's founding. I want them to know how we came to be free—and how we can lose our freedom if we don't defend it.

There's no guarantee that the legacy of freedom we inherited from past generations will endure. Remember Lincoln's warning: The only threat to America is the threat from within.

We need strong moral leadership. We need men and women who will step up and tell the truth about the American Revolution. We need leaders who will defend American freedom and American equality. We can't shrug off our responsibility. America is in trouble and needs courageous, *revolutionary* leaders once again. America needs you and me.

The Seven Sides of Leadership

In the Revolutionary War era, there were no books or seminars on leadership. In fact, the word *leadership* didn't exist in the English language until it was coined by British politician Charles Watkin Williams-Wynn in a letter in 1821.[7] Yet, as we've seen, leadership was profoundly important to the success of the Revolutionary War. Then, as now, the world cried out for leaders. After decades of study and experience, I've concluded that the essence of leadership can be reduced to seven essential ingredients—the Seven Sides of Leadership.

1. *Vision.* To lead people, you must have a clear, inspiring picture of where you want to go and what you want to achieve.
2. *Communication Skills.* You must be able to communicate your vision to your followers so that it becomes their vision as well.
3. *People Skills.* As a leader, you must enable your followers to feel confident, motivated, and empowered to go forth and achieve big goals. People skills are learnable skills.
4. *Character.* Good character is essential to trust. As the life of George Washington shows, if people trust your character, they will follow you anywhere.
5. *Competence.* People want to follow a leader with a proven ability to compete. Competent leaders build competitive armies, teams, and organizations.

6. *Boldness.* Leaders must be willing and able to take coura-geous, reasonable risks to achieve worthwhile goals. Bold leaders are not reckless, but they seize opportunities, act decisively, and avoid second-guessing. Bold leaders inspire confidence in their followers.

7. *A Serving Heart.* A great leader is a servant, not a boss. Servant leaders empower, motivate, and inspire their followers and equip them with everything they need to succeed.

These are the Seven Sides of Leadership. Some people are natu-rally gifted with a few of these traits. No one is born with them all—but we can learn them and improve on them with practice. The more our lives reflect these traits, the more effective we'll be as leaders.

The leadership that won the American Revolution was forged in crisis—and we are living in crisis again today. You're the next community leader, youth leader, spiritual leader, or political leader our world is looking for. You don't need to be perfect. You just need to be willing to do what you can with what you have, right where you are.

The American experiment is ongoing. The story of America is still being written. What part will you play in these critical times? How will you choose to lead?

Notes

Introduction

1. Michele R. Berman, MD, "George Washington, Smallpox, and the American Revolution," MedPageToday.com, February 22, 2011, https://www.medpagetoday.com/blogs/celebritydiagnosis/24996.

2. Andrew Stephen Walmsley, *Thomas Hutchinson and the Origins of the American Revolution* (New York: New York University Press, 1999), 107.

Chapter 1 Samuel Adams: The Father of the Revolution

1. William Vincent Wells, *The Life and Public Services of Samuel Adams* (Bedford, MA: Applewood Books, 1865; repr. 2009), 11.

2. John K. Alexander, *Samuel Adams: America's Revolutionary Politician* (Lanham, MD: Rowman & Littlefield, 2002), 3.

3. Dennis B. Fradin, *Samuel Adams: The Father of American Independence* (New York: Clarion, 1998), 13.

4. Alexander, *Samuel Adams*, 9.

5. Ray Raphael, *A People's History of the American Revolution: How Common People Shaped the Fight for Independence* (New York: New Press, 2016), 22.

6. Raphael, *A People's History*, 23.

7. Library of Congress, "The American Revolution, 1763–1783: First Shots of War: A Proclamation by British General Thomas Gage, June 12, 1775," Library of Congress, http://www.loc.gov/teachers/classroommaterials/presentationsand activities/presentations/timeline/amrev/shots/proclaim.html.

8. Henry S. Randall, *The Life of Thomas Jefferson, Volume 1* (Philadelphia: J. B. Lippincott, 1871), 182.

Chapter 2 Crispus Attucks: The First American Martyr

1. John M. Murrin, Paul E. Johnson, James M. McPherson, Alice Fahs, and Gary Gerstle, *Liberty, Equality, Power: A History of the American People*, Concise

Edition (Boston: Wadsworth, 2014), 117; Eric Hinderaker, *Boston's Massacre* (Cambridge, MA: Harvard University Press, 2017), 324.

2. William Cooper Nell, *The Colored Patriots of the American Revolution* (Boston: Robert F. Wallcut, 1855), 15–16, electronic edition, UNC-CH digitization project, University of North Carolina at Chapel Hill, 1999, https://docsouth.unc.edu/neh/nell/nell.html.

3. Karin Clafford Farley, *Samuel Adams: Grandfather of His Country* (Austin: Raintree Steck-Vaughn, 1994), 8.

4. Martin Luther King Jr., *Why We Can't Wait* (Boston: Beacon, 1963, 1986), 2.

5. Patrick Witty, "Behind the Scenes: Tank Man of Tiananmen," *New York Times*, June 3, 2009, https://lens.blogs.nytimes.com/2009/06/03/behind-the-scenes-tank-man-of-tiananmen/.

Chapter 3 John Adams: The Conscience of the Revolution

1. Anne Husted Burleigh, *John Adams* (New York: Routledge, 2009), 93.

2. David McCullough, *John Adams* (New York: Simon & Schuster, 2001), 68.

3. McCullough, *John Adams*, 68.

Chapter 4 Benjamin Franklin: The First American

1. Clifton Fadiman and André Bernard, eds., *Bartlett's Book of Anecdotes* (New York: Little, Brown, 2000), 216.

2. Benjamin Franklin, *Autobiography of Benjamin Franklin* (New York: Henry Holt, 1916), Gutenberg.org, https://www.gutenberg.org/files/20203/20203-h/20203-h.htm [quoted material slightly edited to conform with modern spelling].

3. Benjamin Franklin, *Poor Richard's Almanack* (New York: Skyhorse Publishing, 2007), 7, 8, 9, 11, 13, 51 [some quotations altered for modern capitalization, spelling, and punctuation].

4. J. A. Leo Lemay, *The Life of Benjamin Franklin, Vol. 1: Journalist 1706-1730* (Philadelphia: University of Pennsylvania Press, 2006), 321.

5. Kenneth T. Walsh, *Celebrity in Chief: A History of the Presidents and the Culture of Stardom* (New York: Routledge, 2017), 152.

6. Barbara Mitchell and Cornelia Gamlem, *The Essential Workplace Conflict Handbook: A Quick and Handy Resource for Any Manager, Team Leader, HR Professional, or Anyone Who Wants to Resolve Disputes and Increase Productivity* (Wayne, NJ: The Career Press, 2015), 55.

7. Ken Blanchard and Sheldon Bowles, *High Five! The Magic of Working Together* (New York: HarperCollins, 2001), 60.

Chapter 5 Sarah Bradlee Fulton: The Mother of the Boston Tea Party

1. Medford Historical Society, *The Medford Historical Register* (Medford, MA: Medford Historical Society, 1898), 1:54.

2. Medford Historical Society, *The Medford Historical Register*, 54.

3. Medford Historical Society, *The Medford Historical Register*, 54–55.

Chapter 6 Patrick Henry: The Voice of the Revolution

1. Ann Maury, *Memoirs of a Huguenot Family* (New York: Putnam, 1853), 421, https://en.wikisource.org/wiki/Memoirs_of_a_Huguenot_Family/Letters_of _Rev._James_Maury.

2. Terry M. Mays, *Historical Dictionary of Revolutionary America* (Lanham, MD: Scarecrow Press, 2005), 290; Gordon S. Wood, *The American Revolution: A History* (New York: Modern Library, 2002), 16.

3. Patrick Henry, "Give Me Liberty or Give Me Death," delivered March 23, 1775, NationalCenter.org, https://nationalcenter.org/GiveMeLiberty.html.

4. 1 Corinthians 14:8.

Chapter 7 Paul Revere: The Midnight Rider

1. David Hackett Fischer, *Paul Revere's Ride* (New York: Oxford University Press, 1994), 20.

2. Central Intelligence Agency, "Intelligence throughout History: Paul Revere's Midnight Ride," CIA.gov, April 30, 2013, https://www.cia.gov/news-informatio n/featured-story-archive/2010-featured-story-archive/intelligence-history-paul-revere .html.

3. National Counterintelligence Center, *A Counterintelligence Reader, Vol. 1: American Revolution to World War II*, ed. Frank J. Rafalko (Washington, DC: NCIC, 2011), 2–7, CIA, "Intelligence throughout History: Paul Revere's Midnight Ride," CIA.gov, April 30, 2013, https://www.cia.gov/news-information /featured-story-archive/2010-featured-story-archive/intelligence-history-paul -revere.html.

4. Kat Eschner, "The Midnight Ride of Paul Revere and Some Other Guys," *Smithsonian Magazine*, April 18, 2017, https://www.smithsonianmag.com/smart -news/midnight-ride-paul-revere-and-some-other-guys-180962866/.

5. Paul Revere, "Paul Revere's Account of His Midnight Ride to Lexington," America's Homepage: Historic Documents of the United States, https://ahp.gatech .edu/midnight_ride_1775.html.

6. Richard Frothingham, *The Life and Times of Joseph Warren* (Boston: Little, Brown, 1865), 307.

Chapter 8 Parson Jonas Clarke: The Chaplain of the Revolution

1. 2 Corinthians 3:17.

2. Charles Eugene Hamlin, *The Life and Times of Hannibal Hamlin* (Cambridge, MA: Riverside, 1899), 13.

3. Hamlin, *The Life and Times*, 13.

4. George Bancroft, *History of the United States from the Discovery of the American Continent*, 4th ed. (Boston: Little, Brown, 1860), 7:293.

5. Bancroft, *History of the United States*, 293–94.

6. Jonas Clarke, "Sermon—Battle of Lexington," WallBuilders.com, December 27, 2016, https://wallbuilders.com/sermon-battle-of-lexington-1776/.

7. Clarke, "Sermon—Battle of Lexington."

Chapter 9 Jonathan Trumbull: The Prophet of the Revolution

1. William J. Federer, *America's God and Country: Encyclopedia of Quotations* (St. Louis: Amerisearch, 2000), 590.

2. Isaac William Stuart, *Life of Jonathan Trumbull, Senior, Governor of Connecticut* (Boston: Crocker and Brewster, 1859), 125–30.

3. Stuart, *Life of Jonathan Trumbull*, 151–52.

4. Jonathan Trumbull, *Jonathan Trumbull, Governor of Connecticut, 1769–1784* (Boston: Little, Brown, 1919), 145–46.

5. Stuart, *Life of Jonathan Trumbull*, 678.

6. Ezra 7:10.

7. Proverbs 22:29.

8. 1 Timothy 3:2.

9. Isaiah 41:10.

Chapter 10 Samuel Whittemore: The Oldest Soldier of the Revolution

1. New England Historical Society, "Samuel Whittemore, The Oldest, Bravest and Maybe Craziest American Revolutionary," NewEnglandHistoricalSociety .com, updated 2009, https://www.newenglandhistoricalsociety.com/samuel-wh ittemore-the-oldest-bravest-and-maybe-craziest-american-revolutionary/; Katie Turner Getty, "Before the Bayonetting: The Untold Story of Capt. Samuel Whittemore," Journal of the American Revolution, June 6, 2017, https://allthingsliberty .com/2017/06/bayonetting-untold-story-capt-samuel-whittemore/; Patrick J. Leonard, "A Veteran Long before the War for Independence, Sam Whittemore Was America's Oldest, Bravest Soldier," TheWhitmoreFamily.com, accessed December 2, 2020, http://dwhitmore.thewhitmorefamily.com/internet/samwhit.htm.

Chapter 11 Henry Knox: The Gold Standard of American Know-How

1. "History of Fort Knox," U.S. Army Fort Knox, September 14, 2020, https:// home.army.mil/knox/index.php/about/history.

2. Thomas Fleming, *Bunker Hill* (Boston: New Word City, 2016), 484–85.

3. Fleming, *Bunker Hill*, 485.

4. George Otto Trevelyan, *The American Revolution* (New York: Longmans, Green, 1921), 1:317.

5. Derek W. Beck, "Henry Knox's 'Noble Train of Artillery:' No Ox for Knox," *Journal of the American Revolution*, February 4, 2019, https://allthingsliberty .com/2019/02/henry-knoxs-noble-train-of-artillery-no-ox-for-knox/.

6. Beck, "Henry Knox's 'Noble Train of Artillery.'"

7. Victor Brooks, *The Boston Campaign, April 1775–March 1776* (Conshohocken, PA: Combined Publishing, 1999), 210.

8. David Hackett Fischer, *Washington's Crossing* (New York: Oxford University Press, 2004), 218.

9. Fischer, *Washington's Crossing*, 153.

10. Encyclopedia Britannica, "Knox, Henry," Encyclopedia.com, November 8, 2020, https://www.encyclopedia.com/people/history/us-history-biographies /henry-knox.

11. Encyclopedia Britannica, "Knox, Henry."

Chapter 12 Esther de Berdt Reed: The Crowdfunder of the Revolution

1. William Bradford Reed, *The Life of Esther de Berdt: Afterwards Esther Reed of Pennsylvania* (Philadelphia: C. Sherman, 1853), 203.

2. Reed, *Life of Esther de Berdt*, 219.

3. Spencer C. Tucker, ed., *American Revolution: The Definitive Encyclopedia and Document Collection* (Santa Barbara, CA: ABC-CLIO, 2018), 838.

Chapter 13 Thomas Paine: The Popularizer of the Revolution

1. "Thomas Paine Blue Plaque | Open Plaques," OpenPlaques.org, accessed August 25, 2020, https://openplaques.org/plaques/1490.

2. Thomas Paine, *Common Sense* (Philadelphia: W. & T. Bradford, 1776), Gutenberg.org, June 24, 2017, http://www.gutenberg.org/files/147/147-h/147-h.htm.

3. David McCullough, *1776* (New York: Simon & Schuster, 2005), 250.

4. Gordon S. Wood, *The American Revolution: A History* (New York: Modern Library, 2002), 55.

5. Christine Gibson, "How One Man Launched a Revolution," *American Heritage* 63, no. 1 (Spring 2018), https://www.americanheritage.com/how-one-man-launched-revolution.

6. Thomas Paine, *The Writings of Thomas Paine*, Vol. 1, ed. Moncure Daniel Conway, https://www.gutenberg.org/files/3741/3741-h/3741-h.htm.

7. Adam Augustyn, ed., *The Britannica Guide to World Literature: American Literature from 1600 through the 1850s* (New York: Britannica, 2011), 44.

8. "11b. Loyalists, Fence-sitters, and Patriots," USHistory.org, accessed August 25, 2020, https://www.ushistory.org/us/11b.asp.

9. History.com Editors, "Thomas Paine," History.com, October 23, 2019, https://www.history.com/topics/american-revolution/thomas-paine.

10. Thomas Paine, *The Essential Thomas Paine*, ed. John Dos Passos (Mineola, NY: Dover, 2008), 55, 87.

11. Christopher Hitchens, *Thomas Paine's Rights of Man* (New York: Grove Press, 2008), 40.

12. Joseph J. Ellis, *Revolutionary Summer: The Birth of American Independence* (New York: Vintage, 2014), 14.

13. Paine, *Common Sense*.

Chapter 14 Thomas Jefferson: The Author of the Declaration of Independence

1. Clifton Fadiman and André Bernard, eds., *Bartlett's Book of Anecdotes* (New York: Little, Brown, 2000), 317.

2. Fadiman and Bernard, *Bartlett's Book*, 317.

3. Fadiman and Bernard, *Bartlett's Book*, 317.

4. Annette Gordon-Reed, *The Hemingses of Monticello: An American Family* (New York: W. W. Norton, 2008), 99–100; Jon Meacham, *Thomas Jefferson: The Art of Power* (New York: Random House, 2012), 49.

5. Meacham, *Thomas Jefferson*, 102.

6. Meacham, *Thomas Jefferson*, 102–3.

7. Martin D. Tullai, "Hatter's Sign Helped Jefferson Accept Changes to Declaration," *The Morning Call*, July 4, 1995, https://www.mcall.com/news/mc-xpm-1995-07-04-3056010-story.html.

8. Jim Zeender, "Thomas Jefferson: Governor of Virginia," National Archives, April 12, 2013, https://prologue.blogs.archives.gov/2013/04/12/thomas-jefferson-governor-of-virginia/.

9. Gaye Wilson, "Jack Jouett's Ride," Monticello.org, September 5, 2006, https://www.monticello.org/site/research-and-collections/jack-jouetts-ride.

10. Thomas Jefferson, *Notes on the State of Virginia, Query XVIII: Manners,* TeachingAmericanHistory.org, accessed August 25, 2020, http://teachingamerican history.org/library/document/notes-on-the-state-of-virginia-query-xviii-manners/.

11. "Interview: Andrew Burstein—Historian," *Thomas Jefferson: A Film by Ken Burns*, PBS.org, http://www.pbs.org/jefferson/archives/interviews/Burstein.htm.

12. Andrew Burstein, *The Inner Jefferson: Portrait of a Grieving Optimist* (Charlottesville: University of Virginia Press, 1996), 61–63.

13. Joyce Oldham Appleby, *Thomas Jefferson: The American Presidents Series: The 3rd President, 1801–1809* (New York: Henry Holt, 2003), 27–28.

14. William G. Hyland Jr., *In Defense of Thomas Jefferson: The Sally Hemings Sex Scandal* (New York: St. Martin's, 2009), 9-15.

15. Newell G. Bringhurst, "Jefferson's Blood: 1974—A Popular but Controversial Biography," *Frontline*, PBS.org, https://www.pbs.org/wgbh/pages/frontline/shows/jefferson/cron/1974brodie.html.

16. Hyland, *In Defense of Thomas Jefferson*, 126.

17. Hyland, *In Defense of Thomas Jefferson*, 17-18.

18. Hyland, *In Defense of Thomas Jefferson*, 32.

19. Hyland, *In Defense of Thomas Jefferson*, 30.

20. University of Virginia, *Alumni Bulletin of the University of Virginia—January 1922* (Charlottesville: University of Virginia Press, 1922), 374, 377–78.

21. Elbert Hubbard with John Jacob Lentz, *Thomas Jefferson: A Little Journey* (East Aurora, NY: The Roycrofters, 1906), 101.

22. Thomas Jefferson Encyclopedia, "Jefferson's Last Words," Monticello.org, accessed August 25, 2020, http://www.monticello.org/site/research-and-collections/jeffersons-last-words.

23. Proverbs 25:3 MSG.

24. Jerry Holmes, *Thomas Jefferson: A Chronology of His Thoughts* (Lanham, MD: Rowman & Littlefield, 2002), 119.

25. Sharon Lynn Pruitt, "6 Countries Where Slavery Still Exists," Oxygen.com, April 9, 2018, https://www.oxygen.com/very-real/6-countries-where-slavery-still-exists.

Chapter 15 John Hancock: The Wealthy Servant of the Revolution

1. John F. Watson, *Annals of Philadelphia and Pennsylvania, in the Olden Time* (Philadelphia: J. F. Watson, 1850), 399, https://archive.org/details/annalso fphiladel01wats/page/398/mode/2up/search/Hancock.

2. Lorenzo Sears, *John Hancock: The Picturesque Patriot* (Boston: Little, Brown, 1912), 233.

3. Frank Moore, *Diary of the American Revolution: From Newspapers and Original Documents* (New York: Charles T. Evans, 1863), 2:11–12; Mary Caroline Crawford, *Old Boston Days & Ways: From the Dawn of the Revolution until the Town Became a City* (Boston: Little, Brown, 1913), 275; Richard M. Ketchum, "Men of the Revolution: 14. John Hancock," *American Heritage* 26, no. 2 (February 1975): part 1, https://www.americanheritage.com/men-revolution-14-john-hancock.

4. Ketchum, "Men of the Revolution."

5. Harlow Giles Unger, *John Hancock: Merchant King and American Patriot* (New York: Wiley, 2000), 272–73.

6. Unger, *John Hancock*, 334.

7. Ketchum, "Men of the Revolution."

Chapter 16 John Paul Jones: The Ranger of the Sea

1. Evan Thomas, *John Paul Jones: Sailor, Hero, Father of the American Navy* (New York: Simon & Schuster, 2003), 16.

2. The Sextant, "Navy Hero—John Paul Jones," Naval History and Heritage Command, July 15, 2015, https://usnhistory.navylive.dodlive.mil/2015/07/15/navy-legend-john-paul-jones/.

3. Thomas, *John Paul Jones*, 6.

4. Thomas, *John Paul Jones*, 89.

5. American Philosophical Society and Yale University, "The Continental Congress: Instructions to Franklin, Silas Deane, and Arthur Lee as Commissioners to France, [24 September–22 October 1776]," National Archives, accessed August 25, 2020, https://founders.archives.gov/documents/Franklin/01-22-02-0371.

6. Joseph Callo, *John Paul Jones: America's First Sea Warrior* (Annapolis, MD: Naval Institute Press, 2006), 42.

7. Callo, *John Paul Jones*, 48.

8. Callo, *John Paul Jones*, 62.

9. John Paul Jones, "Extracts from the Journals of My Campaigns," American Revolution.org, accessed December 2, 2020, https://www.americanrevolution.org/jpj.php.

10. Callo, *John Paul Jones*, 90.

11. Thomas, *John Paul Jones*, 188.

12. Augustus C. Buell, *Paul Jones, Founder of the American Navy: A History* (New York: Scribner, 1906), 1:239.

13. Buell, *Paul Jones*, 239.

14. Edward Sylvester Ellis, *The History of Our Country from the Discovery of America to the Present Time* (Cincinnati: Jones Brothers, 1900), 2:544.

15. Buell, *Paul Jones*, 240, note.

Chapter 17 Sybil Ludington: The Female Paul Revere

1. Willis Fletcher Johnson, *Colonel Henry Ludington: A Memoir* (New York: Ludington Family, 1907), 88–89.

2. Johnson, *Colonel Henry Ludington*, 90.

Chapter 18 Baron von Steuben: The Flamboyant Warrior

1. George Washington, "From George Washington to David Humphreys, 25 July 1785," Founders Online, April 3, 2002, https://founders.archives.gov/documents /Washington/04-03-02-0142.

2. George Washington, "From George Washington to Henry Laurens, 23 December 1777," Founders Online, March 12, 2002, https://founders.archives.gov /documents/Washington/03-12-02-0628.

3. Robert Harvey, *A Few Bloody Noses: The Realities and Mythologies of the American Revolution* (Woodstock, NY: Overlook Press, 2002), 309.

Chapter 19 Nathanael Greene: The Fighting Quaker

1. Thomas E. Ricks, "The Most Underrated General in American History: Nathaniel Greene?," *Foreign Policy*, September 22, 2010, https://foreignpolicy.com /2010/09/22/the-most-underrated-general-in-american-history-nathaniel-greene/.

2. John Buchanan, *The Road to Guilford Courthouse: The American Revolution in the Carolinas* (Hoboken, NJ: Wiley, 1997), 167.

3. James A. Warren, "Nathanael Greene: The Revolution's Unconventional Mastermind," *The Daily Beast*, August 20, 2019, https://www.thedailybeast.com /nathanael-greene-the-revolutions-unconventional-mastermind.

4. David R. Higgins, *The Swamp Fox: Francis Marion's Campaign in the Carolinas 1780* (Oxford, UK: Osprey, 2013), 64.

5. Terry Golway, *Washington's General: Nathanael Greene and the Triumph of the American Revolution* (New York: Henry Holt, 2005), 244.

6. Golway, *Washington's General*, 3.

7. Golway, *Washington's General*, 302.

Chapter 20 Marquis de Lafayette: The Aristocratic Warrior

1. George Washington, "From George Washington to Silas Deane, 13 August 1777," Founders Online, March 10, 2002, https://founders.archives.gov/documents /Washington/03-10-02-0593, note 1.

2. Laura Auricchio, *The Marquis: Lafayette Reconsidered* (New York: Vintage, 2015), 48.

3. Morris Slavin and Agnes M. Smith, eds., *Bourgeois, Sans-Culottes and Other Frenchmen: Essays on the French Revolution in Honor of John Hall Stewart* (Waterloo, Ontario, Canada: Wilfrid Laurier University Press, 1981), 22–23.

4. Jared Sparks, ed., *Correspondence of the American Revolution: Being Letters of Eminent Men to George Washington* (Boston: Little, Brown, 1853), 3:461.

5. Clifton Fadiman and André Bernard, eds., *Bartlett's Book of Anecdotes* (New York: Little, Brown, 2000), 328.

6. Fadiman and Bernard, *Bartlett's Book*, 329.

Chapter 21 Mary Hays, Anna Marie Lane, Deborah Sampson, and Others: Revolutionary Women in Combat

1. Patricia Brady, *Martha Washington: An American Life* (New York: Viking, 2005), 118–19; Erin Blakemore, "Why Martha Washington Was the Ultimate

Military Spouse," History.com, February 4, 2020, https://www.history.com/news/martha-washington-military-spouse-battlefield.

2. Harry Schenawolf, "Firing Field Cannon in the American Revolutionary War," Revolutionary War Journal, September 3, 2014, http://www.revolutionarywarjournal.com/firing-field-cannon/.

3. Joseph Plumb Martin, *The Adventures of a Revolutionary Soldier* (Maine: Hallowell, 1830), Chapter IV, 105, https://en.wikisource.org/wiki/The_Adventures_Of_A_Revolutionary_Soldier/Chapter_IV.

4. "Historic Valley Forge: Molly Pitcher," USHistory.org, accessed December 2, 2020, https://www.ushistory.org/Valleyforge/youasked/070.htm.

5. "Historic Valley Forge."

6. Cengage, "Sampson, Deborah (1760–1827)," Encyclopedia.com, April 25, 2020, https://www.encyclopedia.com/women/encyclopedias-almanacs-transcripts-and-maps/sampson-deborah-1760-1827.

7. Susan J. Smith, "Covered Bridge over the Nashua River, Pepperell," Pepperell Historical Society, January 19, 2007, http://www.pepperellhistory.org/whispers/the-covered-bridge/; Mary L. P. Shattuck, "The Story of Jewett's Bridge," in *Prudence Wright and the Women Who Guarded the Bridge, Pepperell, Massachusetts, April 1775*, Pepperell Historical Society, published May 1900, posted October 2017, http://www.pepperellhistory.org/wp-content/uploads/2017/10/PrudenceWright.pdf.

> Note: Some sources name Pru's brother Samuel and Benjamin Whiting as the spies captured at the bridge; the most reliable sources, however, name Pru's other brother Thomas and Benjamin Whiting's brother, Captain Leonard Whiting of Hollis, New Hampshire, as the spies at the bridge.

8. Shattuck, "The Story of Jewett's Bridge," 43.

9. Carol Berkin, *Revolutionary Mothers: Women in the Struggle for America's Independence* (New York: Vintage Books, 2006), 61.

10. George Pope Morris, *The Deserted Bride: And Other Poems* (New York: Appleton, 1843), 87.

Chapter 22 Alexander Hamilton: The Father of American Prosperity

1. Clifton Fadiman and André Bernard, eds., *Bartlett's Book of Anecdotes* (New York: Little, Brown, 2000), 254.

2. James Hamilton, "To Alexander Hamilton from James Hamilton, 12 June 1793," Founders Online, January 14, 2002, https://founders.archives.gov/documents/Hamilton/01-14-02-0369.

3. Ron Chernow, *Alexander Hamilton* (New York: Penguin, 2004), 153.

4. Lesley Kennedy, "How Alexander Hamilton's Men Surprised the Enemy at the Battle of Yorktown," History.com, November 14, 2018, https://www.history.com/news/alexander-hamilton-battle-yorktown-revolutionary-war.

5. Chernow, *Alexander Hamilton*, 159.

6. Martha Brockenbrough, *Alexander Hamilton, Revolutionary* (New York: Macmillan, 2017), 305.

Chapter 23 James Madison: The Father of the Constitution

1. Clifton Fadiman and André Bernard, eds., *Bartlett's Book of Anecdotes* (New York: Little, Brown, 2000), 366.

2. "Why a Bill of Rights?," National Archives, August 15, 2016, https://www.archives.gov/amending-america/explore/why-bill-of-rights-transcript.html.

3. J. C. A. Stagg, "James Madison: Impact and Legacy," University of Virginia Miller Center, accessed August 25, 2020, https://millercenter.org/president/madison/impact-and-legacy.

4. Michael Reagan, *The New Reagan Revolution: How Ronald Reagan's Principles Can Restore America Today* (New York: St. Martin's, 2010), 177.

Chapter 24 George Washington: The Father of His Country

1. Michael D. McKinney, "George Washington's Rules of Civility & Decent Behavior in Company and Conversation," *Foundations*, accessed August 25, 2020, http://www.foundationsmag.com/civility.html.

2. George Washington, "Letter to His Brother, John A. Washington | Friday, May 31, 1754," George Washington's Mount Vernon, accessed August 25, 2020, https://www.mountvernon.org/library/digitalhistory/quotes/article/the-right-wing-where-i-stood-was-exposed-to-and-received-all-the-enemys-fire-i-heard-the-bullets-whistle-and-believe-me-there-is-something-charming-in-the-sound/.

3. "George Washington Biography," Biography.com, A&E Television Networks, 2014, http://www.biography.com/people/george-washington-9524786.

4. David McCullough, "The Glorious Cause of America" (Assembly address, Brigham Young University, Provo, UT, September 27, 2005), https://speeches.byu.edu/talks/david-mccullough/glorious-cause-america/.

5. Troy O. Bickham, "Sympathizing with Sedition? George Washington, the British Press, and British Attitudes during the American War of Independence," *The William and Mary Quarterly* (Omohundro Institute of Early American History and Culture), January 2002, 101.

6. Thomas J. McGuire, *Battle of Paoli* (Mechanicsburg, PA: Stackpole Books, 2000), 35-36.

7. McGuire, *Battle of Paoli*, 125.

8. Dr. Burton W. Folsom, "George Washington's Unimpeachable Character," Mackinac Center for Public Policy, February 1, 1999, http://www.mackinac.org/1652.

9. Clifton Fadiman and André Bernard, eds., *Bartlett's Book of Anecdotes* (New York: Little, Brown, 2000), 561.

10. Mark Alexander, "The Model for Presidential Character—George Washington," *Patriot Post*, February 23, 2012, http://patriotpost.us/alexander/12704.

11. Paul F. Boller Jr., *Presidential Anecdotes* (New York: Oxford University Press, 1996), 13.

12. Michael Cox and Doug Stokes, *US Foreign Policy* (Oxford, UK: Oxford University Press, 2012), 42.

13. George Washington, "Statement before Delivering Response to the First Newburgh Address | Saturday, March 15, 1783," George Washington's Mount Vernon, accessed August 25, 2020, https://www.mountvernon.org/library/digitalhis

tory/quotes/article/gentlemen-you-will-permit-me-to-put-on-my-spectacles-f-or-i
-have-grown-not-only-gray-but-almost-blind-in-the-service-of-my-country/.

14. George Washington, "Letter to Lewis Nicola," May 22, 1782, Teaching
AmericanHistory.org, http://teachingamericanhistory.org/library/document
/letter-to-lewis-nicola/.

15. Thomas Sowell, "What Kind of 'Experience'?," Creators Syndicate, February 10, 2008, http://www.creators.com/conservative/thomas-sowell/what-kind
-of-experience.html.

16. Donald L. Wasson, "Cincinnatus," Ancient History Encyclopedia, April
4, 2017, https://www.ancient.eu/Cincinnatus/.

17. The Claremont Institute, "Farewell Address 1796," Rediscovering George
Washington, PBS.org, 2002, http://www.pbs.org/georgewashington/milestones
/farewell_address_about.html.

18. Matthew Spalding, "The Man Who Would Not Be King," Heritage.org, February 5, 2007, http://www.heritage.org/research/commentary/2007/02/the-man
-who-would-not-be-king.

19. Ann Rinaldi, *Taking Liberty: The Story of Oney Judge, George Washington's Runaway Slave* (New York: Simon & Schuster, 2002), 260.

20. Rinaldi, *Taking Liberty*, 260.

21. Stephen E. Ambrose, *To America: Personal Reflections of an Historian*
(New York: Simon & Schuster, 2002), 1, 13.

22. Ambrose, *To America*, 10.

23. Peter R. Henriques, *Realistic Visionary: A Portrait of George Washington*
(Charlottesville: University of Virginia Press, 2006), 187–88.

24. Frank E. Grizzard, *George Washington: A Biographical Companion* (Santa
Barbara, CA: ABC-CLIO, 2002), 74.

25. Henriques, *Realistic Visionary*, 194.

26. Henriques, *Realistic Visionary*, 203.

27. John Bartlett, *Familiar Quotations: A Collection of Passages, Phrases, and
Proverbs Traced to Their Sources in Ancient and Modern Literature*, 9th ed. (Boston: Little, Brown, 1905), 445; United States House of Representatives, "President
George Washington's Memorial Service. December 26, 1799," History, Art & Archives, United States House of Representatives, accessed August 25, 2020, https://
history.house.gov/Historical-Highlights/1700s/President-George-Washington
-s-Memorial-Service/.

Epilogue

1. Abraham Lincoln, "Lyceum Address—The Perpetuation of Our Political
Institutions: Address before the Young Men's Lyceum of Springfield, Illinois,
January 27, 1838," Abraham Lincoln Online, accessed August 25, 2020, http://
www.abrahamlincolnonline.org/lincoln/speeches/lyceum.htm.

2. Howard Zinn, *A People's History of the United States: 1492–Present*, 3rd
ed. (New York: Routledge, 2013), 9–10.

3. "An Experts' History of Howard Zinn," *Los Angeles Times*, February 1,
2010, https://www.latimes.com/archives/la-xpm-2010-feb-01-la-oe-miller1-2010
feb01-story.html.

4. Mary Grabar, *Debunking Howard Zinn: Exposing the Fake History That Turned a Generation against America* (Washington, DC: Regnery, 2019), front matter.

5. Mary Grabar, "AHI's Mary Grabar: Why I Wrote Debunking Howard Zinn," Alexander Hamilton Institute, August 20, 2019, https://www.theahi.org /ahis-mary-grabar-why-i-wrote-debunking-howard-zinn/.

6. Mary Grabar, "Howard Zinn's Assault on Historians and American Principles," RealClearPublicAffairs.com, May 26, 2020, https://www.realclearpublic affairs.com/articles/2020/05/26/howard_zinns_assault_on_historians_and _american_principles_486279.html.

7. Richard Marsden, "The Furrow or the Ploughshare: Jeremy Corbyn and the Leadership Question," Off-Guardian.org, July 7, 2016, https://off-guardian.org /2016/07/07/the-furrow-or-the-ploughshare-jeremy-corbyn-and-the-leadership -question/; David Clyde Walters, "Exploring a Definition of Leadership and the Biography of Dr. Frank B. Wynn," 2009, *Graduate Student Theses, Dissertations, & Professional Papers*, 1299, 82–83, https://scholarworks.umt.edu/cgi/viewcontent .cgi?article=2318&context=etd.

Pat Williams retired as senior vice president of the NBA's Orlando Magic in May 2019 to head up an effort to bring major league baseball to Orlando. He has more than fifty years of professional sports experience and has written more than one hundred books, including the popular *Coach Wooden, Coach Wooden's Greatest Secret*, and *Character Carved in Stone*. Find out more at www.patwilliams.com.

Jim Denney is the author of *Walt's Disneyland, Answers to Satisfy the Soul, Writing in Overdrive*, and the Timebenders series for young readers. He has written many books with Pat Williams, including *Coach Wooden, The Difference You Make*, and *The Sweet Spot for Success*. Learn more at www.writinginoverdrive.com.

CONNECT WITH PAT

You can contact Pat Williams at:

pwilliams@patwilliams.com

If you would like to speak with Pat personally,
call (407) 721-0922

Visit Pat Williams's website at:
PatWilliams.com

If you would like to set up a speaking
engagement for Pat Williams, please call his
assistant, Andrew Herdliska, at (407) 969-7578
or email Andrew at aherdliska@yahoo.com.

We would love to hear from you.
Please send your comments about this book to
Pat Williams at the email address above.

Thank you.

12 Core Virtues
THAT LEAD TO SUCCESS

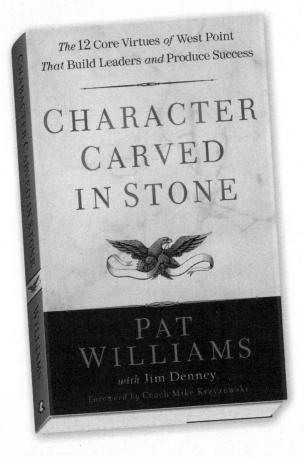

With his signature enthusiasm and insight, Pat Williams shares the incredible stories of West Point graduates, from the Civil War to the War on Terror. He shows you how to develop twelve essential virtues in your life—whether you are in the corporate world, the academic world, the military, the church, or another sphere—so that you can experience lasting success.

Я Revell
a division of Baker Publishing Group
www.RevellBooks.com

Coach Wooden Knew the Long-Term Impact of
LITTLE THINGS DONE WELL

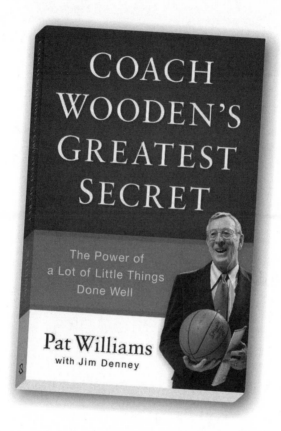

A motivational message filled with life-changing insights and memorable stories—Pat Williams shares why the secret to success in life depends on a lot of little things done well.